THE ENTREPRENEUR'S GUIDE TO
SECOND LIFE®
MAKING MONEY IN THE METAVERSE

DANIEL TERDIMAN

BICENTENNIAL
1807
WILEY
2007
BICENTENNIAL

Wiley Publishing, Inc.

ACQUISITIONS EDITOR: WILLEM KNIBBE

DEVELOPMENT EDITOR: CANDACE ENGLISH

PRODUCTION EDITOR: PATRICK CUNNINGHAM

COPY EDITOR: CANDACE ENGLISH

PRODUCTION MANAGER: TIM TATE

VICE PRESIDENT AND EXECUTIVE GROUP PUBLISHER: RICHARD SWADLEY

VICE PRESIDENT AND EXECUTIVE PUBLISHER: JOSEPH B. WIKERT

VICE PRESIDENT AND PUBLISHER: NEIL EDDE

BOOK DESIGNER AND COMPOSITOR: PATRICK CUNNINGHAM

PROOFREADER: ASHA JOHNSON

INDEXER: TED LAUX

ANNIVERSARY LOGO DESIGN: RICHARD PACIFICO

COVER DESIGNER: RYAN SNEED

COVER IMAGE: DANIEL TERDIMAN AND JONHENRY RIGHTER

■ DEDICATION

To Kathleen, who is my muse, my inspiration, and the one who best gets me, particularly when I'm being silly.

■ ACKNOWLEDGMENTS

Writing a book is a hard thing, particularly a first book, and especially when it's being done on top of a full-time job. So, my gratitude to the many people who helped out with this project is almost beyond measuring.

A very, very big thanks goes to David Fugate, my agent, who helped me take what was an over-ambitious book concept and whittle it down to the essence that is in your hands right now. Willem Knibbe, at Wiley, championed this idea from day one and made it very easy to proceed, and for that I am grateful. I also want to single out Catherine Smith at Linden Lab, who has been great to work with over the years, first when I was with Wired News, then with CNET, and finally on this project. Also, Jim Kerstetter, Scott Ard, Jai Singh, and Elinor Mills at CNET News.com, Evan Hansen at Wired News, and Wagner James Au for being a good friend and for encouraging me to move forward with this project. At Wiley, I want to thank Candace English for her intelligent editing, Janet Chang for her formatting work, and Pete Gaughan for his encouragement. As for the experts I spoke with for the book, I want to thank Alliez Mysterio, Adam Zauis, Nexus Nash, Dana Bergson, Sol Columbia, Lur Sachs, Zee Linden, Hiro Pendragon, Moopf Murray, Twiddler Therian, Munchflower Zauis, Hyasynth Tiramisu, Starley Thereian, Fallingwater Cellardoor, Jennyfur Peregrine, Professor Sadovnycha, Shiryu Musashi, Zabitan Assia, Chip Midnight, Kim Anubis, Neil Protagonist, Foolish Frost, Insky Jedburgh, Aimee Weber, Amethyst Rosencrans, Baccara Rhodes, Genvieve Hutchence, Nyteshade Vesperia, Stroker Serpentine, Giff Forsetti, Andrea Faulkner, Keiki Lemieux, Claudia Linden, BamBam Sachertorte, Francis Chung, Caroline Apollo, Wynx Whiplash, Trinity Cole, Katt Kongo, Ham Rambler, Jenna Fairplay, Deede Debs, Kelly Czarnecki, Nexeus Fatale, Kermitt Quick, Kaeman Demar, Groove Salad, Aesop Thatch, Ming Chen, Anna Normandy, Cory Ondrejka, Qarl Linden, Sibley Verbeck, Jerry Paffendorf, and Sabrina Dent. Finally, a huge thank-you to my parents, Susan Weisberg and Richard Terdiman, and to Phoenix Linden for introducing me to *Second Life* in the first place. And to Izzy for being the best ever.

■ ABOUT THE AUTHOR

Daniel Terdiman is a Senior Writer for CNET News.com who covers the culture of technology, and who has been reporting on *Second Life* since 2003. Daniel has a Master's degree from the Columbia University Graduate School of Journalism and has written and reported for *The New York Times*, *Time* magazine, *Wired* magazine, Wired News, Business 2.0, and other publications. He is also a frequent speaker at such conferences as the Game Developers Conference, the Austin Games Conference, South by Southwest, State of Play, and others. In 2006 Daniel spearheaded the effort to bring CNET into *Second Life*, making it the first mainstream news organization to open a bureau in the virtual world. Daniel lives in Sausalito, California, with his wife, Kathleen.

■ INTRODUCTION

When I've talked to people deeply involved in the *Second Life* community in recent months, especially those who are out speaking in public about it, they tell me that one of the first things that everybody asks them is, "How do I make money in *Second Life*?"

One person, who runs one of the most famous companies building big projects in *Second Life* for outside clients, told me that after giving a talk at a conference in Germany, he was besieged by a flood of attendees asking that question, and he ended up spending more than an hour responding.

So the goal of this book is to provide the answer to the question, and to anyone who wants to know, not just those who have the opportunity to ask it personally of someone in the know. If you read this book, my hope is that you will come away knowing (a) that you *can* make money in *Second Life*, (b) what opportunities exist for those who want to do so, (c) what you have to do to avail yourself of those opportunities, and (d) what the roadblocks are to potential success.

Second Life has been riding a remarkable wave of media attention and public interest since the fall of 2006, and in that time, its population has grown by several orders of magnitude. Some might worry that so many extra people coming into the virtual world might erode the opportunities to make money, but I see the reality as just the opposite: the more people there are, the more potential customers.

There are a few things you should know, though, before you set out on your grand *Second Life* entrepreneurial adventure.

First, despite some breathless press reports that suggest that making money in *Second Life* is as easy as shooting fish in a barrel, that really isn't true, and it would be irresponsible of me to suggest it was. The reality is that conceiving of and running a *Second Life* business is, in many ways, very much like doing so with any kind of business. Those who do well are the ones who come up with a plan, commit to it, put in the time required, and are willing to be flexible as conditions demand.

But for those who do those things, success can follow, whether your goal is to make enough money to pay for your *Second Life* fashion needs or to live on. There are people at every point along that spectrum, and it's vital that you understand that the ones at the more lucrative end of that scale are the ones who have put the most into their businesses, and who have treated them with the most respect.

The *Second Life* community, while an ever-evolving and multifaceted population, universally demands that you take them seriously, and that you offer something new and interesting. Otherwise, why should they patronize your shop? There is another one just around the way.

The point here is just to make sure you understand that you can't simply show up and expect the dollars to roll in. It takes work, and a lot of it. But if you are willing to put in that work, the rewards are there for the taking.

Finally, almost universally, the successful business owners I talked to for this book said that if you're not having fun with what you do, you won't succeed. You have to have your heart in it. Many of them said that what you do for a business should be something that you would almost be willing to do for free, just for the love of it. Because it's hard work, and if you don't love it, you won't enjoy yourself. There are, after all, plenty of other ways to make money.

I hope this book will make it easier for you to find your niche, and to make the kind of money you'd like to be making in *Second Life*. Here's what you'll find:

Chapter 1 is an introduction to the concept of a virtual-world economy like that of *Second Life*. It discusses some of the history of virtual-world economies, as well as the structural underpinnings that keep *Second Life*'s economy afloat—which you'll want to understand before you put any of your real money into a business that exists in an entirely digital environment.

Chapter 2 is a discussion of some of the *Second Life* business basics. It contains business plans for several of the leading segments of the economy written by some of the most successful business owners. It also discusses some financial practicalities, such as accounting and tax issues.

Chapter 3 sets forth some of the most important elements of setting up and succeeding with a *Second Life* business. You'll find industry-specific advice and reinforcements of these basic principles in the chapters that follow.

Chapter 4 covers the *Second Life* fashion industry. This chapter is a primer on what *Second Life* fashion is—including the various subcategories—and covers what people are looking for, and advice on what to do and not to do. Further, it includes a discussion of the technical skills you will need to launch a fashion business, and how to market one.

Chapter 5 covers the *Second Life* land/real-estate industry. It discusses the differences between islands and the mainland, and between selling and renting land. It also talks about technical skills and what it takes to market a land business.

Chapter 6 looks at the *Second Life* building industry, and gives an introduction to the business of constructing everything from small houses to castles to entire islands for clients. It covers both prefab and custom work, and tells you what technical skills you'll need to work in this industry, as well as how to market such a business.

Chapter 7 discusses how to make money in *Second Life*'s adult-oriented industry. It talks about the various segments of the sex industry, and about the skills, both technical and marketing, required to make money there.

Chapter 8 focuses on building a business around *Second Life* gadgets and toys. It lays out the principles of selling toys, weapons, HUDs, and many other items, and explores the vastly different sets of skills that are required to create the many varieties of in-world objects. And of course, the chapter discusses the marketing skills required to build your objects business.

Chapter 9 gets into the many interactive business opportunities, including running bars, nightclubs, and publications. As usual, the chapter includes a discussion of the technical skills required to support such an interactive business, and how to market that business.

Chapter 10 deals with *Teen Second Life*, a teens-only segment of *Second Life* that serves as a training ground for young entrepreneurs. It focuses on some of the specific attributes of *Teen Second Life*, and breaks down the various categories of opportunities available there and the skills a teen will need to succeed.

Chapter 11 looks at the future of business in *Second Life* through the eyes of some of the most important people in the *SL* community and economy. By looking at how *Second Life* is changing and what new technologies are being introduced there, these experts share their thoughts on what opportunities will exist a little way down the road.

Appendix A is a list of additional reading that runs the gamut from the history of virtual-world economies to blogs about *Second Life* and other resources designed to help the budding entrepreneur succeed.

Appendix B is a quick-reference list of prices for items in *Second Life*. This list is by no means exhaustive, but will give you an idea of what to expect to charge (and pay, if you're the purchaser!) for items in-world.

Appendix C is a survey of how much you can expect to earn in each major segment of *Second Life* business.

Second Life is an exciting and vibrant place that is growing quickly and energetically. And it is a land of unending opportunity. I hope that after reading this book you will be ready to embark on your quest to leverage this virtual world to your financial advantage, all while having a great time. Good luck.

—Daniel Terdiman
Sausalito, California

CONTENTS

■ CHAPTER 4: WALKING THE RUNWAY— FASHION IN *SECOND LIFE*   70

■ CHAPTER 5: THE *SECOND LIFE* LAND BUSINESS   104

◼ CHAPTER 6: CONSTRUCTION PROJECTS BIG AND SMALL   104

◼ CHAPTER 10: RUNNING A BUSINESS IN *TEEN SECOND LIFE*   244

◼ CHAPTER 11: THE FUTURE OF OF *SECOND LIFE* ENTREPRENEURSHIP   262

◼ APPENDICES   276

◼ INDEX   298

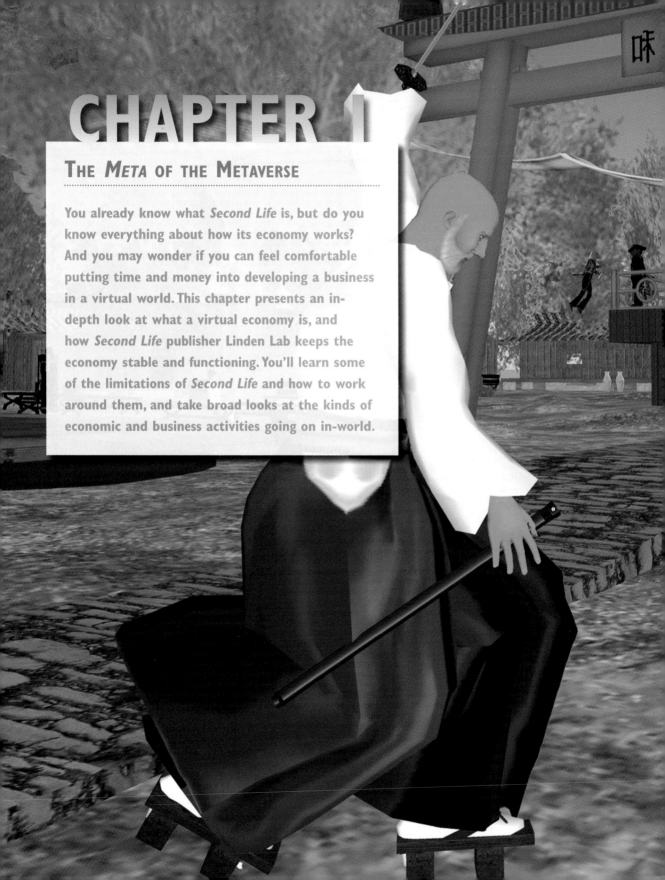

CHAPTER 1

THE *META* OF THE METAVERSE

You already know what *Second Life* is, but do you know everything about how its economy works? And you may wonder if you can feel comfortable putting time and money into developing a business in a virtual world. This chapter presents an in-depth look at what a virtual economy is, and how *Second Life* publisher Linden Lab keeps the economy stable and functioning. You'll learn some of the limitations of *Second Life* and how to work around them, and take broad looks at the kinds of economic and business activities going on in-world.

CONTENTS

UNDERSTANDING *SECOND LIFE'S* ECONOMY

To hear Philip Rosedale (aka Philip Linden, shown in Figure 1.1), CEO and founder of *Second Life* publisher Linden Lab, tell it, he's not creating a game. He's creating a new country. That might be a stretch, but one thing that *Second Life* definitely has in common with any new country is a developing economy.

Of course, some would say that *Second Life*'s economy is actually more stable than that of any new country. After all, its currency, the Linden dollar (L$), has been fairly stable over its lifetime. As of this writing, the L$ trades at 267.7 per US dollar, and historically it has been in the 270 to 300 range. The current state of the Linden dollar demonstrates that it is staying strong, as the fewer Linden dollars it takes to make a US dollar, the stronger *Second Life*'s imaginary currency is.

But although it is a virtual currency, it is also very real. You can hop on over to eBay or to the official LindeX currency exchange and trade in your Linden dollars for US dollars. As noted virtual-economies expert Edward Castronova, author of *Synthetic Worlds: The Business and Culture of Online Games* (University of Chicago Press, 2005), told me recently, a virtual economy "doesn't have to be real to work. Dollars are not real. The value of the Hope Diamond is virtual. Cisco.com has value

*Figure 1.1: Philip Linden, the **Second Life** avatar of Linden Lab founder and CEO Philip Rosedale (Image courtesy of Linden Lab)*

even though it is not real." In other words, if people associate value with a currency, then it has value.

MORE INFO

SPOTLIGHT ON EDWARD CASTRONOVA, VIRTUAL-ECONOMIES EXPERT

CHAPTER 1

CHAPTER 2
CHAPTER 3
CHAPTER 4
CHAPTER 5
CHAPTER 6
CHAPTER 7
CHAPTER 8
CHAPTER 9
CHAPTER 10
CHAPTER 11
APPENDICES
INDEX

(Image courtesy of Indiana University)

I quote virtual-economies expert Edward Castronova several times in this chapter. There's a reason for that: Castronova is considered the leading authority on the subject of virtual economies, virtual currencies, and how those things are related to and correspond directly with users' experiences in virtual worlds and online games.

Castronova's ascendance to his lofty position in this field began in late 2001 when, as a young economics professor at California State University, Fullerton, he published a groundbreaking research paper, "Virtual Worlds: A First-Hand Account of Market and Society on the Cyberian Frontier."

The paper was among the very first pieces of scholarly work that examined the then-nascent subject of economics in online games. This was nearly two years before *Second Life* opened to the public, and at that time few people understood that there could be such a thing as a viable, working, healthy, and developing economy in a game. The rhetorical question Castronova set out to answer was why anyone would care to study the social and economic behavior of what many feel are just silly "games."

(Continued)

With his research and scholarship, Castronova began to make it possible for people beyond the game publishers and a few hundred thousand rabid players to look at MMO games as something more than a "silly" pastime.

Philip Rosedale and his team were already working on *Second Life* when Castronova wrote his paper. And they were already imagining their virtual world of entirely emergent behavior and a wide-open, market-based economy. But without Castronova and his research—not to mention the huge amount of press he has generated—it might have been much harder for Linden Lab to be taken seriously.

One of the chief points of the paper was that a virtual economy can approach real countries' economies, at least in terms of the value of their currency—the total gross national product. He proved that by measuring some of the metrics of *EverQuest*'s Norrath economy. Its currency, he wrote, was more valuable than the Japanese yen; its gross national product was far greater than "dozens of countries, including India and China."

In 2003 Castronova, along with Wharton School of Business law professor Dan Hunter, journalist Julian Dibbell, and Rutgers University law professor Greg Lastowka, launched Terra Nova (www.terranova.blogs. com), which quickly became the most important community blog about virtual worlds. The site is home to regular intellectual and philosophical musings on the implications of these environments and has hosted the writings of nearly every influential figure in the field.

In 2005 Castronova published his first book, *Synthetic Worlds: The Business and Culture of Online Games*, and shortly after the book you're now holding hits stores, he will publish his second, *Exodus to the Virtual World: How Online Fun Is Changing Reality*. Although he has not put much focus on *Second Life* specifically—in large part because *Second Life* isn't a game, per se, his scholarship has affected the environment that any *Second Life* businessperson will deal with every day.

And value is something that many, many thousands of *Second Life* users definitely associate with the nearly endless list of things that you can buy, sell, and own: a gorgeous waterfront piece of land, a shiny red sports car, a stunning evening gown (Figure 1.2), even an office tower. All of these things, while existing only on Linden Lab's servers, belong to actual people. Because those people either put in the time to build whatever they own, or bought their possessions from someone else, there's little question that there is real value.

Figure 1.2: In Second Life, residents can wear fashion of all kinds, including wonderful evening gowns like this one from Paper Couture.

In fact, value is one of the fundamental differences between *Second Life* and other so-called massively multiplayer online (MMO) games. (Those involved with *Second Life* steadfastly insist that it is not a game.) Linden Lab specifically grants property ownership to residents, and thus the ability to do with the property what you will. That decision was made in late 2003, not long after *Second Life* launched publicly. The company announced the policy shift at the first annual State of Play conference in New York, and to anyone familiar with the MMO genre, the decision was a shock. Although many millions of dollars' worth of transactions take place each year for the virtual assets in MMOs like *EverQuest* and *Ultima Online*, those titles' publishers had always maintained ultimate ownership over the goods because, they argued, these were games.

But Linden Lab looked at real-world economies and found that one key to healthy growth was property ownership. If you own what you create, you will be motivated to create more. And creation breeds complex and burgeoning economies. So Linden Lab— aided in part by advice from world-renowned copyright attorney Lawrence Lessig—decided that the best way to foster a real economy in *Second Life* was to buck the MMO trend and give residents the same property rights that people have in real life. The results were instantaneous, and probably beyond any expectations Linden Lab had.

It's difficult to measure the economic impact today because *Second Life* economic data from late 2003 is hard to come by, but the effect of the property-rights decision is apparent in the total user hours for that time period (Table 1.1). Between September and October of 2003, immediately before the policy shift, the total user hours grew by about 9.3 percent. But the next month user hours experienced a 22 percent spurt, and growth of another 14.8 percent the month after that.

Table 1.1: Early Growth of User Hours

MONTH	HOURS	INCREASE OVER PREVIOUS MONTH
Sep '03	51,700	—
Oct '03	56,500	9.3%
Nov '03	69,000	22.0%
Dec '03	79,200	14.8%

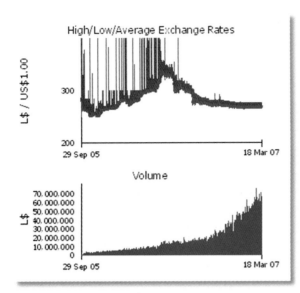

Figure 1.3: In its early days, the LindeX currency exchange was volatile, but gradually it became stable.

And why? Because there was money to be made off an economy in which users owned their creations, and people wanted in. So, very quickly a burgeoning market for the endless supply of *Second Life* goods, services, real estate, and other "property" blossomed. There's no way to calculate the total value of the economy, since the number of objects in *Second Life* numbers in the millions, from T-shirts worth nothing to real estate worth hundreds or even thousands of US dollars. But it is possible to track the total number of Linden dollars in circulation—at least since September 2005, just prior to the launch of the LindeX, the official Linden currency exchange, where residents can buy and sell their currency for US dollars. Figure 1.3 shows how many Lindens have been circulating, and their exchange rate.

In September 2005 there was a total of about 404.6 million Linden dollars in circulation. At this writing, there are roughly 1.8 billion Linden dollars. At 267.7 Lindens to the US dollar, that means the *Second Life* money supply is worth a healthy US$6.9 million.

That's certainly not a fortune, but it should be enough to quiet any skeptic who says that the *Second Life* economy isn't for real. And it should provide justification for anyone who has been thinking about starting a *Second Life* business, large or small, but who has been worried that there isn't a real economy to back up such an operation.

And if you are one of those people, you're hardly alone. *Second Life* is a veritable petri dish for the study of emergent businesses. To be sure, it's hard to measure who is doing what kind of business. But luckily, Linden Lab provides an always-up-to-date list of economic statistics that give general indications about the state of the *Second Life* economy. And by all accounts, that economy is exploding.

For instance, in November 2006 there were 13,788 residents with what Linden Lab calls "positive monthly Linden dollar flow." That's a complicated metric, but essentially it means residents who made more than they spent. By April 2007, that number had swelled to 34,474, of whom 810 were earning in excess of US$1,000 more than they were spending. That was growth of 150 percent. Of course, the size of the *Second Life* population also exploded in that time frame, growing 244 percent. Nonetheless, there can be little doubt that multitudes of *Second Life* residents are making money, with the rate of positive earners growing, month by month, an average of 20.3 percent. That's lower than the growth in population, but still impressive.

Another measure of the size of the *Second Life* economy is how much money is spent each day. Generally, that number hovers at US$1.5 million per day. Not bad for an entirely virtual environment in which human beings are represented by small cartoon likenesses.

CHAPTER 1

CHAPTER 2
CHAPTER 3
CHAPTER 4
CHAPTER 5
CHAPTER 6
CHAPTER 7
CHAPTER 8
CHAPTER 9
CHAPTER 10
CHAPTER 11
APPENDICES
INDEX

THE STRENGTH TO KEEP ON GOING

Today *Second Life* shows many characteristics of a maturing economy—for example, the stable Linden dollar, or the steady growth in the number of people with positive cash flow, or the ever-growing number of products and services available, as well as the nearly endless number of stores operating both in-world and on the Web.

Actually, though, the *Second Life* economy is just a more sophisticated version of what it was shortly after the virtual world was launched. The main difference today is just that there is a whole lot more of everything: Residents, land, buildings, stores—the list goes on. But the structure has been in place all along, and that's noteworthy.

Back in 2003 the people at Linden Lab told me how the company was looking to reward imagination and emergent play and behavior. "Every time someone does something great, we say, let's see how we can help you," Linden Lab engineer Aaron Brashears shared. The idea was to encourage unexpected behavior, especially that which might create some economic activity. Brashears talked about how one resident had hoped to hold regular trivia games. Linden Lab liked the idea, so it donated the Linden dollars for prize money. These days, the incentives for new economic activity are orders of magnitude larger.

Recently, The Electric Sheep Company, the largest of the third-party *Second Life* service-development outfits, sponsored a business-plan contest. The Sheep was looking for the best new business ideas that would represent an entirely new stage of economic and business development than the trivia contests of yesteryear. The winner presented a plan for a *Second Life* market-research service that would help real-world companies decide whether to invest in an in-world presence, and learn how their brands or products would be received by the *Second Life* community.

The other finalists were equally ambitious: a group that conceived of a suite of communications and collaborations tools; a team that wanted to build an in-world music-distribution system along the lines of Apple's iTunes Store; and a pair who had a plan for a value-added search engine that would allow residents to better find the things they were looking for.

These sophisticated offerings show how *Second Life* is growing, but at its core it's the same place it was in the beginning: an environment that fosters emergent behavior, and particularly economic activity. Except unlike the real world, where little things like physics get in the way, in *Second Life* if you have the imagination and the business know-how, you can probably make your concept a reality.

CHAPTER I

UNDER-
STANDING
SECOND LIFE'S
ECONOMY

WHY GET
INVOLVED IN
THE VIRTUAL
ECONOMY

OVERCOMING
SECOND LIFE'S
LIMITATIONS

GAINING THE
NECESSARY
SKILLS

WHY GET INVOLVED IN THE VIRTUAL ECONOMY?

Figure 1.4: Panache, HoseQueen McLean's high-end hair store.

Let's be honest: *Second Life*, though it has many characteristics of the real world—a bustling community, social norms, fancy shops (Figure 1.4), etc.—is still just virtual reality. It's really just ones and zeros, it's stored on servers, its representations of people are often rudimentary, and even its economic activity is conducted in a make-believe currency which, though it can be directly converted to hard currency, is definitely not legal tender. But more to the point, Linden Lab has maintained control over the servers, has retained the right to revoke property ownership rights, and doesn't offer any guarantees that it won't suddenly go out of business or have a catastrophic technology meltdown that results in the loss of everything you've spent hours or even months creating.

To date, of course, there have been no such sudden disasters or unilateral decisions by Linden Lab, and generally speaking, few people have experienced an unexplained or unwarranted loss of their *Second Life* property or businesses. That stability has led thousands of people into *Second Life* and into considering starting a business there. Still, any responsible businessperson has to consider why they're taking the risks they're taking.

So why would anyone want to invest significant time and money in this virtual world? It's a question anyone thinking about setting up a business in *Second Life* should consider, akin to asking whether it really makes sense to open a china shop on a fault line. Fortunately, there are some really good answers.

If you've spent any time in *Second Life*, there's a decent chance you've come across Spin Martin. That's the in-world identity of Eric Rice, a well-known blogger, journalist, and technology maven. In *Second Life*, Spin has invested in four islands and half of a mainland

CHAPTER I

CHAPTER 2
CHAPTER 3
CHAPTER 4
CHAPTER 5
CHAPTER 6
CHAPTER 7
CHAPTER 8
CHAPTER 9
CHAPTER 10
CHAPTER 11
APPENDICES
INDEX

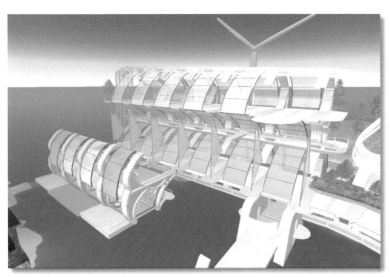

Figure 1.5: Spin Martin's former music-themed sim, Hipcast

simulator and thus is on the hook for more than US$1,000 in land maintenance—or *tier*—fees for his music-themed sim (Figure 1.5).

When asked who would put significant amounts of money on the line in a virtual world, especially one that offers few guarantees, he replied, "There's two types of people. Those that are clearly aware [of the risks]— and those that aren't so consciously aware of it. You don't think Enron-sized [companies] can go away either, but they can."

For Spin, as for many *Second Life* residents and businesspeople, there are any number of immutable draws—attractions that transcend the risks. He says it "isn't chic to talk about since it's not business, business, business," but that a lot of people become invested financially in *Second Life* because it offers a sort of holy trinity of reasons to do so: it's an interesting way to pass a fair bit of time, it's fun, and best of all, there's a chance to make some money.

The fact that *Second Life*'s terms of service grant residents intellectual property rights over what they create was a significant draw for Spin because (save for an unexpected and unlikely change of policy by Linden Lab) he doesn't have to worry about his property being taken away from him. The truth, it seems, is that the odds are in the residents' favor: the earth may indeed shake under that china shop, but probably a long time from now.

There's another intangible reason that people invest in *Second Life*: simply because they believe in it. Alliez Mysterio, who as of this writing controlled one of the largest *Second Life* land empires, with 47 sims—and growing—says she's confident that *Second Life*'s future is bright. "I cannot imagine trying to log in and not having it here," she said to me one day while we toured her magnificent island of huge crystals sculptures, horse paddocks, hidden fireplaces, majestic waterfalls, and romantic gazebos with endless views. "If I did not believe in them, I would not have sim number 47 on order." Alliez, who is now making her full-time living in *Second Life*—as was her former business partner in d'Alliez Estates (Figure 1.6), Tony Beckett, before he sold out to her—has been developing her mini land empire for two years. "Since I arrived, the [Linden dollar economy has] gone up and down as the US dollar has," she says. "As far as I am concerned, it has been stable. *Second Life* has never been in trouble with its economy."

Figure 1.6: Paradise d'Alliez

These are compelling sentiments, but they don't pay the bills, and if Linden Lab were to have a technology meltdown, it could be a serious problem. In fact, in 2006 multiple hacker attacks took down the *Second Life* grid, attacks that eventually resulted in Linden Lab calling in the FBI to investigate.

But Linden Lab CEO Rosedale points to changes that that could protect businesspeople against technology failures. Primarily, those changes have to do with Linden Lab's decision in early 2007 to make its client software open source. Rosedale says the idea is to both make the server code open source and let multiple operators provide *Second Life* services. That could mean that Linden Lab would not be the only party holding on to the many terabytes of data that make up the fabric of *Second Life*. That, Rosedale says, would protect against massive data loss.

MORE INFO

THE MEANING OF AN OPEN-SOURCE CLIENT

In January 2007, when Linden Lab announced its decision to make the *Second Life* client open source, it was, to some members of the community, the most exciting development since the virtual world's launch.

Previously, while users created nearly everything found in-world, they had no control over the basic *Second Life* viewer software and so had no power over some of the software's frustrating aspects, such as poor user-interface choices, heavy lag, and frequent and numerous bugs or bug fixes that broke working features.

By making the software open source, Linden Lab extended users' participation beyond content to the viewer itself, ensuring that they had direct input on and influence over its future, as well as over the creation of standards that will benefit all users.

Ultimately, the change means that Linden Lab will be able to leverage the creativity of thousands of developers outside its own real-world walls for solutions to existing problems, as well as for ideas about new features, tools, and systems.

Rosedale also predicted that Linden Lab would soon be adding—or perhaps the open-source community would add—import and export capabilities to *Second Life*. That means objects created in *Second Life* could be moved to competing platforms, once again protecting residents from losing their intellectual property if Linden Lab ever decided to change its ownership policies.

CHAPTER 1

CHAPTER 2
CHAPTER 3
CHAPTER 4
CHAPTER 5
CHAPTER 6
CHAPTER 7
CHAPTER 8
CHAPTER 9
CHAPTER 10
CHAPTER 11
APPENDICES
INDEX

A STABLE, HEALTHY ECONOMY

To John Zdanowski, Linden Lab chief financial officer, keeping the *Second Life* economy stable is the highest priority. Keeping any economy stable means ensuring that its currency neither suffers hyperinflation nor appreciates too much against other currencies. Thus, the trick is to define a relatively narrow band in which the currency fluctuates—in this case against the US dollar—and do whatever is necessary to stay in that band.

MMO games have not always been able to achieve this. In fact, there's a term specifically for inflation in virtual worlds and online games: *MUDflation*, which comes from early virtual worlds known as multi-use dungeons (or domains or dimensions). Edward Castronova, in his book *Synthetic Worlds*, defines MUDflation as happening when a virtual world becomes overloaded with the many types of weapons, armor, clothing, and the like, and people's inventories clog up. "As the world fills up with these goods, and with cash," Castronova writes, "MUDflation occurs, and item pricing gets seriously out of whack. The prices of many goods collapse, and many others skyrocket."

Part of the problem is that virtual worlds can make it fairly easy for players to accumulate money. And as in any economy, the more money floating around, the more it costs to buy things. In the real world, there are entire governmental bodies designed to handle the health of economies. The United States, for example, has the Federal Reserve, which monitors the strength of the US economy and acts either to rein in inflation or push for it if interest rates are growing too fast.

In a virtual world, the corollary is the publisher—in this case, Linden Lab. Keeping the economy in check requires smart people with a sense of economic history and knowledge of what's behind an economy involving hundreds of thousands or even millions of players, many millions of objects, and millions of dollars' worth of goods.

Part of the equation is what are known as *sources* and *sinks*—tools used by the virtual world's "Federal Reserve" to keep currencies like the Linden dollar within that narrow band of stability. A source is as it sounds: any positive supply of money into an economy. It could be weekly cash stipends or rewards for various activities. A sink is the opposite: it is any method used to pull cash out of circulation. This can be taxes, charges, classified ads, or many other things.

And why is it important to have the right combination of currency sources and sinks? Zdanowski used the LindeX to explain what would happen if there weren't proper sources

UNDER-
STANDING
SECOND LIFE'S
ECONOMY

WHY GET
INVOLVED IN
THE VIRTUAL
ECONOMY

OVERCOMING
SECOND LIFE'S
LIMITATIONS

GAINING THE
NECESSARY
SKILLS

of new money. The LindeX is the primary way that *Second Life* residents can get ahold of new Linden dollars. If, he said, the company hadn't created the LindeX, the Linden dollar would have rapidly appreciated against the US dollar. As a result, residents likely would have begun hoarding Linden dollars, waiting until the right time to sell them, figuring that eventually they would be able to cash out for a big profit. The regularly circulating money supply would have quickly dwindled and created a situation where everyone was doing the equivalent of stuffing their mattresses with Lindens.

Conversely, if Linden Lab didn't provide adequate sinks, the amount of currency in circulation would explode, prices would accelerate, and you'd get the virtual equivalent of the German mark during the 1920s, when prices doubled almost every two days.

OK, that's probably unlikely. But as Castronova puts it in his book, if a virtual world or online game company loses control of its currency, there are real effects on players. "If a player has been planning for months to obtain some item and sell it for a certain amount, she will be distressed if inflation has eaten away that value," Castronova writes.

But fear not. Linden Lab is doing a pretty solid job of managing its sources and sinks, and as a result the Linden dollar has remained stable, particularly since the emergence of LindeX. Linden Lab makes much of *Second Life*'s economic data publicly available in an attempt to be transparent. And that's a good thing for the managers of a developing economy to do, since it can inspire trust as well as give the public a sense of what is going on with the currency. You wouldn't want to get financially involved in an economy without knowing what you were dealing with.

On its economic statistics page (http://secondlife.com/whatis/economy _ stats. php) Linden Lab provides a rundown of sources and sinks. The LindeX Market data chart at http://secondlife.com/whatis/economy-market.php demonstrates that for nearly the first year of the LindeX (while the *Second Life* community was still getting used to it) the Linden dollar mainly stayed stable but still showed many cases of volatility.

Zdanowski explained that that's largely because volume on the LindeX was low. As the community used it more and more, the volatility reduced, and beginning in mid to late 2006, the Linden dollar settled into the value of 260–280 to the US dollar—exactly where Linden Lab wants it to be. Now, among other metrics, Linden Lab provides the current total number of Linden dollars in circulation.

Of course, some fear that a malicious resident with a large supply of Linden dollars could try to damage the currency by dumping their holdings on the open market. Such an event would probably send the currency's value plummeting. But Zdanowski says even that is unlikely, and for a couple of reasons.

First, it would be an expensive operation, as Linden dollars have real value. For someone to dump many millions of Lindens on the market they'd have to be willing to throw away thousands of US dollars. If someone dumped enough currency on the open market, the Linden dollar could collapse against the US dollar. The LindeX features automatic "circuit breaker" trading halts based on movement (positive or negative) of the average exchange rate in any given day, as shown in Table 1.2. Averages are determined for these circuit breakers at least once per hour.

Table 1.2: The Second Life Currency "Circuit Breaker"

TRADING ACTIVITY	RESULT
>10% in any 12-hour period	Projected 1-hour halt
>20% in any 12-hour period	Projected 2-hour halt
>30% in any 12-hour period	Close until at least noon the following day

Second, Linden Lab has imposed limits on how many Linden dollars anyone can sell in a 30-day period. And those limits are designed to protect the economy from an intentional or unintentional hyperinflationary attack.

Linden Lab takes the *Second Life* economy seriously, and has installed mechanisms that protect it. And while there are never any guarantees, as long as *Second Life* is growing, as long as Linden Lab doesn't revoke property rights, as long as the real-world economy stays healthy, and as long as residents keep on creating new things and activities, the economic prospects for newcomers or new business owners look good.

LIMITLESS BUSINESS OPPORTUNITIES

There are plenty of reasons to believe that the *Second Life* economy is for real, that it's stable, and that there's a way to make money in it. But what kind of activity is really going on there? One way to look at it is to examine the many different kinds of things that are being created, sold, and bought in *Second Life*. Still another way would be to think about how much money is being spent. According to Linden Lab, *Second Life* residents spend around US$1.5 million a day. Every day. Sometimes, like on weekends, it's more than $2 million. What are they spending that money on?

A huge number of things. Fashion of all kinds, toys and gadgets, entirely new avatars, futuristic cars, whole islands, and beachfront property on the mainland. And much, much more. And it's good that people are buying so many things, because *Second Life* has a micro-economy in which most goods cost less than US$1. Even some "expensive" items are no more than a couple dollars. And so, to make money in that economy, you need to establish a volume business in which you sell large amounts of your products. But fear not: many people do it, and you can too. And keep in mind that, unlike the real world, the cost of making the second copy of your product is zero.

The following sections touch upon the major categories of products and services, but Chapters 4 through 9 provide much more detail on these industries and more, including selling vehicles, toys, and gadgets, running bars and clubs, developing islands, blogging for money, and much more.

CHAPTER 1

CHAPTER 2
CHAPTER 3
CHAPTER 4
CHAPTER 5
CHAPTER 6
CHAPTER 7
CHAPTER 8
CHAPTER 9
CHAPTER 10
CHAPTER 11
APPENDICES
INDEX

CHAPTER 1

● Under-
   standing
   Second Life's
   Economy

● Why Get
   Involved in
   the Virtual
   Economy

● Overcoming
   Second Life's
   Limitations

● Gaining the
   Necessary
   Skills

FASHION

The biggest *Second Life* industry of all, with the largest number of people making money, including a significant number making full-time incomes, is fashion. This means many things—clothing, avatar skins, shoes, and the like—and the variety is staggering. There are fantastic waistcoats for L$250; men's suits for L$300; entire formal dresses, including skirts, stockings, and trains, for L$500; and so on. There's also fashion for all kinds of specific subcommunities, like furries—fox avatars, anyone?—and others. And there's always room for innovation.

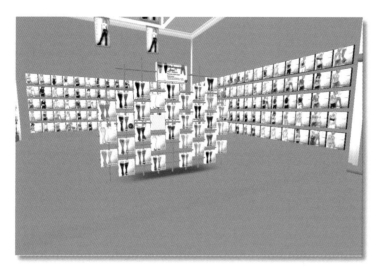

Figure 1.7: The Mischief store, one of the most popular fashion boutiques in **Second Life.**

The stores themselves are almost as varied, running from little hole-in-the wall boutiques in malls on the mainland to giant emporiums on private islands (Figure 1.7).For anyone who can imagine something new and exciting, who has the skills to create something high-quality and innovative, and has the marketing acumen to bring in customers, there is an almost-endless amount of opportunity in the *Second Life* fashion industry.

LAND

While the biggest industry in *Second Life*, by volume, is fashion, the biggest-ticket items (by price) are almost always land. With even small plots going for US$10 and up, mid-sized parcels for several hundred US dollars, and whole islands costing US$1,675 if you buy them from Linden Lab, land is a big money-maker.

That's especially true these days, as the huge influx of new *Second Life* residents is creating a tremendous amount of demand at all levels of size and pricing. There are people making money solely by buying and selling land, but the real way to make money over time, and to stick around as a *Second Life* land baron, is to develop and manage properties, and either sell them or rent them.

Customers of those types of businesses want a variety of things, but chief among them are a sense of privacy and high-quality workmanship. The job of the land developer is to provide the kind of land people want, with a minimum of fuss. For those who succeed at that, there is a lot of money to be made, and a growing number of people are making full-time livings doing just that.

BUILDINGS

If there's one category of products in *Second Life* that can compete with (at least the low end of) the land business for highest prices, it's the building industry. This is all the many beachfront chalets, castles, towers, Japanese teahouses, glass mansions, boutique storefronts, tree houses, and the like—not to mention the themed, full-sim builds that are increasingly popping up—that you see everywhere. In some cases, residents built these structures for themselves, but in many, many other cases, they bought them. As always, prices vary widely, depending on complexity, size, quality, and uniqueness: Some builders create prefab models that they sell again and again. Others do small- to medium-sized custom work, and still others design whole sims for big clients.

Something like a small prefab skybox can sell for around US$3, while a big modern house might go for close to US$15 or $20. Even bigger projects, like a Gothic castle, can fetch as much as US$50. Even at these higher prices, however, it's still necessary to move a high volume of product to make much money, as most people are going to concentrate on the lower end of the price spectrum.

Then, however, there is custom, and full-sim building. And that work tends to be paid by the hour, with lesser-known builders earning around US$15 per hour, and well-known builders fetching upwards of US$60 hourly. And opportunity exists everywhere in between.

THE ADULT INDUSTRY

You may love it, hate it, or ignore it, but there's no escaping the fact that in *Second Life*, the sex and adult-oriented products business is booming. And there's a ton of opportunity there. From beds with built-in animations that allow avatars to engage in simulated adult behavior, to body parts that add realism to that behavior, to sexy fashion, to all manner of toys and gadgets, there is no shortage of goods to satisfy residents' desires. There are even booming escort and nude-dancing businesses. As in the real world, sex sells.

Furniture like beds can run from a US dollar or two all the way up to US$50, depending on who made it, what it looks like, and what it allows avatars to do. Many other products run in the US$0.50 to $2 range, while escorts can earn from US$3 to $14 an hour. Again, over time, and with volume, it adds up pretty quickly.

In Chapter 2 we'll look at many of the business tips and tricks you'll want to follow when starting a new for-profit venture in *Second Life*, and in Chapter 3 I'll cover how to market your business.

MORE INFO

SHOPPING HOTSPOTS FOR FASHION AND TRANSPORTATION

One of the best places to go for male as well as female avatars is Mischief, which also specializes in business outfits and playfully risqué and casual clothing alike. And best of all, Mischief is well-known for a constantly expanding inventory.

If robot chic is your style, Armord is the place to go for the latest in jet-pack fashion. This, of course, is where you might run into *Wired* magazine games editor Chris Baker looking for his latest outfit.

Once you're properly dressed, you might want to find a more advanced way to get around *Second Life* than walking or even flying. If so, there's no end to the kinds of vehicles and vessels you can buy.

One favorite is Jacqueline Trudeaus's Classic Sailing Yachts, a *Second Life* marina where she sells ships like The Defender, a craft reminiscent of an early-1900s yacht. The boat lets you sail on the *Second Life* high seas, and it responds realistically to the virtual world's winds, interacting with the conditions somewhat as would a real ship.

If a car is more your speed, Francis Chung's Dominus Motor Company and its flagship Dominus Shadow, modeled on a Ford Mustang, is a popular choice. It's a ride that fulfills the fantasy of the ultimate muscle car, down to the neon purple lights that you can turn on or off under the vehicle, the many realistic engine noises, and the ability to switch to hovercraft mode.

And another really fun way to get around is on a Slegway, a uniquely *Second Life* version of inventor Dean Kamen's famous gyro-stabilized Segway scooters. And it looks just like a Segway, except it has an added feature: rockets that allow it to fly. They're available from the WhipTech store.

OVERCOMING *SECOND LIFE*'S LIMITATIONS

If you've gone so far as to pick this book up, you're probably aware that *Second Life* is not nirvana. It is not a perfect world, and the daily life of a regular *Second Life* user, let alone someone trying to run a business in-world, can be fraught with technological and practical problems.

Some are rather mundane issues like intermittent software crashes. There's little anyone can do about that, though upgrading to a more powerful computer may be one solution. We'll cover that a little more later in this chapter. But one issue that has come up in the last year has many *Second Life* shop owners—particularly those who create items for sale like clothing, housing, sculpture, and the like—concerned.

The issue is a small piece of software called CopyBot that allows anyone using it to copy any *Second Life* object. It burst onto the *Second Life* scene in the fall of 2006, and many store owners freaked out, worried that CopyBot would mean the death of their businesses. Some shuttered their shops altogether. Many more protested—in fact, there was a series of angry gatherings complete with anti-CopyBot picket signs and plenty of vitriolic language.

CopyBot was created by a group called libsecondlife that had previously worked on creating an open-source version of the *Second Life* client software. To hear the group tell it, CopyBot was just an experiment that got out of control. The press picked up on CopyBot as if it meant the end of *Second Life* altogether, in part because it seemed so scary, particularly in a virtual world where ownership of the intellectual property one creates is so important to fostering a blossoming economy. Linden Lab itself acted swiftly, if only to say that it was aware of the problem and that anyone caught using CopyBot would be banned.

The reality of the situation was not quite as bad as many thought it was. It was true that CopyBot could duplicate may things, but there were limits (as spelled out at `http:// ccslfashionista.blogspot.com/2006/11/copybot.html`). Essentially, it could duplicate fully textured objects attached to avatars in the area near where the CopyBot user was, as well as fully textured objects in the area that were not attached to avatars. But it could not copy object contents, such as animations, scripts, textures, and sounds. Still, while the actual threat from CopyBot was minimal—and there never were any large-scale problems from it—the fear demonstrated to many that *Second Life* had potential problems for business owners that weren't being addressed.

Nonetheless, it is wise to be aware that these kinds of problems do exist in *Second Life*. It is possible that your content could be stolen, in much the same way that a store in real life could be broken into. The best defense? Keep coming up with ideas. The real value of any business is not in the bits; it's in the ideas. It's in making sure that the community knows that your creations are yours. Show your style. Speak through your designs. Then your brand will be valuable even if someone comes along and steals a little bit of it. And don't rest on your laurels—add new items to your inventory frequently, as that is one major way to develop a loyal clientele.

Of course, there are practical solutions, as well—things you can do to ensure that your content, while still copiable, can be identified as yours. One method is to use Photoshop's Digimarc filter (Figure 1.8) to embed a tiny watermark in the digital file that makes up the texture you import into *Second Life*. Ordinarily, it's invisible, but if someone did swipe your hair texture, for instance, you could prove it because the digital watermark would be there, and would be registered to you. You need a registered Adobe watermark account—Adobe keeps records so the watermarks are traceable—but once you do, you are ensuring that you can prove content you create for *Second Life* is yours.

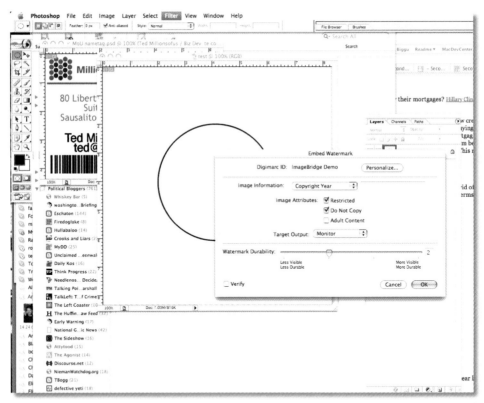

Figure 1.8: Adobe Photoshop Digimarc watermarking

USING A DIGITAL WATERMARK IN PHOTOSHOP

To apply a digital watermark in Photoshop, open your image in Photoshop and, as the last step in the process, apply the Digimarc filter (via Filter ▸ Digimarc ▸ Embed Watermark).

You can apply two different security levels: You can embed information about the image itself, like the copyright year, a transaction identification number, or an image identification. You can also embed image attributes, like whether it's restricted, whether it's not for copying, and even whether it's meant to be adult content.

For the highest level of watermark security, another step in that dialogue box allows you to first register for and then embed a personalized Digimarc ID. You register to get it with Digimarc.com/register. They store your information in a database for easy retrieval. You get an ID and PIN that you can embed in your images.

Then you select a target output so the watermark is an appropriate resolution, be it for a computer monitor, for the Web, or for printing. You can also embed a level of durability—how visible the watermark is. If you're putting thumbnails of your creations on a Web site, for example, you would likely want to have 100 percent visibility. Similarly, in your *Second Life* store, you would probably want a product sign where visitors could see the watermark and some sort of note indicating that everything you're selling is watermark protected. As for the actual content, you probably want it to be invisible.

NOTE

If you do find that someone is using CopyBot or another tool to copy your goods, you can file a Digital Millennium Copyright Act take-down notice against the perpetrator, and Linden Lab may well remove disputed content. But because Linden Lab doesn't play the role of arbiter, the perpetrator can assert that he or she was the creator, and Linden Lab may well restore the content. To prevail once and for all in such a case, a content creator may be forced to take the supposed thief to court, which may be too expensive and time-consuming.

Ultimately, problems like CopyBot are not likely to be a major issue for you or any other store owner. But as mentioned earlier, it's certainly a good idea to be aware of what is possible and to know how to deal with it without overreacting should some new problem arise.

■ BOOSTING *SECOND LIFE*'S PERFORMANCE

By now, you may well be familiar with what a resource hog *Second Life* can be: You've heard the almost never-ending whir of the fan that has to keep your computer cool while running *Second Life*; you've seen how other applications slow down or don't work at all. And you no doubt have seen *Second Life* itself drag to a near-halt as lag overcomes it.

All told, there's no way to get around it: *Second Life* uses a huge amount of your computing power, and even in the best-case scenario, with the fastest computer, the most memory, the fattest Internet pipe, and so forth, you're still looking at software that is waiting for hardware to catch up. But there are things you can do about it, and this section is a primer in how to get the most out of *Second Life*.

To begin with, you have to choose whether you're going to run *Second Life* on a PC or a Mac. In either case, you'll need a high-speed Internet connection and an NVIDIA GeForce2, GeForce4 MX or better, or ATI Radeon 8500, 9250, or better video card.

MORE INFO

SECOND LIFE COMPUTER-SYSTEM REQUIREMENTS AND RECOMMENDATIONS

If you're on a PC, here are your minimum requirements, courtesy of Linden Lab:

- **Windows XP (Service Pack 2) or Windows 2000 (Service Pack 4). As of this writing, *Second Life* doesn't work with Windows Vista, though that could change soon.**

- **An 800 MHz Pentium III, Athlon, or better processor.**

- **At least 256MB of RAM.**

On a Mac, the minimum requirements are as follows:

- **Mac OS X 10.3.9 or higher.**

- **A 1GHz G4 or better processor.**

- **At least 512MB of RAM.**

> Those are the barest of requirements. Running *Second Life* on a machine with these specifications is almost sure to be a slow, frustrating experience, and if you want to run a *Second Life* business, I would recommend upgrading to the best computer and specs you can afford.
>
> But short of that, Linden Lab also offers some recommended system specifications that will ensure that *Second Life* runs at least somewhat better. For both PCs and Macs, the company's recommendations start with an **NVIDIA GeForce FX 5600 or GeForce 6600, or ATI Radeon 9600 or X600 video card.**
>
> For PCs, start with at least a 1.6GHz Pentium 4 or Athlon 2000+ processor. Then make sure you're at 512MB of RAM.
>
> For Macs, the recommendations begin with running at least Mac OS X 10.4.3 (it is not known at this time if *Second Life* will support OS X 10.5 Leopard, which will be installed on all new Macs as of fall of 2007). Linden Lab also suggests a 1.25 GHz or better G4 processor and at least 768MB of RAM.

But practically speaking, running *Second Life* on a computer with those recommended specs is still not likely to blow you away. I am a Mac user, and for years used a PowerBook G4 with a 1.25 GHz processor and 1.25 GB of RAM. And *Second Life* was still very slow. I've now upgraded to a top-of-the-line 2.33 GHz MacBook Pro with 3GB of RAM—and now, finally, *Second Life* performs smoothly.

This is not to say that everyone who wants a good *Second Life* experience needs to spend $4,000 on a new computer. But newer and stronger is certainly better. At the very least, here is what I recommend: more RAM and a better video card. Without question, those are the two most important things to upgrade if you want better performance from *Second Life* or any application. In particular, content creators will want better video cards to best and most quickly render the large amounts of onscreen content they'll be working with.

Ultimately, the lesson here is to be aware that *Second Life* is going to dominate your computer when it's running and you simply want to be able to give it the resources it needs to operate efficiently.

GAINING THE NECESSARY SKILLS

They say it "all starts with a cube." Building objects in *Second Life* that is. And what that means, essentially, is that much of what you see in *Second Life* started out as a single cube-shaped object that was then modified, added to, manipulated and, lo and behold, became that gorgeous beachfront mansion you flew over recently. So at its core, *Second Life* is a collection of modified textures and cubes. And those should be fairly easy to get to do what you want, right?

Alas, it's not quite that simple. And this is where it's wise to pay attention if you want to run a *Second Life* business that depends in any way on creating content. Because what it takes is learning how to manipulate those cubes—*prims*, as they're called—and textures to get what you want. In addition, you'll most likely need to gain some proficiency in Linden Scripting Language (LSL)—the *Second Life* scripting language. This is used for everything from making a door open, to an avatar's dance animation, to a new pose built into a piece of furniture. Of course, we can't cover it in a couple of pages in a book about making money in *Second Life*, but you'll need to master it if you want to make things yourself—hiring someone else to do it for you would take a big cut out of your profit.

The thing is, this is hard work. We're essentially talking about a form of programming, and for many people that is a scary word. And for good reason. But a lot of people I know who do pretty well selling their own content started off not knowing anything about programming or scripting or designing textures. They just started playing with the tools, and before long they were getting somewhere. And you can too.

Still, you're going to need to study and practice. And if you don't have much experience with scripting or programming or working with textures, don't expect to be creating profitable content overnight. Give it some time.

MORE INFO

CHAPTER 1

CHAPTER 2
CHAPTER 3
CHAPTER 4
CHAPTER 5
CHAPTER 6
CHAPTER 7
CHAPTER 8
CHAPTER 9
CHAPTER 10
CHAPTER 11
APPENDICES
INDEX

RESOURCES FOR BUILDING AND TEXTURING

Here are some resources that can help you get started with creating content:

- The *Second Life* Knowledge Base. This is a treasure trove of information, tutorials, and more about everything *Second Life*. The Content Creation section has subsections on modifying avatars and avatar appearance, building, textures and snapshots, and more. This is an essential place to start.

  `http://secondlife.com/knowledgebase/category.php?id=52`

- Nicola Escher's *Second Life* Tutorials, a nice collection of tips and tricks on creating everything from clothing to tattoos to mannequins.

  `http://www.nicolaescher.com/tutorials.php`

- The Ivory Tower of Prims, an in-world, "self-guided, self-paced, comprehensive building tutorial."

  Natoma (210, 164, 27)

- Robin Wood's *Second Life* Tutorials, which offers instruction on texturing, specifically as related to clothing.

  `http://www.robinwood.com/Catalog/Technical/SL-Tuts/`
  `SLTutSet.html`

- The LSL Portal, a Linden Lab-hosted wiki dedicated to community input, discussion, and instruction on the Linden Scripting Language (LSL), the main tool used for creating most objects.

  `http://wiki.secondlife.com/wiki/LSL_Portal`

- *Second Life*: The Official Guide (Wiley, 2006) by Michael Rymaszewski, et al. Chapters 7 and 8 introduce building and scripting and are good primers on how to get started creating content in *Second Life*.

- Creating Your World: The Official Guide to Advanced Content Creation in *Second Life* (Wiley, 2007) by Aimee Weber, et al. This book is designed to give serious content creators an in-depth look at the tips, tricks, and tools necessary to make desirable content.

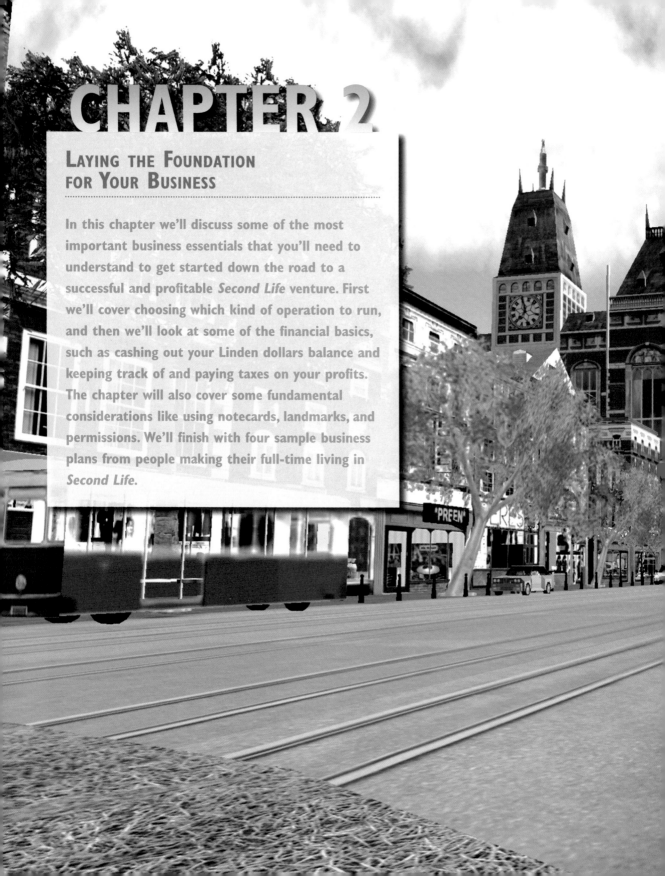

CHAPTER 2

LAYING THE FOUNDATION FOR YOUR BUSINESS

In this chapter we'll discuss some of the most important business essentials that you'll need to understand to get started down the road to a successful and profitable *Second Life* venture. First we'll cover choosing which kind of operation to run, and then we'll look at some of the financial basics, such as cashing out your Linden dollars balance and keeping track of and paying taxes on your profits. The chapter will also cover some fundamental considerations like using notecards, landmarks, and permissions. We'll finish with four sample business plans from people making their full-time living in *Second Life*.

CONTENTS

SETTLING ON A BUSINESS CATEGORY

The very first thing to do once you've decided to start a *Second Life* business is to figure out what category you're going to try. Will you be a fashion maven? Are you interested in developing and renting or selling land? Or do you want to design futuristic cars?

Especially if you're fairly new to *Second Life*, settling on exactly how you want to make money may not be an overnight process. In fact, some of the most successful business owners caution specifically against that.

Before you get set on selling cars or selling specialized furniture or developing land, you may want to try a number of such endeavors to see what really fits your sense of style, your skills, and your business sense.

"I'd suggest that in the beginning, they try many things," says Twiddler Thereian, whose Taunt Hair Shack is one of the best-known purveyors of hair in *Second Life*. "Try making fashions, try making hair, trying making shoes. Try making buildings, and see which of these activities they both enjoy and feel they can make a few dollars at. I've had one or two people come to me asking how to make hair, and a few months later they are making bank in jewelry and they write me, 'I hated hair. I am so glad I tried jewelry.'"

In other words, don't be afraid to fail. It's much better to discover early on that you've gone the wrong direction and that you're not having a good time than to put a great deal of time and money into the project and *then* realize that it's not working.

Finding your niche is key, and before you can be successful, you have to be able to identify what you're good at, what you enjoy creating, and ultimately, what gives you the best chance of turning a profit. After all, that's the point of this, right?

"You aren't going to last long if you don't enjoy what you do," Twiddler says. "You don't have to love it but you should test the waters and see what works best for you."

Of course, another component of deciding what business segment to go into is seeing whether you can compete. There is no shortage of people selling ball gowns or boots or that special hat you think you can sell a million of. So if you want to enter an established field, consider how you would be able to raise the bar and innovate. Think about it from a would-be customer's perspective: she has a ton of choices, so why should she choose your products?

Moopf Murray, who has built a successful business selling roller skates and vending machines in *Second Life*, thinks it is possible to enter into a well-established category, but says you must be careful. And most importantly, don't try to underprice the people you're going to compete with.

"I'll only compete with an existing product if I feel that I can substantially push the functionality forward," Moopf says. "There's two reasons for that. It's an accepted fact of life that you don't solely try to compete on price—that's not a strong, unique selling point. And pushing a product substantially forward also makes it more difficult for it to be the subject of competition as the barrier to entry is [now] higher."

It's fine to try to compete for business, but make sure you're clear on how you're going to attract customers, especially those who have developed loyalties to others. So if you're going to make shoes, develop a style that no one has seen before. If you're going to be a land manager, then find a new and beneficial way to meet your customers' needs.

Most important, you won't be able to distinguish yourself if you don't spend a reasonable amount of time researching your would-be competition. It may sound elementary, but *Second Life* is a big place, with hundreds and hundreds of businesses, many of which are hard to find. So, be prepared to spend as much time as it takes—it could be a day, or two days, or more—researching who your competitors are, what they offer, and how often they add new products.

You'll have to divide your research time between *Second Life* itself and the Web. In-world, familiarize yourself with the Search tool and try out different keywords as you look for competition. When you find a competitor you like, don't be afraid to talk to that business's customers about where else they like to shop. And talk to the owner. In *Second Life*, many business owners are happy to share their wisdom with you even though you may soon be trying to steal their business.

Online, meantime, be sure you spend enough time looking at the websites for some of the more-established competitors. Often their sites will showcase many or even all of their products, and that will give you the best sense of what you're going up against.

On the other hand, if you have identified an entirely new genre of *Second Life* business, kudos to you for coming up with an original idea. But although you may not have to compete with anyone directly, you will still need to establish yourself and convince *Second Life* residents that they want to spend their Linden dollars on what you have to offer. That means marketing your products or services, finding the right place to set up shop, producing an always-evolving inventory, and being as responsive to new customers' needs as possible.

But we'll get to these things later. Many chapters in this book discuss marketing techniques tailored to specific business categories, like fashion or building, and Chapter 3, "Developing a Winning Marketing Plan," focuses on general marketing strategies.

CHAPTER 1
CHAPTER 2
CHAPTER 3
CHAPTER 4
CHAPTER 5
CHAPTER 6
CHAPTER 7
CHAPTER 8
CHAPTER 9
CHAPTER 10
CHAPTER 11
APPENDICES
INDEX

DEALING WITH CASH FLOW

It hardly needs to be said that if you're going into business in *Second Life*, you want to make money. And while it's exciting to have a lot of Linden dollars, you probably are going to want to turn at least some of your earnings into cold, hard cash. First, though, you need to know how your money is going to come in and how you'll collect it.

It's fairly simple, though everyone's system varies. Essentially, when you make a sale, you receive the Linden dollars in your *Second Life* account. As sales accumulate, so will your Lindens total. When you're ready to cash out some of the Lindens, the easiest way to do so is through the official *Second Life* currency exchange, the LindeX (see Chapter 1, "The *Meta* of the Metaverse").

RESIDENTS SPEAK

Sol Columbia on Succeeding in Business in *Second Life*

- Don't expect instant success.

- Consistency and just keeping at it will produce results. If you make quality items, you will get noticed and do well. It just takes time.

- To do well in business in *Second Life*, pick a product that people will buy over and over, not just once, such as clothing, hair, skins, and fashion in general. People don't buy a new couch very often, but they buy lots of clothes.

- Get involved in the sector's community in which you have products. Use blogs and advertise in *Second Life* news sites and anywhere people who care about *Second Life* go.

- Don't take each sale too seriously. Remember you're dealing with pennies in most cases. So don't stress, and help customers out as much as you can.

CHAPTER 1
CHAPTER 2
CHAPTER 3
CHAPTER 4
CHAPTER 5
CHAPTER 6
CHAPTER 7
CHAPTER 8
CHAPTER 9
CHAPTER 10
CHAPTER 11
APPENDICES
INDEX

■ TAXES AND ACCOUNTING

Once you open your business and begin earning income, it's time to start keeping good track of the money you bring in. Partly, that's because you'll want to know exactly how much is coming in and how much you're spending, as that's just a good idea in any venture.

But perhaps more importantly, your government is going to want its share of your earnings—all *Second Life* income is taxable—and you'll need to know exactly how much that is.

■ ACCOUNTING

In an economy where many merchants are paid in both US dollars and Linden dollars, it can get somewhat tricky to keep accurate count of your cash flow. Fortunately, the *Second Life* transaction history (`https://secure-web9.secondlife.com/account/`), which you must be logged in to see, will show you every bit of Linden dollar economic activity on your account within the last 45 days (Figure 2.1).

Figure 2.1: Second Life's Transaction History will show you all the purchases and sales you've made within the last 45 days.

SETTLING ON
A BUSINESS
CATEGORY

DEALING WITH
CASH FLOW

TAKING
ADVANTAGE OF
SECOND LIFE'S
AUTOMATED
SYSTEMS

BUSINESS
MODELS:
THE KEYS TO
SUCCESS IN
SECOND LIFE
BUSINESS

It's imperative that you keep track of this data—and that you maintain these records for the future, as well as figure out the US-dollar equivalent of your Linden-dollar transactions. To maintain the highest degree of accuracy, you'll want to track that number at the time of the US-dollar/Linden-dollar exchange in question. And, because only 45 days' worth of transaction history is provided, you must be sure to track the data at least that often.

The transaction history won't, of course, tell you anything about economic activity that takes place outside *Second Life*'s systems—such as US-dollar payments for land rental or for completed custom building projects—so you'll need to stay on top of that history as well.

Many people involved in the *Second Life* economy use PayPal for such transactions, and that's good for a number of reasons, not the least of which is that PayPal can provide you with a recent history of cash flow (Figure 2.2).

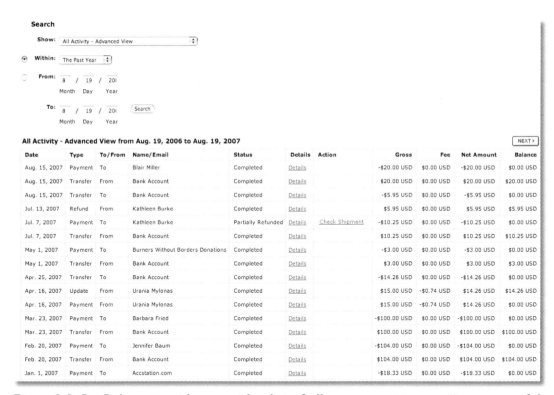

Figure 2.2: PayPal can provide you with a list of all your recent transactions—a useful thing when keeping track of your business's cash flow.

Once you've gathered all your data, you'll need to keep track of it in a way that can show you, at a moment's notice, what's going on economically with your business. How you do that may depend on the complexity of the situation. If it's not all that complicated, then you may be able to use a simple spreadsheet to keep track of sales and income data. If you think a homemade spreadsheet won't cut it, consider using accounting software such as Quicken.

CHAPTER 1
CHAPTER 2
CHAPTER 3
CHAPTER 4
CHAPTER 5
CHAPTER 6
CHAPTER 7
CHAPTER 8
CHAPTER 9
CHAPTER 10
CHAPTER 11
APPENDICES
INDEX

TIP

Many business owners, when they're ready to cash money out, use the LindeX to convert Lindens to US dollars, and then transfer money from the LindeX to a real-world bank account via PayPal.

TAXES

Although running a *Second Life* business revolves around a virtual world and a made-up economy, you need to report your income and expenses—both those that were directly in US dollars and those that were converted from Linden dollars—as self-employment income.

But because U.S.-based *Second Life* publisher Linden Lab won't be sending you a 1099 (non-employee income) form, it's crucial that you keep track of your cash flow as described in the preceding section. Then, when filing your taxes, you will need to report Schedule C, Profit or Loss from Business (Sole Proprietor), income in the United States. In Canada, self-employment income from *Second Life* is reported on lines 135 to 143 of the T1 General Return.

The best way to deal with the taxes may be to use software like TurboTax or H&R Block's online tools. That way, you can simply plug in the numbers you've accumulated with your accounting tools, and the tax software will figure out what you owe or are owed.

TIP

Well-known Second Life builder Foolish Frost suggests setting aside a portion of your income each quarter, say 20 percent, to account for the taxes you will owe. Of course, you'll want to consult a tax professional to figure out the exact numbers, but it's much better to set money aside as you go than have to come up with it all on tax day.

Further, self-employed people in the US must file quarterly taxes. Consult the IRS (in the United States) for more information on quarterly payments (www.irs.gov). In Canada, consult the Canada Revenue Agency (http://www.cra-arc.gc.ca/) for questions related to self-employment and sole proprietorships, or visit the CRA's website on the topic (http://www.cra-arc.gc.ca/tax/business/topics/solepartner/menu-e.html).

Additionally, if you have anyone working for your *Second Life* business, you need to account for their income and report what they made. That means—in the US, at least—

you'll need to send each of them 1099 forms in January stating what they made during the year, and you'll need to report that income to the government.

One complication to all this can be Linden-dollar payments to contractors. For example, many business owners use Linden dollars that come in from sales and pay their employees with those monies. Linden-dollar transactions are not (yet, at least) officially tracked. But to be on the safe side, it's worth reporting that income and those payments to the government, even if you find that you can get away with not doing so.

Finally, if you have people working for you, it's highly probable that some of them will be in other countries. That's another place where a service like PayPal can come in handy. Kim Anubis, for instance, pays her UK contractors through PayPal because it means she gets records of the payments in US dollars, and the contractors get paid in their own currency.

TAKING ADVANTAGE OF *SECOND LIFE'S* AUTOMATED SYSTEMS

Second Life has a number of automated systems, and using them effectively is a necessity for any successful business. So it's in your best interest to understand them, or at least know what they are, from the get-go rather than trying to catch up with them later on.

■ VENDOR SYSTEMS: THE KEY TO EASY SALES

In a sense, a *vendor* (Figure 2.3) is just a functional part of a store. In a real-world store, you would have merchandise displayed on shelves, and a customer would pick up the item they want, take it to the cash register, and the salesperson would ring them up. But in *Second Life*, it's more like shopping on the Web, in the sense that the actual purchase is almost always self-serve. A vendor is the mechanism for that.

There are lots of different styles of vendors, but the bottom line is the most important part: a vendor is a scripted device that displays merchandise or, at the very least, a selection of the names of merchandise, and allows a customer to select an individual item and purchase that item. The vendor script accepts Linden dollars from the customer, deposits them in your account, and then triggers the delivery of the purchased item to the customer's inventory. The final step in that automated process requires the customer to acknowledge that they want to purchase the item and accept receipt of it.

CHAPTER 1
CHAPTER 2

CHAPTER 3
CHAPTER 4
CHAPTER 5
CHAPTER 6
CHAPTER 7
CHAPTER 8
CHAPTER 9
CHAPTER 10
CHAPTER 11
APPENDICES
INDEX

There are many different kinds of vendors. Some are free from places like YadNi's Junkyard, or you can search for them on `http://slexchange.com/` or OnRez (`http://shop.onrez.com`; see the following section). Ultimately, the best idea is to do some comparison shopping and see what features you might want.

A free vendor is likely to be suitable for someone starting out, because it can handle the basic requirements of sales transactions. But what might make a vendor

Figure 2.3: Vendors make it possible for Second Life businesses to sell items automatically, either at one store, or at many.

something you'd want to pay for is better ease of setting up, and also a better experience for your customers. The more you are willing to pay, of course, the more features you're likely to get, and the better it will work for your customers.

Complex vendors might include features like networking, which would allow you to link vendors in multiple stores so that when you want to add new merchandise to your offerings, you have to do it only once from a central location.

But regardless of whether the vendor you use is free or not, you'll need a little know-how to set it up. Most require understanding notecards (which I'll cover in a moment). Many vendors look like an ATM or a computer; they display what looks like a screen where you can see the item, as well as some text describing the item, and some sort of simple interface that lets the customer make their purchase. But many other vendors are simply scripted to attach to what appears as a poster on the wall or to items on a stand.

Ultimately, setting up your stores to sell your products can be time-consuming, and one of the most important elements of that is how you use your vendors. The better the system, the easier it will be to set prices, add items, and make it easy for customers to buy things.

USING SL EXCHANGE AND ONREZ

While a significant amount of your business may well be conducted in your store, you can also hope that your customers will buy your products or services through the two main *Second Life* product aggregators, SL Exchange and OnRez.

Settling on
a Business
Category

Dealing with
Cash Flow

Taking
Advantage of
Second Life's
Automated
Systems

Business
Models:
The Keys to
Success in
Second Life
Business

These services allow *SL* merchants to sell their goods via centralized websites. And because many residents know that they can search for specific kinds of items on these sites, they often choose to do their shopping there rather than visiting store after store in-world. In addition, both services allow merchants to set up in-world kiosks that customers can use to search for the items they want. However, when customers want to buy something, they still need to do so through the websites.

To sell things through SL Exchange or OnRez, first you need to set up a verified account. Then you get a free vendor box from the site. You have to rez it in-world from your inventory and put it in a place where it can stay. So it has to be on your own land, or on a place where you have permission to keep it.

In your free vendor box you place one copy of each item you wish to sell. Once you've done that, you can go back to the SL Exchange or OnRez website and finalize each listing for each item. That means adding a picture and some descriptive text and perhaps a link to your blog, or your own website, if you have one.

However, getting set up to sell on SL Exchange or OnRez is not something you should expect to be able to complete in a day. It's a complex process. Look at their websites for help on how to complete setup, and if you're having trouble, ask for assistance from someone who has succeeded at it. Both services offer in-world help, as well, at their respective headquarters.

■ WORKING WITH NOTECARDS

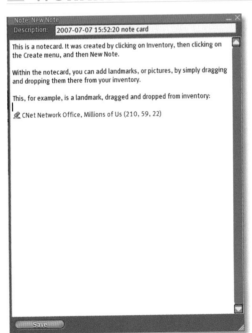

A *notecard* is simply a way of handing out text, as you would a brochure or instructions for something you would sell in the real world. For a *Second Life* store, a notecard might include things like policies, who to contact for customer service, information about other stores you might have, and even images or landmarks (which I'll cover in a moment).

To create a notecard, open your inventory and choose Create ▸ New Note. Once you've created the notecard (Figure 2.4) and saved it, you'll see it show up as a new note in the Notecards folder in your inventory. To rename it, right-click it and choose Rename. To add a notecard to a vendor, drag and drop the notecard into the Inventory folder of the item you're selling.

Figure 2.4: A notecard allows you to explain instructions, policies, and anything else you want to a potential customer.

Again, this is complicated stuff and you will want to experiment with it before opening your store.

CHAPTER 1
CHAPTER 2
CHAPTER 3
CHAPTER 4
CHAPTER 5
CHAPTER 6
CHAPTER 7
CHAPTER 8
CHAPTER 9
CHAPTER 10
CHAPTER 11
APPENDICES
INDEX

◼ USING LANDMARKS

As mentioned previously, you can add landmarks to the notecards that you give your customers. This is important because it allows your customers to look at the notecard days or months after they've received it and see where your store is. Otherwise, they may not be able to remember, and might not be able to find you again. And if that happens, you're losing sales.

It's also worth putting a landmark in the folder the customer gets that contains the item they've bought, in addition to in the notecard, because you can't assume a customer will look at the notecard, much as you can't assume someone is going to read the manual for a product.

Figure 2.5: By adding a landmark to a notecard or an item's inventory folder, you ensure that your customers can find you again.

To create a landmark, go to the exact location where you want people to arrive—whether that's standing in the doorway of your shop facing inward or directly in front of an item that's on sale. Then go to the World pull-down menu and click Create Landmark Here. You'll see the landmark open up on the screen, showing you the option to teleport or show on map (Figure 2.5). But that landmark will also show up in the Landmarks folder of your inventory.

The default name of a landmark is the place name, the sim name, and then the map coordinates, as shown in Figure 2.5. But you can go to that landmark in your inventory and rename it to anything you want. That's a good idea if you want to make it obvious what it is a landmark for, like your store.

You can take that landmark from your Landmarks folder and drag and drop it into the folder of an item you're selling, a notecard, or even a group notice. The latter can be useful for alerting update group members of a sale you're having, for example (see the "Update Groups" section of Chapter 3, "Developing a Winning Marketing Plan").

CHAPTER 2

SETTLING ON
A BUSINESS
CATEGORY

DEALING WITH
CASH FLOW

TAKING
ADVANTAGE OF
SECOND LIFE'S
AUTOMATED
SYSTEMS

BUSINESS
MODELS:
THE KEYS TO
SUCCESS IN
SECOND LIFE
BUSINESS

■ PERMISSIONS

Figure 2.6: This dialogue box allows you to set the permissions for any item you create.

If you make something, you can choose what the next person who gets it can do with it. This is called granting *permissions*, and which permissions you grant can have a big impact on your business.

Permissions govern whether a person can copy, modify, or transfer your creation. For example, if you set permissions for an item to Copy, No Modify, and Transfer, you allow the buyer to copy the item and to transfer it to someone else, but not to modify it.

Since in theory every single avatar in-world can be a different size, people who sell fashion items very often sell them with modify permissions so that buyers can fit the items to their avatars. When you sell something with modify permissions, it's most often paired with copy permissions so that any modifications can be done on a copy, and so that if the buyer makes a mistake in their modification, they can start over.

Increasingly, customers are requesting items to be sold with transfer permissions so they can give them as gifts. For instance, if you're selling statuary or trees for a garden, you might set one price for a tree without copy permissions, and a higher price for the same tree with copy permissions. If you grant copy permissions, people can landscape their whole garden with that one purchase.

Ultimately, the idea is to see what makes the most sense for your item and your store. So look at similar businesses and see how they've set their permissions. It's crucial that you choose the right combination of permissions (Figure 2.6), as it's one of the things customers care the most about, largely because it determines how they can use the item.

WARNING

If you grant copy and transfer permissions for an item, be warned that a buyer can make multiple copies and sell them.

CHAPTER 1
CHAPTER 2

CHAPTER 3
CHAPTER 4
CHAPTER 5
CHAPTER 6
CHAPTER 7
CHAPTER 8
CHAPTER 9
CHAPTER 10
CHAPTER 11
APPENDICES
INDEX

BUSINESS MODELS: THE KEYS TO SUCCESS IN *SECOND LIFE* BUSINESS

Many people think that running a business in *Second Life* is a game, and that it's possible to succeed by just taking a stab at it. Nothing could be further from the truth. In fact, successful *Second Life* businesses are well thought out and often meticulously planned. And the people running them know a great deal about what they're doing.

It's not that they necessarily knew everything going in, of course—many learned a lot along the way. But most successful *Second Life* business owners have a plan, and they follow it. And while every one of those businesses is run differently, there are many similarities that distinguish the successful operations from those that don't make money.

The remainder of this chapter consists of sample business plans from leading entrepreneurs—all of whom earn their full-time living in the virtual world. The business plans cover the four most profitable segments of the *Second Life* economy: fashion, real estate, building, and the adult industry, but the principles can be extended to almost any other field. No matter what your business goals, the four business plans that follow can help you get started.

FASHION: SHIRYU MUSASHI OF MUSASHI-DO

Figure 2.7: Shiryu Musashi's Musashi-Do specializes in men's and women's fashion, often with a Japanese flair.

Shiryu Musashi runs Musashi-Do (Figure 2.7), a leading purveyor of women's and men's fashions. His styles are distinctive—often with a Japanese flavor—and he is known as an innovative designer with a cultured aesthetic. Here is his sample fashion-industry business plan.

1. **Define your target as precisely as possible**. Pick a gender to focus on, an age range, a social group, even a niche, if that's what you find fitting.

Women's fashion has stronger initial sales, but competition is much fiercer. In the men's fashion market it is harder to reach widespread recognition, but it's easier to grab a consistent slice of the market when you get there.

Subcultures [like furries, Goreans, etc.] are also sometimes easier to target, but they require good knowledge of their traditions and styles to succeed, so be prepared if you go that way.

2. Once you've defined your target market it's time to **begin working on your product range**. Initially, try to stick to the style that's most appropriate to that target as strictly as possible. That will help in developing your brand identity and help your customers identify your shop with what they need. It's much easier to remember "X sells tuxedos" than to remember "Y sells clothes." You'll have time to differentiate your range of products later, once your brand identity is settled and solid.

3. Once your initial range of clothes is ready—you'll need at least 10 items before thinking about opening a decently sized shop—you'll need to **set your prices**. This is where your choices about a target social group comes in. If you target oldbies— experienced residents that have been on *Second Life* a while—you'll be able to set higher prices. They have more money available, and are willing to spend a little more [on quality] in dressing their avatars.

Of course, you can target experienced residents and people with a lot of money to spend only if you are very confident in your skills. If you can't offer top quality, then you might want to choose a little lower target and price range until you get better.

4. Now that your inventory is ready, you have to **build and open yourself a shop**. An ideal situation is an already established friend willing to offer a corner in his/her shop. That would give you a big advantage in initial visibility and will make communicating your brand much easier. But that's not always possible, so also think about having to start from scratch.

Avoid placing your first shop in a mall. Malls are too confusing, and even if they can give you an initial spur in visibility, they will choke your brand identity between tens of others, and your recognition will suffer in the long run.

Assuming you're going to start small, get a nice shop space in a good-quality commercial district that fits your target market. First, though, scout them all, and find the one that looks the best to you. It doesn't need to be big, but it has to be nice. Don't be afraid of using lots of time in designing and building your shop; it's very important to offer a nice and pleasant shopping environment to your customers.

Also put your clothes for sale on web portals like SL Exchange and OnRez. They're very good ways to reach customers that don't know you.

5. After your shop opens it's time to **think about marketing**. Many beginning designers think that advertising in *Second Life* isn't needed; that *Second Life* is some sort of marketing heaven in which everyone will notice their talent automatically. This isn't true. *Second Life* is a shark pond in which the competition long ago became extremely fierce. Without the right advertising your brand will not be noticed, and your venture will fail.

Post your grand opening and every product release in the Classified sections of all the *Second Life* forums you can find. Also send copies of your clothes to the owners of *Second Life* fashion-related blogs and magazines. Hopefully they'll notice you and begin blogging and writing about your fashions. That will raise your visibility dramatically.

If you have enough time, start your own blog and subscribe it to a site like Fashion World of SL (`http://fashionplanet.worldofsl.com/`) that aggregates the latest postings of dozens of blogs, then post about every new release in your shop.

When your budget begins to get bigger, you can think about placing paid ads and banners on websites and on fashion-related magazines.

6. **If possible, never photosource**. Paint your clothes yourself. People will recognize your creativity and will reward it. Photosourcing basically means stealing someone else's creativity and using it to earn money. If you avoid that your brand will seem professional and creative. It's not important if initially your painted clothes aren't perfect. They are the fruit of your imagination. This is, basically, what makes you a designer.

CHAPTER 1
CHAPTER 2
CHAPTER 3
CHAPTER 4
CHAPTER 5
CHAPTER 6
CHAPTER 7
CHAPTER 8
CHAPTER 9
CHAPTER 10
CHAPTER 11
APPENDICES
INDEX

■ REAL ESTATE: ADAM ZAIUS OF AZURE ISLANDS ESTATES

Figure 2.8: Azure Islands, which is run by Adam Zaius and Nexus Nash, is one of the biggest real-estate businesses in Second Life.

As the successful co-owner of Azure Islands (Figure 2.8), Adam Zaius is one of the largest land developers in Second Life. Here, Adam shares a basic business plan for setting up and starting a new Second Life real-estate business.

1. **Work out your target market**—niche markets [like Japanese- or Goth-themed] are significantly easier to start in than the main market.

However, niche markets can be small, so the size of your planned estate will strongly influence which markets you should target. You should have been in *Second Life* for at least a few months by now to understand the nature of these niches and all the key factors in running an estate.

2. **Plan out your estate**. If you are designing a larger estate you will likely need some assistance on the art side of things, so make sure to lock down a tight design document that you can hand out to potential contractors. Get at least three quotes and make sure to look at prior work before settling on a designer.

3. **Arrange your finances**. Some credit-card providers do not like carrying large positive balances on credit cards and have issues when processing large payments in these circumstances. The best option for buying land is to use a wire transfer, which Linden Lab is happy to arrange on larger transfers. Create a PayPal account—most users prefer to use PayPal or Linden dollars to pay for their tier fees, and PayPal integration with Linden Lab's billing system allows for some convenience. Having a separate account with your estate's finances makes it easier to track your position and makes taxes and accounting a lot easier to manage.

4. **Go buy some sims**. Find a nice spot on the land store map where there isn't much around. If you cannot find a spot large enough for your planned estate, contact the Linden Lab Concierge and they can arrange an area for you. You will want to take advantage of the reservations system to plan out future growth area and keep your estate isolated from its neighbors.

5. Initially, new sims will take you a while to design or build. When we started it took around seven days to **get each new region designed**. These days it's closer to three hours. I'd probably write off your first month as a miscellaneous expense while you get things built. If you hired contractors to assist you, they should have started before you got your first sims delivered (most of the major ones have their own development regions which they can work in). The average sim delivery can take up to two weeks, so get as much of this done during this time as possible.

6. **Write a covenant** which explains the rules and acts as a terms of service for your estate. It should include information such as when payments are due, how much leeway you give on late payments, and what happens when a payment is late. Make sure to include terms covering removal from the estate for violating said covenant and any kinds of refunds given. It is also worth listing your tier (subscription) prices and support contact details.

7. **Launch.** Put up a classified ad or two and list your estate parcels in the land directory. Keep careful logs of everything that happens for future reference, and make sure to keep a backup of this. Put in place some protections so that if you are incapacitated for a period of time, someone else can take over and manage your estate temporarily.

BUILDING: INSKY JEDBURGH

CHAPTER 1
CHAPTER 2
CHAPTER 3
CHAPTER 4
CHAPTER 5
CHAPTER 6
CHAPTER 7
CHAPTER 8
CHAPTER 9
CHAPTER 10
CHAPTER 11
APPENDICES
INDEX

If you've been around Second Life *for awhile, there's a very good chance you've seen Insky Jedburgh's castles (Figure 2.9) somewhere. Insky sells both prefab and custom castles, and since he began his business, he has become one of the most successful builders in the virtual world. Here's his sample building business plan.*

Figure 2.9: Insky Jedburgh's prefab and custom Gothic castles are well-known throughout Second Life.

1. **Purchase and acquire building supplies**. Before setting out to build, it is good to have a few basics in your inventory to help you make a nice structure.

   The number-one set of items to have is textures. They can make or break the appeal of your builds. You can buy textures at texture stores in *Second Life* or in some cases find free collections online that you can then upload to the virtual world.

   Deciding what style of builds you are going to make will help determine which texture sets you will purchase. One good set is all you need to start. Ideally, it should have wall, floor, ceiling, roof, trim, and door textures all in one set. But often, you will have to find each of those kinds of textures in different sets and match them.

   Other items you may want to consider are door scripts, or prefab doors. Later on, more elaborate things like shower and hot tub systems, pose furniture, etc. might be worth adding. Or, you can create your own.

   Textures and doors should be full permissions (modify/copy/transfer) to allow you to sell your finished product without any problems.

   Finally, for very large builds, it's a good idea to have some kind of rezzing device like Rez-Faux (`http://www.slexchange.com/modules.php?name=Marketplace&file=item&ItemID=65607`) to help you not only rez a huge build, but maneuver it as a whole, and package it for sale.

Settling on
a Business
Category

Dealing with
Cash Flow

Taking
Advantage of
Second Life's
Automated
Systems

Business
Models:
The Keys to
Success in
Second Life
Business

2. **Create some stock to sell**. First, find out what you like building. If you like building a wide range of structures, great, but if you prefer sci-fi, medieval, industrial, or modern, focus on that style, and perfect your skills in that style of design.

Most of all, build something. People will want what you can make once they have seen an example or perhaps bought something from you. Build to match all types of use. Some people will want huge buildings to fill their sim, others will want one that fits a 512-square-meter parcel. A range of building sizes and prim amounts will foster more sales.

3. **Provide information with your products**. People want to know a few things before they buy, and even after they have purchased, your build. I include basic information like how many prims are in my build, what the footprint of it is (like 20x20 square meters), what permissions the purchasers will get (i.e., modify/copy/ no transfer), and of course the price.

For products that come in a rezzer, instructions on setup should be included; instructions for lockable doors are good to include. Often, those products, if made by others, will have instructions you can copy and paste into your own.

I create a notecard with all the info about the build in it. I include pictures, instructions, a landmark to an example of the product or my store, all the stats (prims, footprint, permissions, cost, etc.), and a description of any special features of the build. This notecard will become useful for the next step.

4. **Advertise your builds.** The biggest task of selling what you make is making people aware that it exists. *Second Life* provides a Classified-ad service in the search window. It has a weekly cost, which is L$50 minimum per week. Paying more will get your listing higher up the list, where it might be seen by more people.

There are also marketing websites that will sell your prefabs, like SL Exchange and OnRez. Finally, using your Picks tab in your profile will help people find your prefabs or services.

Using the information from your notecard in the last step can really help in creating ads on all these services.

Any or all of these options will increase your chance of connecting to the right customers, but you need to use them to their fullest advantage. One of the single most effective ways to help people that want your product to find it on the classifieds or market sites is *keywords*. This is basically a list of search terms that people might use to find a product like yours, from descriptive words, to activities, to style. Keywords should be included in the body of your product description text on classified ads, and on marketing websites. Create a section with just a list of words that might attract the searches of your preferred customers.

Any extra attention-grabbers you can add to your advertising, like nice pictures of your products, or even machinima [video made in-world] of your products will help increase the sense of value. Always include at least one picture, as people like to see what they are getting.

5. **Get some land for a store.** Whether you buy it or rent it, having a store and display area is essential for getting people to seriously consider buying your builds. Land should either allow commercial activity or be no-covenant land so that you can sell freely. Even space in a mall for a couple vendors will be a huge aid to selling your product.

   If you set up demonstration models of your builds, do not furnish them unless the furnishings come with the build, since people will often think they are getting more than they actually get when they see so much stuff in a display.

   Have good signage at your store that gives all the critical information, whether that signage is on a vendor, or on prims nearby.

6. **Get a vendor.** If you have a store of any kind, a vendor will be a real help in organizing and selling multiple builds from a single point.

   When you advertise your store, make the landing point near the vendors, or make it obvious where the vendors are in display areas. There are many kinds of vendors you can get; some are stand-alone and contain the products in their local contents. Others are linked to a server—a prim with your products in its contents that updates multiple vendors—so that you can have multiple vendors at different locations selling the same thing. And some are even linked to online market websites like SL Exchange.

   Vendors help streamline your inventorying process, and give your customers an obvious place to make a purchase. Some even allow you to control the vendor network from an online website outside the virtual world.

   As you expand, networked vendors become the obvious choice since making changes to products in the server automatically updates to each of the many vendors you may have out, saving time running around.

7. **Custom builds.** People may want you to design a build for them specifically, and this requires coming to some agreements. Besides having a floor plan you both agree on, you need to establish whether this build will be "one-of-a-kind" or something you can make into a prefab for multiple sales after the job is done.

   One-of-a-kinds should be more expensive to make up for some of the potential extra revenue a prefab would get you. For example, I built Fizzdrake Castle with the understanding that I would be selling copies of the original as prefabs. I sold the copies at a lower price than the original, and at first it seemed not to be making much money.

● SETTLING ON
   A BUSINESS
   CATEGORY

● DEALING WITH
   CASH FLOW

● TAKING
   ADVANTAGE OF
   SECOND LIFE'S
   AUTOMATED
   SYSTEMS

● BUSINESS
   MODELS:
   THE KEYS TO
   SUCCESS IN
   SECOND LIFE
   BUSINESS

But over almost a year, it has made thousands of US dollars in sales. I could never have sold a one-time build for as much money as I have made selling it repeatedly at a lower price.

This should be a factor in your pricing of building services when doing a custom build. When negotiating such a contract you should have clearly established how many prims the buyer wants in the build, how much area it will take up, a basic floor plan you both agree on for the design, and what if any furnishings, etc. will be going into the build at your expense. It is inevitable that as you build they will request new changes to the design, and it requires a fine balancing act to keep those changes and reworks to a minimum and keep your client happy too.

8. **Customer-service policy.** People will have all kinds of issues, from *Second Life* malfunctions wrecking their buildings, to rezzers not being properly used, to them simply trying to modify a prefab and destroying it.

Be prepared to have a customer-service policy to follow up on these kind of things. If you are going to charge for house calls to make repairs, be up-front about the costs and work you will do.

Many people just need information, so have your information notecards ready for that. Include "all sales final," if needed, on all advertising. If you have made a mistake in packing a rezzer or putting a building together, get an update out to your customers as soon as you can. Word of mouth will work wonders for your business, and many people want to know that someone will back them up if they lay down money for a product.

If your buildings appear whole and attractive, people will click on them to see who the creator is, and then click on your profile. That may well be another customer in the making.

■ THE ADULT INDUSTRY: NYTESHADE VESPERIA OF XCITE

Not everyone in Second Life *participates in the adult industry, obviously, but many, many do. And for those who do, Xcite (Figure 2.10) is a household name and one of the leading creators of adult goods. Its co-owner, Nyteshade Vesperia, agreed to share her sample business plan.*

1. **Decide if you *really* want to be in the *Second Life* adult business.** The adult industry is not always a very good place to be. Hazy legal standing, ever-changing Linden Lab policies, social stigma, and outright hostility from certain segments of the population—all these things contribute to making the adult industry something of a minefield that must be trod carefully.

Figure 2.10: Xcite is one of the leading adult-oriented businesses in Second Life, and one of its most profitable ventures.

CHAPTER 1
CHAPTER 2
CHAPTER 3
CHAPTER 4
CHAPTER 5
CHAPTER 6
CHAPTER 7
CHAPTER 8
CHAPTER 9
CHAPTER 10
CHAPTER 11
APPENDICES
INDEX

If you want to be successful, the adult industry is as good a place as any to be. If you want to be famous, you might want to choose a more socially acceptable market.

2. **Have something worth selling.** It sounds obvious, but apparently it's not. The adult industry is chock-full of people who simply build what other people are already building, or who outright steal other people's ideas and figure by underselling they will get ahead. They certainly may make some sales, but all they will ever be is a knockoff.

If you want to succeed you need to own your market, and that means coming up with an idea that fills a previously unserved niche, or creating a new market and then serving it. Adding to an already flooded market will not get your brand recognized and will ultimately be a waste of your time and resources.

3. **Get Organized.** Take a moment to realistically look at what your talents and abilities are and determine where your energies will be best spent, and where you may need some help.

Does your planned product or service involve programming? Graphic design? A special sales methodology? If you can't fill all of your own needs, get some help and get it early.

Also be realistic about your time commitment to this project, as well as the time commitments of any partners you may have. Your success may require you to dedicate a significant amount of time, energy, and resources—so, do you have them to give?

Finally, do not think that your business ends with simply making product. Customer service can make or break your business's reputation, so will you have the resources to handle it?

A solid infrastructure, such as sales tracking, expenses tracking, vendor technology, customer communication paths, etc. may mean the difference between fast, easy solutions and a lot of extra work. Know what your business is going to need at every step of the way and don't set yourself up to get overwhelmed or caught off-guard.

4. **Build It.** Design it, build it, refine it, test it, test it again, beta-test it—no, *you* cannot beta-test your own items—fix it, and test it again. Just do what it takes to get it right.

Keep good revision notes at each stage to save yourself trying to rethink your steps later. Set goals and stay on target. Don't get sidelined by shiny nifty new projects that ultimately will only distract you.

Finally, have a development list that makes sense given your abilities and resources. Know where you are going before you get there—control your path; don't be led down it.

5. **Buy some land.** Building your brand should be your focus, and one of the best ways to do that in *Second Life* is to build a presence with which your brand will be associated. This can only really be done effectively on your own land, over which you have creative and security control.

Land ownership also allows you to list your business in the Search tool with keywords of your own choosing, and can be the staging point for events and activities that will draw interest to your products.

It is generally a good idea to supplement your main store with well-placed vendors in a variety of targeted locations around the grid. But using these alone does very little for building your brand's identity and gives you very little control over your business's destiny.

And don't get suckered into renting or leasing land. If you don't own the land you don't control it, and don't let anyone tell you differently. Once you have some land, take as much care in building your shop as you did building your product. A shop is not just a place to sell your items. It's a place to tell your story, to interface with customers, and is a physical representation of yourself and your brand even when you aren't online.

6. **Advertise**. Even a minimal amount of targeted marketing will give most *Second Life* entrepreneurs an advantage given that the landscape is filled with people who have no idea what effective marketing really is, or how it can help them.

Do what it takes to get your brand name out and repeated. There are quite a few advertising avenues available to the *Second Life* business, but the best by a long shot is good old-fashioned word of mouth. Take the time and effort to get to know who your customers are and how to get your message out to them.

CHAPTER 3

DEVELOPING A WINNING MARKETING PLAN

From building a brand to choosing where to put a store to using the Classifieds, forums, and blogs, this chapter covers what can help any *Second Life* business owner attract—and keep—customers. While Chapters 4 through 9 cover marketing techniques specifically applicable to the many different areas of the *Second Life* economy, this chapter discusses marketing methods that work generally across the board.

CONTENTS

CHOOSING WHERE TO SET UP SHOP

Not everyone who operates a *Second Life* business needs to have a storefront in-world, but most will. For those who do, it's crucial to select the proper place to set up shop and determine how much land is required, whether to buy or rent that land, and how much to pay for it.

The two top-level choices for where to set up are the mainland and on an island. Each has its own set of advantages and disadvantages. One of the advantages of being on the mainland is that there's likely to be more foot traffic wandering through naturally, as people tend to pick a spot on the mainland and then just go prowling around. On islands, people tend to teleport in, check things out, wander a little bit, and then move on. On the other hand, it's much, much harder to control your surroundings on the mainland because it is much more like urban sprawl and because Linden Lab is not adding much new land there.

Islands offer the ability to either have space entirely to yourself or to share it with a small number of people. You're much less likely to have an unknown neighbor on your border doing who knows what and who you may find to be an ongoing annoyance.

There are plenty of other things to consider as well. You have to think about what you want from your immediate surroundings. If you want a quiet area where your shop will be the focus of attention, then you probably want to look for space on an island. If you want to take advantage of foot traffic from other businesses, it might make sense to look for space in the middle of a shopping district because residents tend to walk around and browse shops to see what's available. In that case, it matters less whether you're on an island or the mainland, just whether you can find a spot around similar merchants.

To take advantage of residents wandering from shop to shop in commercial districts, first-time business owners will be best off putting a store in a high-traffic area. The caveat is that you must think carefully about what kind of shopping district it is (Figure 3.1). Shopping districts can vary significantly in style and tone, which can make a difference in the type of would-be customers who wander by.

"If you're selling adult toys and can find a plot right next to an adult store or a brothel, that's fantastic," said Sabrina Doolittle, owner of the furniture emporium Chez Petite. The same wouldn't hold true, on the other hand, if your products have nothing at all to do with sex.

From Sabrina's perspective, it doesn't matter where your shop is, so long as you can place it in the right environs. She cautions to be as careful as possible about looking before you choose.

Figure 3.1: By putting your store in a shopping district or mall, you give yourself a better chance of higher foot traffic.

There are a million different places to pick from, and although locale isn't the most important factor to consider, it is certainly one of them.

Sabrina also says there's a lot of value in putting your business near others because many customers will follow a Classified ad to one store and then walk across the street to see what else is around. It's a great way to pick up extra business and works well if your store is attractive.

TO RENT OR OWN; THAT IS THE QUESTION

Once you've decided to open a store, you have to decide whether you're going to buy the land to put it on or rent it. The primary advantage of renting is that it's easier. You simply find a land owner who has property you want, figure out the right piece of land, make a deal, and voilà. You don't have to deal with the complications of paying tier—or maintenance fees—to Linden Lab, though you will have to make regular rent payments to the land owner. Also, you don't have to deal with any of the management issues related to owning. Your landlord should take care of all problems.

However, renting on the mainland has a serious downside—one that's not necessarily found on islands. Renting means you won't be the deeded owner of the land and, therefore, you won't show up in resident searches made using the *Second Life* Find ▶ Places tool. That tool, which is available via the Search button, allows users to look for locations, but only deeded locations show up. On islands, however, landlords can hand over the deed to the renter, which means that stores on such property would show up in a search.

Another consideration when deciding where to put your shop and how much space to use is how many prims—the fundamental building blocks of *Second Life*—you need. There's no direct formula for figuring out how many prims various objects take, but it's something you need to learn, as you will not be able to exceed the prim limit for your space. The more space you have, the more prims you can use.

CHAPTER 3

CHOOSING
WHERE TO
SET UP SHOP

MAKING AN
IMPRESSION

GETTING
THE MOST
OUT OF
CLASSIFIED
ADS

BLOGGING
YOUR WAY
TO BUSINESS

POSTING ON
THE FORUMS

SUCCESSFUL
SECONDARY
ADVERTISING

GETTING
BIGGER AND
MOVING UP

Sometimes, residents end up getting adjacent plots of land because it's possible to combine prim limits between two pieces of land owned by a single person.

Table 3.1: Prim Limits

LAND PARCEL	PARCEL SIZE	MAXIMUM NUMBER OF PRIMS
Full region	65,536 m2	15,000
1/2 region	32,768 m2	7,500
1/4 region	16,384 m2	3,750
1/8 region	8,192 m2	1,875
1/16 region	4,096 m2	937
1/32 region	2,048 m2	468
1/64 region	1,024 m2	351
1/128 region	512 m2	117

Some business owners can start on the smallest piece of land—512 square meters, or one 1/128 of a region. As their business grows, they grow the amount of space they need. Figuring out how you will display your product if you have a store is a good way to understand how what prim limits you need. Experts like Sol Columbia have figured out that one of the best way to save prims—and also a great way to display products like clothing or smaller items—is to put up lots of pictures of your products around your store, tastefully and prominently displayed. The advantage of this approach is that customers can easily see what you're selling, and it requires fewer prims than actually putting the products themselves on display. Many fashion boutiques in *Second Life* follow this method.

If you're selling things like furniture, cars, plants, homes, or large decorations that customers will want to try out on the spot or see in their actual size, you'll need to have display models. To do so will take more prims, and you'll likely need to have a somewhat higher prim limit.

MORE INFO

THE "SHOTGUN" APPROACH OR A SHARPER FOCUS?

Sol Columbia, the co-owner of the store Luminosity, thinks there are two real estate strategies for setting up an initial business.

"You could rent lots of mall spaces, and put down stores all over. This is the 'shotgun' approach," says Sol. "Or you can do one better, well-done store and use advertising by doing lots of Classifieds."

The approach you choose just depends on your desire. The shotgun approach likely means less work initially, because each shop could be more or less a copy of the first. However, it might take longer to develop a strong customer base.

CHAPTER 1
CHAPTER 2
CHAPTER 3

CHAPTER 4
CHAPTER 5
CHAPTER 6
CHAPTER 7
CHAPTER 8
CHAPTER 9
CHAPTER 10
CHAPTER 11
APPENDICES
INDEX

MAKING AN IMPRESSION

If you happened to wander into the clothing boutique Luminosity on Luminous Island, the first thing that might strike you is that the store just looks good. You immediately get a feeling that you're in a shop run by a professional, that you're going to find what you need there, and that you'll get the service you require. Never mind that Luminosity is a *Second Life* business, the brainchild of Sol Columbia and Lur Sachs, and not a fancy Rodeo Drive establishment. It almost doesn't matter because, inside and out, its presentation is top notch: It makes you just want to wander around, browsing for what's new, for hours.

Figure 3.2: Visitors to Luminosity are instantly impressed with how well the store is laid out and how professional it looks.

Of course, that's exactly the kind of environment that transforms browsers into customers. They feel comfortable and at ease, and that makes them want to open their purse strings. Luminosity is an example of a *Second Life* business that seems to have found the right formula for attracting customers, keeping them around, and getting them to return again and again (Figure 3.2).

Naturally, Sol and Lur didn't just show up in *Second Life*, decide to start Luminosity one day, and open its doors the next. Rather, they took it slowly, built organically, and learned as they went—just like any real-world business owners would.

■ MAKING A NAME FOR YOURSELF

The names of *Second Life* businesses are as diverse and varied as the people who run them. You've got names like ASpiRE!, Taunt, BabyDoll's, Armord (Figure 3.3), Dominus Motor Corporation and Sweet Leaf Creations. They're sometimes catchy, sometimes indicative of their corresponding businesses, and sometimes neither.

Figure 3.3: To many longtime Second Life residents, just the tall black-and-green towers of Armord are enough to recall the store's brand.

The point is that although a commanding business name may well stick in residents' memories, it is not the be-all, end-all that some would have you believe. That's not to say you shouldn't try to come up with a name that people will remember. But when you're thinking of a catchy name, also think about how that name relates to your business. "Skin Deep" is both memorable and implies a connection to avatar skins. Be careful with what you choose. The name will stick with your business for a long time.

BUILDING CUSTOMER LOYALTY

Figure 3.4: Sabrina Doolittle's Chez Petite specializes in low-prim furniture.

According to Sabrina Doolittle (Figure 3.4), your first worry shouldn't be the name of your business. It should be the quality of your products.

She explained that one store she had visited wasn't memorable for its name or even for the way it looked. In fact, she said, the store itself was ugly, looking like a children's nursery. Yet the owner of this store had a large roster of loyal customers who return again and again because they like her products. Naturally, Sabrina wasn't touting the ugly store/good products approach. Instead, she was making the point that impressing visitors with what you can offer them matters hugely in *Second Life*, because word of mouth is more powerful there than just about any other form of information sharing.

CHAPTER 1
CHAPTER 2
CHAPTER 3

CHAPTER 4
CHAPTER 5
CHAPTER 6
CHAPTER 7
CHAPTER 8
CHAPTER 9
CHAPTER 10
CHAPTER 11
APPENDICES
INDEX

Figure 3.5: When Elikapeka Tiramisu's ETD shop releases a new product, dozens of customers are sometimes waiting outside to be among the first to buy it.

Although there are many popular designers of clothing, furniture, shoes, buildings, and the like, there's no Jimmy Choo or Manolo Blahnik, designers whose products everyone just has to have to feel special. But loyalty can be visceral. It's common that when a top fashion designer like Elikapeka Tiramisu (Figure 3.5) closes her shop to update her store's inventory, she'll have dozens of customers standing and waiting nearby when she re-opens.

"Brand comes from the loyalty of your customers," Sabrina says. "There will be a mob of 35 women waiting to walk in. These people are seriously loyal, and there are any number of retailers who have that loyalty."

Clearly, that kind of loyalty is something to shoot for, because it almost guarantees repeat customers, regardless of what your business is.

RESIDENTS SPEAK

MOOPF MURRAY ON BUILDING CUSTOMER LOYALTY

- Research your competition and ensure that what you offer compares well with that [market's] competition.

- Don't compete solely on price. It's never a good unique selling point. Be aware that prices for similar items in *Second Life* vary wildly.

- Ensure that your store looks professional. It's the first thing many prospective customers will see, so make sure it's polished and well-organized. First impressions count a lot.

- Be prompt, courteous, and helpful with your customer service, no matter how stupid or ridiculous your support or pre-sales questions are. They may be stupid or ridiculous to you, but they won't feel that way to the people asking them.

- Think carefully about quality of product rather than quantity. A quality product will have a much longer shelf life and be more likely to be successful.

CHAPTER 3

Choosing
Where to
Set Up Shop

Making an
Impression

Getting
the Most
Out of
Classified
Ads

Blogging
Your Way
to Business

Posting on
the Forums

Successful
Secondary
Advertising

Getting
Bigger and
Moving Up

So how can you start to build loyalty, right from the get-go? There are several ways to head in that direction.

The best thing to do is to develop great products, right off the bat. The better your stuff is, the more people will want to come back. Of course, it's hard to know what is going to resonate, so that's something that you'll have to learn over time. But if you concentrate on making things that are of the highest quality possible, it's a good start.

Although business in real life often precludes going to competitors for feedback, *Second Life* is different. If you are new and sensitive to other people's needs to focus on their own things, most will talk to you. It's commonplace for those in the same business to turn to each other for feedback on what they're creating. As a resource, your peers will be able to see, much more quickly than most residents, what works and what doesn't about your products. You can win them over by giving them review copies of your creations, something that won't cost you anything but that will demonstrate your generosity.

RESIDENTS SPEAK

HIRO PENDRAGON ON BUILDING CUSTOMER LOYALTY

Hiro Pendragon is one of Second Life's most accomplished developers, and he makes swords that are well known in the community. He is now a principal at Infinite Vision Media, a large developer of Second Life projects for corporate clients. If Hiro knows one thing, it's how to keep customers happy.

- **Your products need to be new or the highest quality, or both. You're either the first or the best.**

- **Respond to all of your customers' instant messages. If you can't, hire managers who can.**

- **Fix your products if they break from a *Second Life* patch. Support your products.**

- **Eat your dog food. I wear my swords. I like my swords.**

- **Thank your customers and make them feel special, either with notecards or freebies.**

Beyond ensuring that you're creating high-quality products, there are other things you can do to foster customer loyalty.

Figure 3.6: A shop bell allows a store owner to be elsewhere in Second Life. When rung, it sends an instant message to the owner or another store worker.

As Moopf Murray says, good customer service is key. At the very least, you want to be as responsive as is possible, answering questions whenever you can and operating on a solid "the customer is always right" philosophy. Truthfully, isn't that how you'd like to be treated? Even if you spend only a couple hours a day logged in, you should try to be available for questions most of the day. *Second Life* allows you to receive instant messages sent from in-world at your email address. The advantage of this is that your customers can IM you whenever they need to and you can—especially if you link your email to your mobile phone—see those messages at any time of the day. Another option is a "shop bell" (Figure 3.6), which can be installed in any store or business. If you're online, the bell alerts you when it's pressed, allowing you to teleport back to your store to talk to whoever pressed it. This L$35 item, available from Robbie Dingo or through SL Exchange, gives you a way to be much more responsive to customer requests for help.

Another thing that helps, assuming you are not the only one running or working for your store, is to install a board showing everybody involved and whether they're online. This feature lets customers know who they can get in touch with if they have a question and is a nice touch, given that many stores in *Second Life* don't offer such a thing.

The point here is to get noticed, as soon as possible, for having both great products and great customer service. One is worth a whole lot less without the other. But let's assume for a second that you do have products people will line up for and you offer stellar customer service. There's still more you can do to build the loyalty that leads to repeat customers and then to money coming in consistently.

UPDATE GROUPS

One important way to build loyalty is to follow the lead set by real-world supermarkets, casinos, and hotels: Create a loyalty club. In *Second Life*, that takes the form of an update group (Figure 3.7). When customers join your group, you give them special treatment going forward.

Figure 3.7: An update group allows you to automatically alert your members about new or updated products.

At the very least, they get a notice whenever you have a new product. You also can offer free trials of your products or special deals, or whatever it is that you can think of that makes them feel like you're earning their loyalty. It's well worth the cost of giving away some free product and taking time out of your day to cater to these customers because when they're happy, they're going to tell their friends—and that just means more money for you.

EVENTS WITH FREEBIES

Another technique that many successful *Second Life* business owners tout is throwing events at your store or on your land, with the aim of bringing potential new customers in who you can then impress and, hopefully, convince to come back in the future. One way to impress them and build some instant loyalty is to give out free copies of your products. Doing so can very easily make residents happy because everyone in *Second Life* likes to get things for free, and it costs you nothing because there are no additional costs of production once you've created something. By giving out freebies, you're gaining goodwill with your visitors and showing them the kinds of products they could be buying from you in the future. So be sure the freebies you give out are high quality and unique to your business.

Saturday, June 30, 2007

Add Event   Category: All

Time	Event	Host
8:00PM	OVERDRIVE GRAND OPENING...2000L to give away	Cookie Munro
8:00PM	12 Free Business in a Box sets	Sarina Georgette
8:00PM	Mischief Cove - Tip Jar Class	Betty Curry
8:00PM	FREE MONEY ! FREE LINDENS ! CAMPING ! HIPPIEPAY ! MYLINDE...	Jay Mahoney
8:00PM	~*~ Club Xstasie ~*~	Anesthasia Lyon
8:00PM	OVERDRIVE GRAND OPENING...2000L to give away	Cookie Munro
8:00PM	2000L give away. Launch party	Cookie Munro
8:00PM	***Zyngo! L$25,000 - 10 Ways to WIN!!***	Paulie Sputnik
8:00PM	Sploder Madness	Seth Newman
8:00PM	Formal event at Atlantic Waves	Sue Saintlouis
8:00PM	PARTY MUSIC, FREE MONEY & JOBS	Precious Messmer
8:00PM	Saturday Night's All Right for Fighting	Nachtengel Reisler
8:00PM	YARD SALE AND FREEEEEEEBIES	Sara Lukas
8:00PM	**MASSIVE YARD SALE** CLUB STUFF COUPLES DANCES NEW HUDS ...	Alberta Cao
8:00PM	(((ADULT POSEBALLS, FURNITURE POSEBALLS-ANIMATED)))	mantras Jie
8:00PM	Tringo@Sam's w/Sam!!!	Samblue Dougall
8:00PM	Tarot Group Forming!	Scarlett Qi
8:00PM	LAND FOR SALE EXOTIC ISLAND	Kristina Rosca
8:00PM	Mythica Writer Live at the swank Lounge	Distilled1 Rush

Figure 3.8: Posting to Second Life's official live events calendar allows anyone looking for something to do to find your gathering.

CHAPTER 1
CHAPTER 2
CHAPTER 3
CHAPTER 4
CHAPTER 5
CHAPTER 6
CHAPTER 7
CHAPTER 8
CHAPTER 9
CHAPTER 10
CHAPTER 11
APPENDICES
INDEX

Exactly what kind of event you throw doesn't matter, as long as you make an effort to ensure that a number of people show up. When planning your event, tell as many people as you can think of about it, consider hiring a DJ or some other form of entertainment and, if you've got an update group, be sure to send out a notice informing the members. Additionally, you may want to post the event on the official *Second Life* events calendar (Figure 3.8).

To do that, go to the events section of the *Second Life* website (www.secondlife.com/events/), click Add Event, log in, read and agree to the event listing rules, and then fill out the form. Be sure to list the correct date and time (in *Second Life* time) and the location. If you're going to be hosting an event, it's a good idea to get it on the calendar as soon as you can. Either way, the advantage of listing it is that anyone perusing the calendar looking for something to do can come across your event and choose to attend, even if they've never heard of you before. Do your best to make it sound compelling.

ALWAYS INNOVATE

To Twiddler Thereian, the most important factor in the success of your business is constantly introducing new, high-quality products. He calls it "nine out of ten important." The idea is to produce new content regularly and, in the process, develop a following. It's hard work and requires a regular schedule and a determination to be coming out with something new every day or every few days like clockwork. But it can pay off in a customer base that is always ready to stop by and see what is new.

"If you look at some of the more successful merchants in *Second Life*, a high percent of them are two years old," says Twiddler. "One of the reasons they are doing well is that they have been producing excellent products for 18 months to 24 months and have stores jam-packed with selection and choices. The more you produce, the better you will do, especially in the beginning. Customers want new products and they want choices."

CHAPTER 3

CHOOSING
WHERE TO
SET UP SHOP

MAKING AN
IMPRESSION

GETTING
THE MOST
OUT OF
CLASSIFIED
ADS

BLOGGING
YOUR WAY
TO BUSINESS

POSTING ON
THE FORUMS

SUCCESSFUL
SECONDARY
ADVERTISING

GETTING
BIGGER AND
MOVING UP

GETTING THE MOST OUT OF CLASSIFIED ADS

The most basic form of *Second Life* marketing is using keywords tied to Classified ads. That way, when someone does a search for the kind of thing you're selling, they can find you. Sabrina Doolittle thinks classifieds are one of the less-well utilized marketing methods in *Second Life*, yet are a valuable system for luring new customers.

The *Second Life* Classifieds system is essentially an auction for placement in a list of competing ads that will come up when a resident does a keyword search. The more you bid for your keywords, the higher they will appear in the list of results. Bidding starts at L$50 per week, and can go much, much higher.

To place an ad, click on the Search button in *Second Life*. Do this when you're at your store or business, because it will assume that the ad is for the place where you are when you create the ad.

Then click on the Classifieds tab, press the Place an Ad button, click New, choose OK, and then fill in a title and the text for your ad. Next, choose a category: shopping, land rental, property rental, etc. Then hit Publish, and the tool will prompt you about how much you want to pay for your ad. The more you pay, the higher it will be placed in the listings (Figure 3.9).

Though you can spend a lot on Classifieds, Sabrina recommends starting small, with maybe a series of L$50 keyword purchases. But she says it's crucial to not be too generic. If you're selling shoes, for example, don't just use the keyword *shoes*, because anyone searching on that term will get hundreds of results. Instead, focus in. So, for example, *green stilettos* would likely bring your business to the top of the search results—assuming you're selling green stilettos.

"Use very specific keyword phrases," Sabrina says. "I guarantee you'll see a return on your investment. If one person is searching for green stilettos, you'll have made your money back on a customer you wouldn't have had otherwise."

The idea is to think of all the different keywords that could plausibly be used to describe what your business is, and buy as many of them as you can afford. Don't pay too much for them, particularly if you're using phrases that few others are using, because they will rise to the top regardless. On the other hand, if you want to use a common phrase, you'll likely have to pay more to get your advertisement placed higher in the listings. Also think about ways that you can tie your keywords and products to holidays, special events, and the like. For example, around Valentine's Day, if you introduce some especially romantic products and buy keywords that are linked somehow to love or romance or sexiness, there's a good chance someone will try searching for those words and then find you. Just like that, more business.

Figure 3.9: Purchasing a Classified ad increases the odds that residents can find you when they use the Second Life search tool.

Another approach is to put your eggs in a smaller number of baskets and bid high for your keywords, which essentially ensures that you will get higher-placed results. The payoff may well be worth the extra investment. It may take you some time to figure out how to make the Classifieds system work for you. But, given that it can be pretty cheap to buy simple keywords, it's worth a bit of trial and error.

"The best thing you can do is test, test, and test again," says Twiddler Thereian. "Use as many keywords as you can think of that apply to your product. But don't use words that don't apply because you will end up with cranky customers."

Twiddler also says that one way of testing the effectiveness of your keywords is to buy a low-priced keyword and then check the teleport count. That's a method where you can see how many people have actually teleported to your store or business after reading your ad. To see this count, after you have ads running, go into the Classifieds tool, as described previously, click on Place an Ad, and you'll see all your ads. If you click on any individual ad, you'll see the current teleport count.

"Because of the great tracking online and in-world, test, test, and test some more," Twiddler repeats. "Try new things, check the stats, and keep dialing your business in."

CHAPTER 1
CHAPTER 2
CHAPTER 3
CHAPTER 4
CHAPTER 5
CHAPTER 6
CHAPTER 7
CHAPTER 8
CHAPTER 9
CHAPTER 10
CHAPTER 11
APPENDICES
INDEX

BLOGGING YOUR WAY TO BUSINESS

If you really hope to get anywhere with your business, you'd better be prepared to start blogging. By that, I mean blogging regularly. There is a huge *Second Life* blogging ecosystem, and within the various genres of *Second Life* business—fashion, land, vehicles, and the like—the bloggers and many of your potential customers voraciously read and link to each other. So, by participating in this network, you can quickly and without too much effort build up significant brand-name recognition. There are several approaches to blogging, but to be successful you must be committed to putting up new content regularly and religiously, just like you should be doing with new products.

According to Moopf Murray, you shouldn't count on getting that audience just by blogging about your products, although you certainly want to post any time you have something new available. It's hard to get noticed at first, but the best way to do so is to start blogging about your general *Second Life* observations, especially those related to the kind of business you're running.

"It's difficult to get the eyeballs to your own blog, especially one that just talks about your new products," says Moopf. "So it's important to keep people reading by blogging about other issues of more general interest."

If you are running a custom car business, for example, try blogging about your experiences in *Second Life* related to others' cars as well as your own. Include other kinds of related observations that will interest readers. Anything that gets people reading your blog makes it more likely that they will want to do business with you. You'll also need to read the other *Second Life* blogs about your kind of business to stay informed about the latest trends, gather fodder for your own entries, and help you become better educated about where your business might go. You'll want to use your own blog as a way to keep a (hopefully) wide audience apprised of what you're thinking about and doing.

Ultimately, what matters is the content. In addition to keeping readers apprised of your thoughts and observations related to your type of business, your blog is also a fantastic way to let your existing and would-be customers know about your new products. Ideally, any time you have a new product to sell, you'd make a post about it. Since you're going to offer an RSS feed, anyone who subscribes will instantly know that you've got something new. If you think about it from the customer's perspective, you can see that that is a terrific way of advertising that costs nothing except a little bit of your time.

DEALING WITH RSS FEEDS AND BLOGGING SOFTWARE

It's difficult to always be looking for new postings on a lot of other peoples' blogs, but a good solution is to start using an **RSS** reader to keep up with all the blogs about your field. They're usually free or cheap, and you can subscribe to as many blogs as you want—as long as they offer **RSS** feeds. If they do, they'll have an **RSS** or **XML** button that you can click to subscribe. Then, each time those blogs have new postings, you'll be notified via your **RSS** reader. It's a fantastic way to manage what can be an otherwise unmanageable flow of information.

There are many options for blogging software. Google's Blogger (`www.blogger.com`) software is free and fairly easy to use. Many *Second Life* bloggers are using Wordpress (`wordpress.org`) because it offers more features. If your traffic justifies it, you should consider moving to a premium Wordpress account to get more control over the templates that govern the way your blog looks.

No matter which software you choose, it's crucial to offer an **RSS** feed. Just as you can use the feeds to keep up with others' blogs, if you offer **RSS**, others can easily keep up with what you're doing.

As you set up your blog, you should consider whether you want a more traditional website, as well. The chief advantage is that you can maintain an exhaustive list of product or service offerings, including pictures, pricing, colors, sizes, etc., which is very useful for would-be customers, particularly if they're searching on the Internet rather than in *Second Life*. If you're well versed in designing and building websites, this is a good way to go and will probably be fruitful. If this isn't a skill you have, you may want to skip this part, as you will either have to put in a great deal of time getting going or have to pay someone else do it for you. For someone just starting a *Second Life* business, it may not be cost effective.

NOTE

Unlike websites for regular online businesses, there's no simple way to actually sell your Second Life *products or services on your own website. Thus, one key advantage—and in fact, necessity—of having a full-fledged site is absent for* Second Life *businesses.*

POSTING ON THE FORUMS

Another good way to get your business or new products in front of large numbers of *Second Life* residents is to post in the official forums. To read or post to the forums, you need to sign in. Once you've done that, you'll see that there is a section just for Classifieds that is used specifically for marketing purposes: `http://forums.secondlife.com/forumdisplay.php?f=107`. This section has subsections for shopping, land sales and rentals, property sales and rentals, and an entire subsection for new products.

Using the forums is crucial, many business owners say, because bloggers and many residents read them regularly, looking for things to write about or new products to check out. Thus, if you use the forums wisely, you have a free method to reach the most influential residents and bloggers with hardly any effort. As always, if you're going to use the forums for these purposes, you need to be sure you're ready for whatever onslaught of people may come. Be certain your store is ready, your products are in order and are high quality, and that you can handle any customer service issues that might arise.

SUCCESSFUL SECONDARY ADVERTISING

One more important and lucrative way to build and sustain a business in *Second Life* is placing ads in one or more of the many popular blogs or *Second Life*-specific publications or product aggregators. Placing an ad on a blog can be a very efficient way to build business, especially in the fashion industry, says Sabrina Doolittle. "For people marketing things for avatar vanity, like clothing, shoes, skins, and hair," says Sabrina, "the clickthrough rates can be as high as 10 percent, which is extraordinarily high."

The key is to research the best blogs in your niche. It may take some time, but once you find the right ones, putting together a small ad could pay quick and lucrative dividends.

WARNING

It's important not to pick a blog in the wrong category to advertise on, as you will get poor response and you will seem a bit amateurish. Pick and choose wisely to get the most bang for your buck.

CHAPTER 1
CHAPTER 2
CHAPTER 3
CHAPTER 4
CHAPTER 5
CHAPTER 6
CHAPTER 7
CHAPTER 8
CHAPTER 9
CHAPTER 10
CHAPTER 11
APPENDICES
INDEX

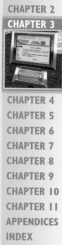

Figure 3.10: An SL Exchange terminal allows residents to search for products for sale. OnRez provides a similar service.

Another valuable place to advertise is on one or both of the major product marketplace sites, SL Exchange (www.slexchange.com; Figure 3.10) and OnRez (http://shop.onrez.com). Both of these sites are basically huge databases of what's available from hundreds of *Second Life* businesses, arranged by categories, such as avatars, body parts, buildings, clothing, fashion, furniture, and more. These sites allow anyone to list items for sale, commission-free. Because both are extremely popular with residents, it's a great way to reach a broad audience.

It's also worth considering whether to advertise in *Second Life* publications like the *Metaverse Messenger* (www.metaversemessenger.com). Although this Web-only newspaper doesn't have a giant circulation, its readers are committed *Second Life* residents who are more likely than most to respond to ads they see. *The Second Life Herald* (www.secondlifeherald.com) is another, as is *Second Style* (www.secondstyle.com). The good thing about these publications, from an advertiser's point of view, is that they should be able to give you statistics on your ads. Those statistics allow you to get a pretty good idea of how well your ads are doing so that you can decide whether to continue using a specific ad in a specific publication or whether to try something different.

One factor to consider when determining whether your ad is paying off is how much it costs. Each publication has its own rates, and you should be aware of the going rates so you don't pay too much. Each site should have a section devoted to ad rates. Check a few to see what a fair rate is. For example, full-page ads in the *Metaverse Messenger* and *Second Style* run L$7,000 and L$9,000, respectively. A horizontal banner in *The Second Life Herald* costs L$6,000 a week or L$22,500 per month.

GETTING BIGGER AND MOVING UP

Expanding your business almost always means moving locations. Unless you have a whole island or a significant amount of one that you're not using yet, it's not very likely that you'll be able to get an adjacent piece of land at fair market prices to the one you have already. If your neighbors know you're planning on expanding, they're not likely to sell to you without driving the price way up. So, moving somewhere else entirely is the best way to get the land you need at a fair price. Moving isn't that big a deal, but it is probably worth keeping your original plot of land for a month or so—and thus paying double rent for that period—so that you can put up a sign informing customers who are used to just dropping by where you've gone.

As your business gets bigger, you'll also have to think even more about prims and make sure that you're working within your limits. Sabrina has made a business out of this by selling low-prim furniture that caters to residents running up against those limits.

Many people discount how important marketing is to a business's success. *Second Life* is crowded with businesses and competition is tough. Thus, you have to find ways to make your business and your products or services stand out, and quality in and of itself may not be enough.

CHAPTER 4

WALKING THE RUNWAY—FASHION IN SECOND LIFE

Fashion in *Second Life* is big. Really big. It's the single biggest segment of the virtual world's economy, and no wonder: There are countless thousands of residents for whom the most fun thing to do is to dress up in outlandish, fantastical outfits. And since fashion includes more than just clothing, it is a nearly limitless industry whose most successful entrepreneurs are the real celebrities of *Second Life*. This chapter discusses the ins and outs of succeeding in fashion, including the skills you'll need, the financial considerations, and how to market your new business.

CONTENTS

THE BIGGEST BUSINESS OF ALL

If there's one common experience that just about everyone in *Second Life* has shared, it's customizing the appearance of our avatars. It's no wonder—the stock avatars, skins, and clothes we get when we sign up are, to be nice about it, boring. Useful, sure, because we have to have something when we go in-world for the first few times, but remember: the defaults tend to make people assume you're a newbie.

The nice thing about *Second Life* is that we can do just about anything we want and express ourselves any way we want. It's so easy, and relatively cheap, to change our avatar's looks, that each element of that look becomes a significant expression of individuality. And customers are clearly having a lot of fun with the *Second Life* fashion industry offerings, which are well priced for a little guilt-free retail therapy.

Figure 4.1: Starley Thereian is one of the best-known designers of skins in **Second Life.**

Whether for male or female avatars, furry or Goth, hugely tall or amazingly tiny, there's fashion for just about every taste, budget, and desire. But as with nearly everything else in *Second Life*, this is an industry created by the community, not by Linden Lab. All that haute couture—ball gowns straight from the court of French kings, shoes that Manolo Blahnik would envy, delicately freckled skins for redheads, and so much more—was created because the *Second Life* community wants to look sharp and is willing to pay good Lindens to do so. "In *Second Life*, anyone can have their ideal body type, and everything fits," says Starley Thereian, a famous designer of skins (Figure 4.1). "People can wear whatever they want, wherever they want. And it's a lot cheaper to buy a designer dress [in *Second Life*] than in real life."

More to the point, *Second Life* fashion is a huge business opportunity. It's the biggest-volume business—and the most profitable. Well-known designer Munchflower Zaius offers a reason: "The first thing you see when you come into *Second Life*? Other people wearing hot skins, hot clothes. It's instant peer pressure. You want to look as good as everyone else. In a world where everyone can be a sex god or goddess, why wouldn't you want to? I'm just catering to it."

WHAT IS THE *SECOND LIFE* FASHION BUSINESS?

Fashion in *Second Life* is a wondrous world where everyone can wear what they want, assuming they can find someone selling it or can design it themselves. And it's not just clothes. It's skins, as well, enabling any avatar to enjoy a Superman-fast change from an everyday boy- or girl-next-door to the fashion model's gala night out look (Figure 4.2), to the exotic fairy tale shimmer of scales in a mermaid's skin.

Figure 4.2: At a club, a sexy female avatar with an enhanced skin dances away the evening.

With millions of registered *Second Life* users, it's no wonder that nearly everywhere you look in-world, there is a boutique. Popular stores develop a unique style, catering to specific tastes and to loyal customers who return again and again to buy whatever is new.

■ DESIGNING WOMEN'S OR MEN'S FASHION— WHICH WAY TO GO?

When going into the *Second Life* fashion business, the first question to ask yourself is whether to go after the women's market, the men's, or both.

It's worth noting that designing fashion items for males in *Second Life* is very different from designing ones for females, and because of that most people choose one or the other. Some designers cater to both markets, but they are definitely exceptions. So, how to choose?

Figure 4.3: Female avatars outnumber male avatars, and most people choose young, attractive body types.

Figure 4.4: Shiryu Musashi, of Musashi-Do, is a well-known designer of men's fashions.

One way to look at the question is from an economic standpoint: There's simply more business for women's fashion in *Second Life*. Even though about 60 percent of registered users are men, among active users, about 60 percent are women or use female avatars. And where image-conscious women go, so goes the fashion business (Figure 4.3).

There are also technical reasons that women's fashion has grown more than men's. Much of that has to do with the fashion-design templates that Linden Lab and others make available to aspiring designers of clothing, skins, and more. Women's fashion in *Second Life* has "always been bigger," says Munchflower Zaius. "My personal take on that is that the templates cater to the female form. It's just easier to make female clothing and items."

Jennyfur Peregrine, another well-known fashion designer, agrees that because the templates were created seemingly with the female form in mind they lend themselves more to creation of female fashion items. In fact, she thinks that some of the in-world controls for designing fashion aren't very well-geared toward males. Thus, she thinks designing for male avatars can be harder.

Shiryu Musashi (Figure 4.4), who owns the Musashi-Do boutique on Anton, agrees. He says that the biggest part of the problem is that male avatars tend to be bigger than female ones, so clothes are stretched out over a larger area, making it more difficult to design textures crisp enough to look good on the male body. To ensure that clothes fit properly, it is essential to pay serious attention to detail. "Most men wear the same suit much more than most women wear the same dress," says Shiryu, so quality is of the utmost importance. For instance, Shiryu offers male and female versions of his polo shirt, as hand-painted details simulating folds in fabric, shading, and highlights need to be placed differently for a curvy female shape than they do to show off the male physique. And Shiryu knows male avatars are likely to be wearing the shirt long enough to notice if it doesn't look good.

Jennyfur agrees. She says that her husband, Flipper Peregrine, famous in his own right in *Second Life,* "changes his outfit maybe four times a year at best . . . The demand [for men's clothing] is not going to be as large as, by comparison, [a woman who may change clothes] four times a day."

Men's Clothing on the Rise

That said, men's fashion is clearly in a growth period. It's not entirely clear why, but Fallingwater Cellardoor, whose *Second Life* shoe designs are some of the most sought-after, thinks the men's fashion industry is blooming because it reflects the population coming into *Second Life* these days. "I suspect more of the men joining now are more fashion-conscious, social, and less geeky. I happen to like geeks—and am one—so that's not an insult, but the stereotypical guy [in *Second Life*] wears the same outfit for six months and just doesn't care." *Second Life* fashion blogs are also writing more about men's fashion, which could lead to increased sales. Additionally, the blossoming *Second Life* population means there are simply more male avatars wandering around, looking for better clothes, skins, hair, shoes, and the like.

MORE INFO

DESIGNER FROM MILAN, ITALY, BUILDS HIS FASHION LINE ON MEN'S CLOTHING IN *SECOND LIFE*

It should come as no surprise that in the real world's fashion capital—Milan, Italy—Shiryu Musashi is building a reputation as one of *Second Life*'s best men's clothing designers.

Many think that there is more profit in higher-volume sales of women's fashion, and so many more designers are catering to that market, but Shiryu thinks that is the perfect reason to focus his attention on dressing *Second Life*'s male avatars.

CHAPTER 1
CHAPTER 2
CHAPTER 3
CHAPTER 4
CHAPTER 5
CHAPTER 6
CHAPTER 7
CHAPTER 8
CHAPTER 9
CHAPTER 10
CHAPTER 11
APPENDICES
INDEX

(Continued)

CHAPTER 4

THE BIGGEST
BUSINESS
OF ALL

WHAT IS THE
SECOND LIFE
FASHION
BUSINESS?

THE
FINANCIAL
SIDE OF
FASHION

SKILLS AND
PLANNING:
WHAT YOU
NEED TO
KNOW

SETTING
UP SHOP

COMPETING
AGAINST
OTHER
BRANDS

FASHION
MARKETING:
BRINGING
IN THE
CUSTOMERS

INVENTORY
MANAGEMENT
AND
CUSTOMER
SERVICE

"There's the other side of the coin," Shiryu says of the dominance of the women's fashion business. "Being much bigger, there's also *much* more competition. And I do think that men need some style help in *Second Life* given the low number of men's designers."

Although Shiryu is Italian in real life, he is a Japanese stylist. His store, Mushashi-Do, on Anton, is filled with Japanese-themed clothes and art, and it makes for a very pleasing aesthetic. Shiryu got his start designing fashion in *Second Life* when, after he acquired a degree of expertise with texturing, a friend convinced him to try the new virtual world. He decided to design something as a birthday gift. "[The birthday party] was a pajama party, so I made a Chinese-like outfit that could pass as pajamas," Shiryu says. "[The gift recipient] liked it and persuaded me to start designing. And here I am. It's been two and a half years since then."

In a case of real life imitating *Second Life*, Shiryu is now enrolled in fashion school in Milan.

THE FINANCIAL SIDE OF FASHION

To evaluate your chance for success in the fashion business, you probably want to know the answer to a couple of key questions: How much can you make? And how much do you need to invest to get into the fashion business in *Second Life*?

HOW MUCH YOU CAN MAKE

It's tough to get anyone who's making real money in this business to give exact figures, but one thing is clear: If you are committed to putting in the time to build your name, reputation, and skills, and you market intelligently, you can make a full-time living in fashion.

"I've been quite successful, but it took a while to build up," says Fallingwater. "I think it took a year before I could really say I had a real income that I could live on." Munchflower is even more succinct: "I'm supporting myself and two kids on my income," she says. "It's my only income. This *is* my job."

Most people aren't going to make a full-time living at this business. But there is money to be made. Of course, we're talking about a business in which goods sell for very small

Figure 4.5: Mischief, with new releases every week, has long reigned as one of the most popular fashion-design stores. It has a regular clientele and attracts customers from all over Second Life.

prices—from about thirty cents to a couple of US dollars, at most. Specialty items or complete outfits may sell for the Linden dollar equivalent of as much as three US dollars. Regardless, the small prices mean that to make even a modest amount of money, you have to move a hefty amount of product. That's not a problem for some of the bigger designers, such as Mischief's Janie Marlowe, (Figure 4.5), ETD's Elikapeka Tiramisu, Fallingwater Cellardoor of Shiny Things, and others. But for someone starting out, it can be a challenge.

The amount you can make, then, depends on your ability to create attractive and alluring designs, to market them effectively, and to always be thinking about how to update your line of products.

■ THE REQUIRED INVESTMENT

You're going to need some capital to get started in the fashion business. There's no way around it. On the other hand, the amount of money you need is laughably small, especially compared to, say, the Second Life land business. In that arena, experts say you could need more than US$10,000 to begin and that it could take you nearly a year to make the money back.

But authorities on Second Life fashion say that to get started in their business, you need only about L$10,000, or around US$37. That's assuming, of course, that you already own the software you'll need for designing. If you don't, add several hundred US dollars in software expenses to your startup budget.

According to Starley Thereian, your initial investments would include a prefab store (most likely in a mainland mall), a good skin, and a few accessories to gussy up your own avatar. After that, you'll need to factor in rent on your store, texture-upload fees, and Classified ads.

Not bad at all, right? But the truth is, your initial investment includes not just money—it's also your time and energy. No matter how talented you are, you're going to have to invest some serious time into learning the ins and outs of the fashion business before you start to make money. That's no surprise; it's the same in any business, whether in Second Life or real life. But don't be discouraged. If you take the time to learn what you need to learn, by the time you get your business going you'll be ready to create great stuff that will be known throughout the virtual world.

But more on that later.

RESIDENTS SPEAK

MUNCHFLOWER ZAIUS'S ADVICE ABOUT GETTING STARTED IN THE FASHION BUSINESS

Munchflower Zaius, who is known in *Second Life* as one of the most talented designers of skins, has been in the business long enough to learn what works and what doesn't. Here she shares advice on things to do and things to avoid as you start your business.

- Be able to use an imaging program to some degree. [See the "Skills and Planning: What You Need to Know" section for more.]

- Do not give up. The fashion business takes a while to learn.

- Read tutorials. [See Appendix A at the back of this book for references.] They help massively.

- Ask around for places that charge little or no rent, and try to set up there. Exposure is really helpful.

- Learn how to build. Spend some time in a sandbox [a special region where everyone is allowed to build, practicing their skills]. This is good advice for anyone who comes to *Second Life*.

- Don't always listen to what everyone else has to say. Not everybody knows what they're talking about.

- Don't beat yourself up too much. *Second Life* has a learning curve, and if you keep at it you'll get better.

- Don't spread yourself too thin. If possible, get one main location and spread out from there.

- Don't do everything you're asked to do. People can and will take advantage of you mercilessly in *Second Life*.

- Don't bite the hands that feed you. If someone helps you out, don't turn around and stab them in the back.

■ FOCUSING ON A SUBCOMMUNITY

CHAPTER 1
CHAPTER 2
CHAPTER 3
CHAPTER 4

CHAPTER 5
CHAPTER 6
CHAPTER 7
CHAPTER 8
CHAPTER 9
CHAPTER 10
CHAPTER 11
APPENDICES
INDEX

One way to carve out a niche in the fashion business is to cater to a specific subcommunity. Although *Second Life* has many residents who don't consider themselves part of any one group, significant numbers do.

One identifying factor of those groups is that they have certain styles of dress. For example, there's a sizable Japanese-themed community whose members dress in various forms of Japanese fashion. Goreans dress in styles set forth in the *Gor* science fiction books by John Norman. Their role-playing wear includes full dresses for "free" women and silks and scanty outfits for "slave" girls. Other stores offer stylish business clothing to the growing numbers doing business in *Second Life*, while others offer fashion tailored to Goths, to the very small avatars known as "Tinies," or to the Victorian Era denizens of the quasi-historical region known as Caledonia.

There are many others, too. If there's a subcommunity in the real world, it probably has a presence—and a fashion—in *Second Life*. If you're inclined to cater to them, these subcommunities can offer substantial markets, steady clientele, and the opportunity to become known within that niche—even aspire to be the big fish in the pond.

Of course, to successfully design for one of these groups, you'll need a really good feel for their style or at least the commitment to learn it. It helps if you are a member of the community and can follow trends within the group.

If you succeed in creating a line of fashion that appeals to a specific community, you may find you have a steady source of sales as you build your repertoire.

SKILLS AND PLANNING: WHAT YOU NEED TO KNOW

As you've no doubt noticed in your meanderings through *Second Life*, there are hundreds of people selling fashion. The thing is, the quality of their products ranges from the barely worth mentioning to the transcendent.

Although not everyone can do transcendent work, my hope is that as you seek to leverage the *Second Life* fashion business as a way to bring in some money, you will make your products of the highest quality.

This section offers insights on the technical skills you'll need to proceed and suggestions for deciding on the kinds of images to use in your designs.

■ PHOTOSHOP AND BEYOND

If there's one thing that every expert in the *Second Life* fashion business agrees on, it's that you need to develop some technical skills before you can do anything. This isn't surprising, given that every bit of fashion you see in-world was created using software tools that take some time to learn.

The consensus is that the one software program everyone should learn is Adobe Photoshop. Beyond that, there are many different programs, such as GIMP (the free GNU Image Manipulation Program), that can help. Be prepared to spend several hundred dollars US on software if you don't already have it.

"I use Photoshop and LightWave for texturing," says Starley Therian. "I think it takes some natural talent or a good eye for style, as well as at least some degree of proficiency in your software." If you don't already have that proficiency, consider taking a class—your ability to create the fine textures is what will make your fashion products stand out. "I taught myself how to use Photoshop," says Starley, "but it took me at least a year or two to be really comfortable in it, [and] I'm still no expert by any means."

Figure 4.6: Jennyfur Peregrine, of Indigo, is well-known as a designer of Goth fashions in **Second Life.**

Jennyfur Peregrine (Figure 4.6), whose designs are well-known and who specializes in Goth and Victorian fashion, among other types, says you need a high degree of understanding of layering and manipulating the templates inside the graphics program you choose. Further, she says you need to have basic *Second Life* photographic skills for framing and composition for all of your box images, store modeling, and the like. "Packaging is a big part of the design process," Jennyfur explains. "I probably spend just as much time imaging my items as I do creating them, from photo shoots to careful editing in Photoshop to branding, logo design, and making advertisements."

Equally important is learning 3D texturing, which involves learning how to use the many different *Second Life* fashion templates. Linden Lab provides a whole series of them for free (http://secondlife.com/community/templates.php), and members of the community also offer some.

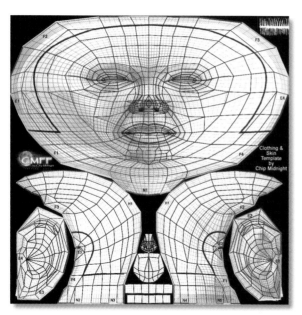

Figure 4.7: Linden Lab provides free fashion templates, but many designers find Chip Midnight's much easier to use. (Image courtesy of Chip Midnight)

CHAPTER 1
CHAPTER 2
CHAPTER 3
CHAPTER 4

CHAPTER 5
CHAPTER 6
CHAPTER 7
CHAPTER 8
CHAPTER 9
CHAPTER 10
CHAPTER 11
APPENDICES
INDEX

To start, you may want to use the Linden Lab templates, but to those with more experience, they are limiting. Hyasynth Tiramisu recommends the free templates provided by Chip Midnight (Figure 4.7) (http://www.slboutique.com/chipmidnight), saying they offer more flexibility than the ones from Linden Lab. Either way, you must import the templates into Photoshop or a similar program that can read Photoshop 7.1 PSD files.

It's also worth spending some time taking classes in *Second Life* that teach you how to make clothing or other fashion items. There is a wide variety of such classes, taught by many experts. Classes are listed in the Event Calendar (http://secondlife.com/events/); click on the Category box and choose Education to see a list of the available classes for the current day or for whichever day you select on the calendar.

Also, learn how to import the textures you've created in your graphics program into the templates and how to manipulate them there. Acquire a good understanding of how prims—the basic *Second Life* building blocks—work. Prims are discussed briefly later in this chapter, but more-thorough primers are available as classes in-world.

TIP

Don't sidestep learning about prims. "Technical knowledge of prim work and prim texturing for fashion design is crucial," says Jennyfur Peregrine. "Fabrics on textures do not always look the same as the fabric you uploaded on a template. Sometimes it takes extra editing time to get them to match. The most common glitches are pattern repeats, alpha transparencies, and darkness/lightness of the fabric."

Alphas are transparency maps that can be manipulated in Photoshop. Using alpha channels, as they're called, can take even the most skilled designers time. Hyasynth Tiramisu, for example, said it took her five months to figure out how they worked. Her advice? Stick to it, and keep trying to learn. Eventually, you will pick it up, and then you can make your designs much more sophisticated.

Finally, to make up for the fact that *Second Life* doesn't actually render light and shadow (so any shading and highlights on your clothing have to be painted in), some go beyond painting them with graphics software, instead using 3D software for these effects. Whether created in Photoshop or Maya, fabric textures with such effects rendered or painted and saved as part of the image are referred to as "baked" textures. Modeling software includes LightWave, Maya, or Blender.

Munchflower Zaius says that it's not essential to have 3D modeling skills, given that the fashion templates are flat, but that it can be good to understand how the templates will turn out in 3D once you've uploaded textures onto them and you've brought them into *Second Life*.

■ PHOTO-SOURCED OR HAND-DRAWN IMAGES?

One choice to make as you move forward with your fashion business is whether to use photo-sourced or hand-drawn images. In the beginning you'll likely want to use photo-sourced ones—textures based on existing images—because it's simpler. After all, you'll be working with images that you have acquired from somewhere, such as all the minute details of an outfit. If you decide to go hand-drawn, you must create the textures from scratch, by hand.

It sounds hard, but for those who are good at it, it's more than worth it. Discriminating *Second Life* residents can tell when something is hand-drawn and often don't want anything else.

Figure 4.8: Many designers use pre-existing images to design their clothing, but Hyasynth Tiramisu has built a reputation as one of the best designers of hand-drawn fashions.

Hyasynth Tiramisu is one of the best-known designers of hand-drawn clothing. She says she draws manually (in Photoshop and Illustrator) the buttons, the collars, the shading, and much more in each of her designs. "I didn't source an image of a button or an image of (an) entire jacket," she explains to me while wearing one of her signature designs (Figure 4.8). "Most of my designs are from my imagination alone. I didn't go to a website with pictures of a men's waistcoat and apply their images onto the template. Everything is built layer by layer, piece by piece."

Though it takes her much longer to create a new item, it means a creation of hers is unique and often instantly distinguishable from clothes designed by others. "It has my touch and my personal sense of design," she says proudly. You might think that her clothes would command a premium, given how much time she puts into creating them. In fact, her prices are about the same as many other designers'. Still, she has created a niche market, and her customers wear her clothes proudly, knowing that other residents who know *Second Life* fashion will recognize her work. It's a status symbol, and that's why she has been able to make a good living from her creations.

CHAPTER 1
CHAPTER 2
CHAPTER 3
CHAPTER 4

CHAPTER 5
CHAPTER 6
CHAPTER 7
CHAPTER 8
CHAPTER 9
CHAPTER 10
CHAPTER 11
APPENDICES
INDEX

RESIDENTS SPEAK

HYASYNTH TIRAMISU'S ADVICE FOR NEWCOMERS TO THE FASHION BUSINESS

A leader in the Second Life *fashion business, Hyasynth Tiramisu is well known for her hand-drawn clothing. Here she shares suggestions for newcomers to the business, as well as mistakes to avoid.*

- **Be persistent. Don't let the technical aspects of fashion creation in** *Second Life* **keep you from making your dream clothing.**

- **Make friends with other designers. It's really important to have a support network. Other designers will teach you more than any book or website.**

- **Do something different. Be unique. People will notice.**

- **It's all about branding in** *Second Life*, **just like in real life. Pick a name and a look and stick with them.**

- **Provide excellent customer service. Your customers will remember you replacing that dress that was eaten by the inventory monster and return to buy more. It's better to make customers happy than to worry about the one person who might be scamming.**

- **Don't sell your product before it's the best. People remember quality, and you want them to remember yours is the highest.**

- **Don't stick with a rental location if it isn't pulling its weight. I spent a lot of money on losing spaces in the beginning out of some false sense of responsibility to the location.**

- **Don't set up shops without a friend to help you reality-check your permissions and sales prices. We are people, and we make mistakes. I let many dresses go for L$0 a year ago until someone was honest enough to tell me.**

- **If it's too good to be true, it probably is. Just like in real life, not everyone is honest or out to help you.**

UNDERSTANDING PRIMS AND MESHES

If you're a *Second Life* fashion designer, you need to understand the difference between the two elements that make up fashion items: meshes and prims.

Prims are the *Second Life* base objects, building "blocks" that are somewhat like LEGOs. They come in a variety of shapes and can be stretched and even cut. As with LEGOs, you combine them into groups to make a larger or more detailed item.

The surface or finish that makes one prim cube look like wood and another like metal or fabric is just an image, imported into *Second Life* as an image, called a texture, which is applied to one or more sides of the cube's surface.

Thus, a sofa would be made out of a collection of variously shaped prims, with textures added to make the couch seem upholstered with leather, for example.

The default prim is a cube, but they also come in circle, donut, cone, and various other shapes. So, combining various prims, stretching and cutting others, you could create a lamp, a car, a house, even a very elaborate shoe. To complete the illusion, good textures are vital, adding depth, shading, and detail, often making the item seem much more complex ("prim-heavy") than it really is. Fashion items frequently made from prims include jewelry, eyeglasses, hats, handbags, and, last but far from least, prim hair, which are worn like wigs and are a welcome relief from the default "system hair."

Prim items are worn by an avatar as attachments. For instance, a ring might be attached to the left hand, and sunglasses to the bridge of the nose. *Meshes* describe items, such as clothing or skins, that are textures stretched directly over the avatar body, rather than over a prim. In fact, most clothing is made this way. To create such an item, you would draw or paint it in your graphics software and then import it as a texture into *Second Life*.

To make the texture into clothing an avatar can wear, the key step is to actually import the texture onto the desired layer and position, for instance the shirt layer or the pants layer. Elements like sleeve length are selected at this stage. Then you can save the desired item of clothing and give it a name. Once saved, your "Awesome Tee Shirt," can be worn by other avatars (see "Permissions" for details on how to share, or prevent sharing of, an item).

Mesh items appear as if they were painted onto an avatar. You'll want to import the Mesh template as one layer in your paint or illustration software, so you can see how elements like weave or pattern will wrap around the avatar. While this grid of squiggly lines might look scary at first, it is the key to professional quality work.

The mesh lines will help you decide where to place simple elements like a pocket or buttons, but most importantly, it's essential to making sure your seams match, very important with fabric texture or pattern. (The Mesh template is available at http://secondlife.com or at Cristiano Midnight's website, http://www.sluniverse.com/php/.)

To make your designs look more realistic, consider including details like folds of cloth and shading, all painted into your texture as though you were an illustrator working on a flat canvas. The trick is making a 2D illustration look good when worn in a 3D environment. Since *Second Life* doesn't render shadows, you'll need to paint them in yourself.

Mesh items are worn on a few available layers (designated by Linden Lab as part of the Avatar Edit Appearance controls, in the *Second Life* user interface). An avatar might very well be wearing a skin, with a T-shirt and a jacket, as well as jeans on the pants layer. Tattoos are likewise worn as clothing layers, and a smart tattoo creator will include the same tattoo as a T-shirt and as a jacket so that they can be paired with whatever clothing an avatar customer prefers to wear.

As you can imagine, clothes that look painted on can't provide the silhouette of a high collar or a long skirt or cape. So, prim objects are used to enhance mesh clothing. For example, the top of a formal dress might be mesh clothing, and the inverted bell of the skirt made from prims (Figure 4.9).

Figure 4.9: (a) Prim object clothing and (b) mesh textures

You also have the ability to set a prim to be flexible. With *flexiprims*, you can make a piece of clothing that moves. The degree of flexibility can mimic, for example, a skirt that seems to have the heavy sweep of velvet or a flutter of light silk.

Ultimately, to make impressive fashion designs, you must truly nail down your skills in your graphics program and get meshes right. Creating good prim objects requires mastering the prim and texturing tools in *Second Life*.

MORE INFO

PRIM LIMITS DO NOT IMPACT FASHION CUSTOMERS DIRECTLY

In *Second Life*, there is a great deal of emphasis on prim limits. You cannot go over the prim limits for a particular parcel of land, and getting close to the limits affects performance. This is certainly a concern as you build your store and decide how to display your merchandise, but what about the number of prims in the items you sell?

Many wonder if an avatar wearing prim objects, from the hundreds of flexiprims that might be in a wig, down to the dozens that could easily make up an attractive pair of shoes, contributes to server slowdown, otherwise known as lag.

Prim limits do not apply to fashion items worn by an avatar, according to Linden Lab's former head of production, Chris Lassonde, and prims worn as attachments don't contribute to lag.

On the other hand, scripted items can affect performance because anything with a script—like a typing override, a multi-gadget, or the animated "bling" on jewelry—causes drag on the server. So if there is an event with a lot of avatars and many of them have scripted items, performance may drop, but not because of prim limits.

■ SKINS: THE MOST PROFITABLE FASHION BUSINESS

When you think of fashion, you may well think first of clothing. But as in real life, in *Second Life* fashion has many elements: clothing, jewelry, shoes, hairstyles, lingerie, etc. One you may not think of, however, is the most profitable of them all: skins.

In *Second Life*, a skin is what covers your avatar underneath (or, sometimes, instead of) clothes. Residents can select from a few basic skins when they first sign in, and can change a skin's look using the Appearance tools.

For many residents, the path to good looks must include a designer skin. There are freebie skins available, but the best skins created by the most-talented designers, with realistic tone, shading, and detailing, can cost more than L$1,000.

And because so many people want different skins and want to have a collection of different skins to suit their mood and their clothing, a booming and highly profitable market has emerged.

Indeed, pricing for skins can be substantially higher than for clothing. That's because, the experts say, it is substantially harder to design them and have them look good.

Munchflower Zaius is well known for her skins, and she says it's no wonder that they are the most profitable fashion item. "Most people charge more for skins than clothing, and they seem to be a higher priority than having cool clothes," Munchflower says. People "must look good naked first, I guess."

Figure 4.10: **Second Life residents can chose from a wide variety of different skins at Munchflower Zaius's store Nomine.**

A male avatar may only own one or two skins, with variations in tan or facial hair, perhaps. However, female avatars will routinely purchase a new skin simply to get different eyebrows, freckles, or cosmetics options (Figure 4.10). Skins are often sold in six-packs where the only variation is in the makeup, so that it's easy to keep the same base look while swapping the pale lips and light blush day-at-the-beach-in-her-favorite-bikini-makeup for the bright lipstick and glitter eye shadow that goes with that new ball gown.

But Munchflower also acknowledges that skins are significantly more work to create than clothing is. That's because skins require stitching three separate templates together into a single skin. To get it right, you have to work hard to ensure that details like eyebrows and toes are placed correctly in reference to the different templates, and that no seams show. Starley agrees. "While a shirt or pants has natural seams ... skins don't. A lot more time is spent on a skin to make it as seamless and flawless as possible," Starley says. It's very hard to treat seams properly, so a quality skin justifies the higher prices.

To do well at creating skins, you must become highly proficient in using your graphics software, and you should be prepared to spend quite a long time learning how to match the templates properly so that you can ensure that your skins are clean.

But once you do, the market for them is nearly unlimited. That's because a skin is something that virtually every avatar buys at least once to replace their first default skin. But female avatars take skins very seriously, upgrading every time their favorite designers do. With some female avatars owing upward of 100 skins, at L$1,000 or more, it's easy to see why this is such a strong market, and can add up to some serious money.

CHAPTER 1
CHAPTER 2
CHAPTER 3
CHAPTER 4
CHAPTER 5
CHAPTER 6
CHAPTER 7
CHAPTER 8
CHAPTER 9
CHAPTER 10
CHAPTER 11
APPENDICES
INDEX

MORE INFO

DESIGNING CUSTOM SKINS

A true custom skin is an exclusive, one of a kind skin, intended to be a good likeness of the human behind the avatar. These skins are paired with a custom-sculpted avatar shape, made with careful attention to every detail, especially facial features. With the default *Second Life* avatar editing tools, this is no easy task. While some designers do both, the shape may be sculpted by an expert who works with the skin designer.

Customers for custom skins tend to be those humans who retain their real world identity in *Second Life*, famous actors, musicians, authors, politicians, business people, and the like. Notable examples have included Suzanne Vega, Bruce Willis and Jay Leno.

Like any skin, the style may be photo-realistic, literally based on a photograph of the subject, or hand drawn, in an artistic or cartoon-like manner.

Custom skins and shapes are expensive. This is a business opportunity only for the most proficient, as they require a great deal of skill to make. As with any one-off, custom product, you have to keep attracting new customers. It's also more difficult to predict when the next order will come in. For those with enough skill, however, custom skins can be a fun and profitable sideline.

SETTING UP SHOP

Now that you've got your skills down and you know what kind of fashion you want to design, it's time to think about how to sell it. This means setting up a store or stores, establishing prices, deciding how to display your merchandise, whether to create limited editions, and other important decisions.

IT'S YOUR STORE

If you're going into the fashion business in *Second Life*, you need a store. There are other ways to sell your wares, but a store (Figure 4.11) is the best and most frequently used

method because it offers the ability to showcase your various designs, to impress your customers with demos to try on, to show off your overall style and store-layout sensibility, and to create a sense of place that customers will enjoy visiting, hopefully again and again.

CHAPTER 1
CHAPTER 2
CHAPTER 3
CHAPTER 4

CHAPTER 5
CHAPTER 6
CHAPTER 7
CHAPTER 8
CHAPTER 9
CHAPTER 10
CHAPTER 11
APPENDICES
INDEX

Figure 4.11: Fallingwater Cellardoor's Shiny Things store as seen from above

RENTING LAND FOR YOUR STORE

The easiest option for setting up your first store would be to rent a location and set up shop there. There are several ways to find such a space.

One of the best ways is to identify where you'd like to be and see if a store is available for rent there. Look for a For Rent sign so you can contact the owner of the space and make a deal.

To do this, you'll need to explore possible locations. You're more likely to find malls on the mainland, though some do exist on islands. Exploring various malls is a good thing to do anyway, as a way to find out what other designers are doing with their stores. You can see what looks good and what doesn't, and which kinds of stores people seem to be attracted to and which ones don't pull in customers.

Another way to find stores for rent is to peruse the *Second Life* land sales and rentals forums: (http://forums.secondlife.com/forumdisplay.php?f=114) or (http://forums.secondlife.com/forumdisplay.php?f=115) to see if there's anything attractive there. Third-party sites also have forums, such as SL Exchange (http://www.slexchange.com/modules.php?name=Real _ Estate).

Regardless, if you're going to rent, make sure that once you have struck a deal with the landlord he or she grants you the permissions to build and script on the land. Otherwise, you won't be able to modify the space at all. Be sure any land you rent allows commerce; some land agreements limit use to residential, banning stores.

So, why would you want to rent?

One reason is that if you rent, there's a pretty good chance you'll be able to find a spot that is set up as a store and can move right in. That's not to say that you couldn't rearrange things or add things to make it your own, but at least you don't have to start from scratch.

Hyasynth Tiramisu says that renting is a simple matter of flexibility, which is something you want when you're getting started. "Renting is easier.... If the location isn't working, you can always move," Hyasynth says, "unlike buying and selling land, which can get messy and pricey."

Hyasynth also recommends renting on an island rather than on the mainland, largely because there is likely to be less lag on an island, where there tends to be much more control over how much is built near your store. "The first instinct is to want to rent next to the new hot club. But the quieter the better," she says. "Your customers will actually be able to shop for your clothing ... [Mainland malls are] frustrating, slow-loading nightmares, usually."

She also points out that when you own the store, you can list it so that it comes up under Find Places, in the *Second Life* search interface. That's a bit like listing your store in the phone book, though in *Second Life* customers can search for the name of the store and get a teleport link directly there.

When you're looking for a rental, consider the price. It's not very expensive to rent a small location, but it's not free either. Make sure you've set aside enough for rent each month—a 512-square-meter location can go for a relatively low fee, almost certainly less than US$20 a month. Just make sure you have enough budgeted to keep the store open, while you build inventory and clientele needed for the store to pay for itself.

Getting Free Vending Space from Another Designer

Many successful designers like to help newcomers to the business by giving them free vending space in their stores. The idea is that they are helping out someone they consider promising, and in many cases they're paying back an old debt: someone likely helped them the same way.

Basically, you benefit by getting exposure to the clientele of famous designers; customers walking through their stores will see your displays. The store benefits too, giving clients another reason to drop by the store to see new designers, but you get the substantial benefit of all those shoppers looking at your work. Of course, this is definitely not something you can expect, and if you're lucky enough to get such an offer, make the most of the opportunity by showcasing your very best work and offering landmarks back to your store.

Most vendors who offer the space do so for people they have met and become friendly with, and whose work they admire and want to help promote. Some, however, have a more codified process. One such designer is Elikapeka Tiramisu, who offers a free month of display space at her ETD shop (Figure 4.12). She has a selection process that allows anyone to apply for space.

Figure 4.12: Some designers, such as Elikapeka Tiramisu, offer newcomers free display space in their stores.

CHAPTER 1
CHAPTER 2
CHAPTER 3
CHAPTER 4

CHAPTER 5
CHAPTER 6
CHAPTER 7
CHAPTER 8
CHAPTER 9
CHAPTER 10
CHAPTER 11
APPENDICES
INDEX

Others only rent space to friends. Once you've got some designs under your belt, you may want to seek out designers who provide such space, then work to become their friends—or organize a group of your friends to share a store.

For Fallingwater Cellardoor, the location isn't the most important element. Instead, she thinks it's crucial to have your own store, rather than relying on being able to showcase your designs in someone else's store. "It's your best chance to make your shop a destination," she says.

BUYING THE LOCATION FOR YOUR STORE

One of the basic ways to locate land to buy is through the official *Second Life* forums mentioned earlier in this chapter, where you can seek land to rent or purchase. Alternatively, you can look in the Classifieds by clicking on the Search button in the *Second Life* viewer, and then clicking on the Land Sales tab. Then you can choose whether you're looking for land at auction by Linden Lab or for private land for sale on either the mainland or an island.

Experts like Starley Thereian and Munchflower Zaius recommend waiting a little while before buying a store location—most likely until you've got your business going. But Starley says that a strategy that worked for her was to set up a main store in a desirable location—and then rent locations for satellite stores in other places as a way of getting your name out there a bit more. This is a short-term strategy, she explains, designed to build a clientele. "As your business grows," Starley says, "you'll have less time to maintain satellite locations, so you can reduce them as you attract more visitors to your main store, and eventually be left with just the one to take care of."

BUYING YOUR OWN ISLAND

The ultimate *Second Life* location, as you might guess, is an island of your own. There are plenty of reasons to buy your own island, probably summed up best by Munchflower as: "Control. Private islands offer far more control of the land to their owners. You can set things better, you can [transform] the land far more easily. It's just a better deal."

Of course, buying an island is not likely something you need or even want to do when you're getting started. First of all, you almost certainly won't have enough items for sale to justify the size of store you would want to put on your own island. More importantly, an island is a pricey proposition. As of this writing an island costs US$1,675 plus a monthly fee of US$295. That's a lot of overhead for a business that you could get off the ground for less than US$50, And if you're not a builder, you can easily spend much more than the cost of the island paying someone to build and landscape a whole sim for you.

Figure 4.13: Hyasynth Tiramisu, of Silent Sparrow, is a leading designer of hand-drawn clothing.

But once you've been in business long enough to develop a reputation and a loyal clientele, it's definitely something to think about. Take the case of Hyasynth. She had just moved her operation, Silent Sparrow, (Figure 4.13) onto her own island when we first talked. And she could barely contain her enthusiasm. "It's been a dream," she said at the time. "To be able to control texture size, script use. To keep lag as low as possible. It's something I've wanted for a long time, and it still feels unreal." She also said that her sales had gone up, at least a little, once she moved onto her new island. "There is an implied prestige to owning your own sim," Hyasynth says.

In other words, it's a sign you've made it. That you're a success. And that will breed more success as customers will find you and, hopefully, be impressed by your location and your ability to have your own island.

WARNING

Buying an island is not something to take lightly. Even after your initial outlay of US$1,675 or more—since the price of islands could well go up over time—you will also need to come up with US$295 or more each month in land maintenance, or tier, fees.

For her part, Starley—whose Celestial Studios is on her own island, Celestial City—has a formula she uses to advise people about whether they're ready to get an island. It's certainly not scientific, but it's worth thinking about when you're pondering the expense. "When people are considering purchasing an island, I usually tell them to figure out how many days' profits it takes to pay the island fees each month and decide if it's worth it," Starley says. "If the fee is going to be 50 percent of your monthly income, I probably wouldn't suggest it."

RESIDENTS SPEAK

CHAPTER 1
CHAPTER 2
CHAPTER 3
CHAPTER 4
CHAPTER 5
CHAPTER 6
CHAPTER 7
CHAPTER 8
CHAPTER 9
CHAPTER 10
CHAPTER 11
APPENDICES
INDEX

STARLEY THEREIAN'S ADVICE FOR NEW FASHION DESIGNERS

*Starley Thereian is known as one of the best designers of skins in **Second Life**. From her store, Celestial Studios, she sells huge numbers of skins and a wide range of clothes.*

*As indicated by her last name "Thereian," she joined **Second Life** after first spending time in the competing virtual world, There.com. But after trying designing in **Second Life**, she never left. Now, one of the most successful designers, Starley shares what she has learned about what to do and what not to do.*

- Look around. See what's out there. What appeals to you? Is there a market for it?

- Surf the Web for tutorials on Photoshop and other graphics software.

- Create a distinctive and recognizable brand name and logo.

- Shop around for good locations to set up shop. Compare rents and traffic.

- Be original. Make what you love. You'll have more fun, and other people will love it too.

- Don't put out an inferior product that is not ready to be sold.

- Don't resell unauthorized works like freebies to try to turn a quick profit.

- Don't spread yourself too thin between too many locations.

- Don't forget to take advantage of free advertising. Post your new store and items on the forums if you want to be found.

■ PRIMS AND LAG AND NEIGHBORS, OH MY

When you're considering where to set up your store, consider a handful of essential practical matters: prim counts, lag, and neighbors. These are particularly important things to think about if you're starting out and are going to be putting your store on someone else's land. Without the control that you get from having your own private island, you have no choice but to deal with whatever conditions exist, or develop, around you.

It all starts with prim counts. Linden Lab has set limits on the number of prims—the basic building blocks of *Second Life*—that can be used in any particular space. The total prim limit is determined by the size of the land parcel in question.

If you're familiar with the costs of maintaining a website, you can think of prim limits and land costs as being similar to bandwidth costs. Those with more traffic and storage space, measured as bandwidth or as prims, pay a larger fee than do those who only use a small amount of server space (see Table 3.1 in the preceding chapter).

One problem is that when a parcel of land begins to approach its prim limit, it creates lag problems additional to whatever is happening in *Second Life* generally at that time. As a store owner, you definitely want to avoid lag as much as possible, because it makes for a poor shopping experience for customers. If your customers decide that the lag problems are related to your store rather than to something going on in *Second Life* at large, they may never return.

You can increase prim count on your parcel of land to minimize problems with sims. That's because prim limits can be shared among two or more parcels that are owned or controlled by the same person. Thus, a common solution to prim limits is to have a store on one parcel and nothing or almost nothing on another parcel on the same sim.

Additionally, lag—a store owner's worst enemy—can come from server load caused by too much going on in your neighborhood. That's why most successful fashion designers make sure to not put themselves on the same sim as big, popular clubs. The number of avatars who visit such sims, combined with various scripts they have attached, as well as scripts that are part of the club, drag down performance across the sim. The busiest areas are usually ones to avoid when looking for your store location.

MORE INFO

MAKE IT EASY TO SHOP: BASIC STORE-DESIGN PRINCIPLES

When you're setting up your store or stores, consider implementing these basics to make your customers' shopping experience as good as can be while maximizing your sales opportunities.

- Always think ease of use. People need to have room to walk around.

- Use viewable ads, but don't use up all your wall space with large posters.

- Put new and popular items, especially if you've been lucky enough to have one reviewed by a blogger, right near the entrance, in the front of the store.

CHAPTER 1
CHAPTER 2
CHAPTER 3
CHAPTER 4

CHAPTER 5
CHAPTER 6
CHAPTER 7
CHAPTER 8
CHAPTER 9
CHAPTER 10
CHAPTER 11
APPENDICES
INDEX

- Put less-popular or sale items in the back or on the second or third floor.

- Keep prominent space available for your best-sellers.

- Make sure your sales displays are clear and well-lit and show the product honestly, attractively, and with easy-to-understand information about permissions, just what comes "in the box" with purchase, and any options, like color variations.

- Make sure your store directory and signs make it easy for customers to find what they're looking for.

INCREASING SALES

Where else will your customers shop and what else can you do to get their attention?

Consider listing your merchandise on SL Exchange (http://www.slexchange.com/) or OnRez (http://shop.onrez.com/). These websites are online stores where your customers can browse at work, or during times they can't log into *Second Life*, such as during updates. Purchases are delivered in-world, directly to the avatar customer. Note that you may get more sales from these listings than may be obvious at first; customers may very well browse online, but make their purchase in-world at your store.

Remember to offer a nice freebie or two as a sample of your work. And, no, you're not going to impress anyone with Yet Another Tee Shirt. Consider offering some free items in the stores that cater to new *Second Life* residents, like the GNubie store or the DOVE store, or at YadNi's Junkyard.

TIP

*When your budget allows, think about placing ads in the Second Life fashion media—fashion blogs (see below) as well as magazines like Second Style (*http://www.secondstyle. com/*) and Aspire (*http://www.aspiresl.com/*).*

COMPETING AGAINST OTHER BRANDS

If you've been following the news about *Second Life*, you may have heard that some real-world companies have come in-world and are selling versions of their real-life clothing.

It would be natural to worry about competing with such big brand stores when you're just starting up. But don't fear. *Second Life* offers no advantages for big companies going head-to-head with smaller businesses. That's because the economies of scale in-world mean that it costs nothing to create your second (or millionth) copy of an item, regardless of whether you're Reebok or a newcomer to the *Second Life* fashion business. So your costs are no higher than those of a large brand.

Similarly, the advertising and marketing environment puts every designer, big or small, on more or less a level playing field; there are no TV ads to buy and Classified ads don't cost enough to price out smaller businesses.

■ THINK ABOUT PRICING

In *Second Life*, designers don't really compete on price. They compete mainly on style and quality, and word of mouth is the currency of business development. That doesn't mean you can charge whatever you want for your products. If you look around, you'll see that prices for fashion items are fairly standardized, from less than L$100 for things like T-shirts to a few hundred Lindens for more-substantial clothing and upward of L$1,000 for good skins. If you charge too much, you risk pricing yourself out of the market. Look around to see what others with similar items are charging, and try to win over their customers by making a more attractive product.

That said, once you are established and your designs are in demand, you can charge more, albeit not a huge amount more, for limited-edition items. *Second Life* fashionistas will notice when someone is wearing a limited-edition design and will likely be willing to pay a little more for exclusive items.

■ PERMISSIONS

One other thing to consider when putting your designs up for sale is what permissions you will grant. There are three to consider: modify, copy, and transfer. Just ask yourself what you'd like your customers to be able to do with something they buy from you. Is it OK with you if they give it as a gift to someone else? What if they want to re-size it a little so it fits better? Are you willing to let them re-sell the item?

You probably won't want to sell something set with "full permissions"—which means it can be transferred to another avatar, copied, and even sold to a third party. You may, however, want to offer a selection of different permissions to your customers.

CHAPTER 1
CHAPTER 2
CHAPTER 3
CHAPTER 4

CHAPTER 5
CHAPTER 6
CHAPTER 7
CHAPTER 8
CHAPTER 9
CHAPTER 10
CHAPTER 11
APPENDICES
INDEX

MODIFY

Modify rights boil down to whether you want to let people change your item. Customers might want to be able to modify a prim object, such as hair or jewelry, resizing it for a perfect fit.

COPY

Copy can go hand in hand with modifying. If customers screw up while making a change to a copy, they can revert to the original and start over. Generally, that's the best reason to allow copying: to let customers recover from a mistake they made in modifying an item.

TRANSFER

Giving a customer the right to transfer an item allows them to buy something and give it to someone else as a gift. Many female avatars buy clothing for male friends, for instance. On the other hand, if you're dealing with a specialty item that you don't want people to sell, you probably don't want to offer transfer permission.

NOTE

The most common permission settings are:
- *Copy and Modify OK, but no Transfer.*
- *No Copy, No Modify, but Transfer OK.*

FASHION MARKETING: BRINGING IN THE CUSTOMERS

The best thing about marketing in *Second Life* is that some of the most effective ways to do it cost nothing. You are on a level playing field with the big real-world companies that are coming into *Second Life* to sell fashion: they can't win the marketing wars with dollars. In the preceding chapter you read about the general marketing suggestions that all *Second Life* business owners should follow. But some marketing tips apply specifically to the fashion business. The following are some of those specifics.

FRIENDS WHO TELL FRIENDS WHO TELL FRIENDS

One kind of marketing is building a reputation as a hot designer and having your customers do your advertising for you. You'll see it all the time: people will be gathered in a store, happily looking at some item, and seconds later a friend of one of the customers will teleport in. That's because the customers instant-messaged the friend to invite them to come shopping.

Of course, you don't have direct control over word of mouth, but if you make good products, replenish your inventory frequently, and offer good customer service, it will happen. (For more detail, see "Inventory Management and Customer Service" later in this chapter.)

BLOGS

One of the most important marketing efforts you can make is to blog, and to do so regularly. Post every time you have a new release, a sale, or an event, and make sure you post images of each new release. You can use the same image you will use on the box or poster in your store. It's fine to start out with one of the free blogging services, like Blogger. What's important is that your blog makes it easy for people to follow your work. "I have a blog now because everyone has to," says Fallingwater Cellardoor.

Also, and perhaps more important, *Second Life* fashion has inspired a vibrantly active community of third-party bloggers who review and comment on the twists and turns of fashion, interview designers, and generally focus a spotlight on the fashion business as a whole.

MORE INFO

THE FASHION PRESS

No, *Vogue* hasn't seriously started covering *Second Life* fashion, at least, not yet. But the influence of those who do write about in-world style is very real, and a positive review from them can be a tremendous boost, with a direct impact on your sales and reputation. These blogs can get hundreds of thousands of page views a month. And if you're serious about your business, you need to read enough to know about trends and issues in your industry. Some of the best known include:

🖐 **Second Style** (http://blog.secondstyle.com)

🖐 **ASpiRE!** (http://www.aspiresl.blogspot.com/)

🖐 **StyleDisorder** (http://www.styledisorder.com/)

CHAPTER 1
CHAPTER 2
CHAPTER 3
CHAPTER 4

CHAPTER 5
CHAPTER 6
CHAPTER 7
CHAPTER 8
CHAPTER 9
CHAPTER 10
CHAPTER 11
APPENDICES
INDEX

- 🔹 **Linden Lifestyles** (`http://www.LindenLifestyles.com`)

- 🔹 **For a more comprehensive list of existing fashion blogs, visit** `http://del.icio.us/secondlife/fashion`

- 🔹 **How can you get the fashion bloggers to write about your work? Ask them to! (See "How to Generate Buzz.")**

Send a set of your newest items to the fashion bloggers regularly (perhaps monthly or seasonally). Be sure to include a notecard with any particulars, including prices. The key: most blogs will tell you exactly how they'd like review items to be sent. Ignore their preferences at your peril.

Bloggers enjoy reading and commenting on each others' blogs, so it's a great way to get noticed and written about by others.

FORUMS

Don't overlook the forums, the official place where *Second Life* residents can post new items for sale (`http://forums.secondlife.com/forumdisplay.php?f=194`). "Always post in the forums," reminds Hyasynth. "Fashion blogs get huge readership traffic, and they usually pull their information from the forums."

UPDATE GROUPS

Another important way of getting word out about your designs, the new ones in particular, is to create an update group. A group lets you easily send messages, including objects or landmarks, to a group of subscribers. If people are loyal customers and join your group, then every time you put out a new product, you can alert them immediately. And they will come.

Reward those who join your group with special sales and freebies only available to group members. Be careful not to overdo it with too many messages—you want to send your customers welcomed updates, not spam!

Keep in mind that *Second Life* allows residents to join only 25 groups, so people are careful about which groups they join. You may have a hard time building membership, but doing so is important and will become easier as your reputation grows.

MORE INFO

HOW TO GENERATE BUZZ

You need to get the word out that your store exists, and then regularly get the attention of potential customers. Here's how to get noticed.

Figure 4.14: The Fashion Consolidated group gives designers a way to alert customers who want to know about new fashion products from many stores, but may be approaching their group limits.

- **The Fashion Consolidated Group.** The idea's simple: a shared group, Fashion Consolidated. Designers can post their announcements (Figure 4.14) to a wide, opt-in audience of those who are interested in fashion. This group is a great platform for smaller, new businesses whose own groups don't yet have a large membership.

- **Generate excitement** with regular updates, freebies, sales, limited edition items, and so on.

Remember, you want to keep giving customers reasons to come to your store. Make sure there's always something new to see.

■ YOU GOT THE WORD OUT, BUT CAN THEY FIND YOUR STORE?

Though your goal as a fashion designer is certainly to develop a loyal and regular clientele, you'll have a significant number of walk-in customers—especially in the beginning. They'll buy something, leave, and then forget where they bought their new favorite shirt or dress or skin. If they can't remember where your shop was, that means lost sales.

Your job is to make sure customers can find you when they get that inclination. One essential way to do that is to include a notecard that provides a landmark to your store in the packaging for your designs. (To create a notecard, go to your inventory, click the Create menu, and choose New Note; Figure 4.15.) That way, people can look in their inventory,

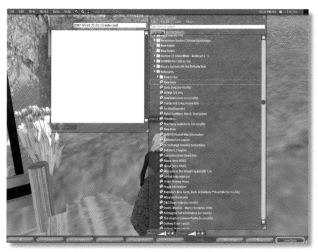

Figure 4.15: You should include notecards with landmarks as part of the packaging for your fashion designs. Here, you can see how to create a new notecard.

see the notecard, and find the landmark. Voilà! They're back. You should also make sure your store is listed in Find Places, and in the Classifieds, and in your Pics (see the Marketing chapter for more information.)

INVENTORY MANAGEMENT AND CUSTOMER SERVICE

The last two things to keep in mind as you develop your business are how inventory management can encourage visits to your store and whether your customer service practices will gain you loyal customers or drive away the very folks who buy your goods.

INVENTORY MANAGEMENT

Inventory management is key for anyone who takes *Second Life* seriously, and especially for someone running a store. That's because residents usually acquire so many different items that if they don't work hard to keep order, it can become nearly impossible to find what they need. A clean inventory is a useful inventory.

YOUR STORE INVENTORY

Inventory is critical. Think of how boring a real-world store would get if it never had any new products and never changed how it displayed its products.

"I try to introduce a new item every week," says Hyasynth. "You need to stay fresh in people's minds. And it's a great challenge as an artist." For Starley, shifting inventory is even more radical. While she doesn't profess to change things up as frequently as Hyasynth, when she does, she doesn't mess around. "An average-size clothing release now is probably [around] 20 items," Starley says. "And a skin release could be anywhere from 30 to 300."

Whatever your frequency is, introducing new items is a great way to bring customers into to your store. Cycling out old, slower selling items also opens up display room for newer, more exciting designs. Of course, you can't forget to do what it takes to get the word out that you have new items in the store.

YOUR CUSTOMER'S INVENTORY

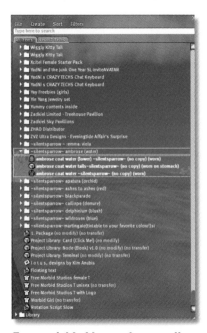

Figure 4.16: Notice how well-named items from one store are grouped together in this inventory screenshot. It's easy to find something bought from this store, even if you can't remember the item name.

Inventory is also the name for the virtual closet where *Second Life* avatars keep their goods. Thinking about your customers' inventory management is a smart business practice: Make sure it's easy for your customers to find and wear the fashion they buy from you. And make sure your store name is no mystery. Don't make your customers wonder where the heck they bought that pretty "Purple Dress." Start by naming every item, including folders, with the name or initials of your store. Then, make sure each item has a helpful descriptive name. (Figure 4.16)

If your badly named item gets lost in a client's inventory, they won't wear it. You've lost any word of mouth marketing, because others won't see your work being worn. And no matter how great that item was, it won't have much chance to become a favorite, the kind that keeps customers returning to your store to see what else you'll make that they will love. So, do yourself a favor. Set up your naming conventions right away, and use them wisely.

CUSTOMER SERVICE

Customer service is key. The two most important things you can do are to answer any and all customer instant messages and to be helpful about replacing customers' items that get lost in the technical glitches that are regular parts of the *Second Life* experience.

All told, providing excellent customer service could take as little as 30 minutes to an hour a week. Don't neglect it! "It's crucial," says Munchflower Zaius. "You still want people to come back to your store [and] you want return customers and devotion to your product." As Starley puts it, "I think any reputable merchant will take their customers seriously and do whatever they can within reason to keep them happy."

But beware. Some customers want the moon and have no problem harassing merchants with all kinds of requests and problems. It's important to keep things in perspective.

MORE INFO

CUSTOMER-SERVICE TIPS

Anything proactive you can do to keep your customers happy is going to be much easier than dealing with unhappy customers.

- Let your customers know who to contact for customer service. Some busy stores hire customer service help and even include a monitor in the store that informs customers who is online and available to answer questions.

- If you keep hearing the same question, think about what you can do to make the answer clear ahead of time. For instance, if customers frequently ask you about permissions, review your signs and any ads or posters to make sure they clearly state your policies.

- Keep your cool. Don't hit the send button when you're upset. Sometimes the best thing you can do is take a break before you respond, or respond with a simple pre-written response explaining your policy.

- You may want to designate specific times in your schedule to answer customer service questions, so they don't feel like constant interruptions.

- Make sure you get your messages! When you're not logged into *Second Life*, you can have any IMs forwarded to your email account. To change this preferences setting, log in at www.secondlife.com and go to your Account Preferences.

CHAPTER 5

THE *SECOND LIFE* LAND BUSINESS

What is land in a virtual world? There's no actual dirt, and more land can be created by Linden Lab. So why is it valuable? Land is necessary to anyone who wants a home or business in *Second Life*, and so the real-estate business, generally based on adding value to the land it deals in, is thriving. In fact, *Second Life* already has produced its first millionaire "land baron."

In this chapter, we'll look at the tips and tricks of the most successful *Second Life* real-estate developers. We'll discuss the first decision a would-be land-related business owner has to make—whether to sell land or rent it—and then go into other key decisions, such as whether to develop on the mainland or on islands. We'll also look at how much you need to invest to start a business, the skills needed to go into business, and how much time it will take to learn what you need to know.

CONTENTS

WHAT IS THE *SECOND LIFE* LAND BUSINESS?

In many ways, the economy in *Second Life* mirrors that of real life: There are innumerable opportunities—some more lucrative than others, some of which are saturated, and some of which still have significant room for smart, motivated people with a plan (see the sidebar "The Schoolteacher Turned Land Baron").

Land is always going to be one of the best of those areas because, as in the real world, it is a limited resource. Although land can be created or added to the grid in *Second Life* in a way that cannot happen in real life, each new piece of land is tied irrevocably to a server. This means that growth is limited and is tied to costly hardware, making land a scarce resource. Also, as the early land barons demonstrated, real estate in *Second Life* works best as a service business. Their services make it easier for residents to find what they want, such as turnkey communities with homes or condos where avatars can move in the minute they pay the rent. Others provide the variety of landscapes, cultures, and thoughtful community development that make it possible for residents to let go of the fear that their neighbors will suddenly start building hideous, lag-tastic eyesores that will render neighborhoods uninhabitable, ruining property values and driving people away.

MORE INFO

THE SCHOOLTEACHER TURNED LAND BARON

(Image courtesy of W. James Au)

On November 28, 2006, a Chinese former schoolteacher named Ailin Graef held a press conference in her private *Second Life* theater and announced to a room full of reporters, bloggers, and others that she was a millionaire.

Graef, who is better known as the avatar Anshe Chung, likes to talk about how she turned a $10 investment in 2004 into what is without question the largest *Second Life* business empire. She is, everyone would agree, the first true *Second Life* land baron.

It's hard to overstate how big a player Anshe Chung is in the *Second Life* land business. At her press conference, she spelled it out in cold, hard numbers: The 550 sims she owned, plus stakes in other *Second Life* businesses and her Linden-dollar holdings were worth more than $1 million—in US dollars.

After entering the *Second Life* land market in summer 2004, Anshe became the most astute player in one of the most lucrative segments of the *Second Life* economy. She embodied smart business: She bought low and sold high, again and again. She learned the market and figured out how to leverage her initial capital into a growing business. Her business soon became focused on buying and developing custom estates, and renting them to *Second Life* residents searching for an easy way to hang a shingle in the virtual world. In the process, she became the standard-bearer for a small flood of competitors who have followed in her footsteps.

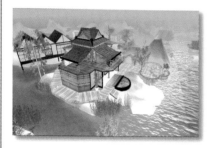

Anshe Chung is likely the biggest real-estate owner in *Second Life*, having developed hundreds of sims with specific themes (like the one shown here).

Today, Anshe Chung has real competitors, though they pale in size compared to her now-incorporated Anshe Chung Studios (ACS). In fact, while some of the other land outfits are nearing double-figure headcounts, ACS has set up shop in the Chinese metropolis of Wuhan and has more than 30 full-time employees, with an additional 20 expected to be added to the payroll in the coming months.

Indeed, Anshe Chung has ambitions to transform the market for modern, high-tech employment in central China. She is leveraging her teaching background and hiring trainees, many of whom she hopes will soon be able to join her team, and who provide her with a low-cost way to remain one of the most powerful presences (if not *the* most) in the explosive *Second Life* economy.

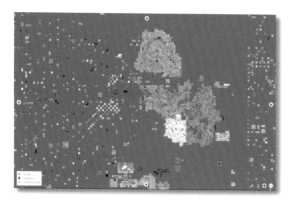

In *Second Life*, land is divided into two categories: the mainland and islands (Figure 5.1).

*Figure 5.1: The **Second Life** world map on April 15, 2007, showed several large areas of mainland and countless islands.*

Those who prefer islands say they offer more privacy, the ability to control borders, a higher likelihood of waterfront property, and the opportunity to name the island. When buying a new island from Linden Lab, you can select from a variety of default topographies or create a specification of your own. Islands are regions corresponding to a square on the map grid, roughly 16 acres, or 65,536 square meters. Some projects require more than one sim, and so are spread over two or more islands. Islands can be grouped together into an estate, either as a cluster of islands or joined to make a larger land area. It's possible to reserve the exact spot on the grid where your island will be placed and, for a fee, reserve specific areas on the grid where you think you'd like to expand later—very handy for an expanding business with limited budget. Those who prefer the mainland enjoy lower prices, as well as a feeling of being in the middle of a large and growing community.

Figure 5.2: Japanese-themed land in Second Life

In either case, land is often developed according to a theme: winter, Japanese (Figure 5.2), New York City, adult, and many others. Because of that, *Second Life* residents in search of existing land tend to look for developers who specialize in the theme they're interested in for their homes and businesses.

Land must be owned by a single individual, although the owner can designate helpers (either as a group or specific individuals) who have the right to build or otherwise exercise some of the estate owner's powers. The estate owner has the ability to make very specific divisions of those powers, for instance creating one set for event managers (who may need to send out notices and set the number of avatars allowed in an area) and a different set for builders (who can be given the ability to build and landscape, for instance).

THE FINANCIAL SIDE OF THE LAND BUSINESS

Sticking it out in the land business is not cheap. An island costs US$1,675 as of this writing, with an additional US$295 per island each month for maintenance fees. Full mainland sims can go for more than that on the open market. The days of getting started for a few hundred dollars are long over.

Figure 5.3: Dana Bergson is the principal owner of the Otherland Group, one of the largest real-estate businesses in Second Life.

CHAPTER 1
CHAPTER 2
CHAPTER 3
CHAPTER 4
CHAPTER 5

CHAPTER 6
CHAPTER 7
CHAPTER 8
CHAPTER 9
CHAPTER 10
CHAPTER 11
APPENDICES
INDEX

In fact, Dana Bergson (Figure 5.3) estimates that you shouldn't even bother making a serious go of it without being able and willing to put up at least US$10,000 to get started. "The land business is cash intensive," Dana says. "When you start, you have to put in at least some five-figure sums; otherwise it's just too slow."

Dana suggests that to get a land business off the ground—renting or selling—you need several sims and the resources to manage them. Regardless of how good you are, it's going to take a while to recoup your investment. Anyone who goes into the *Second Life* land business thinking they can make their investment back overnight is in for a serious shock.

Adam Zaius (of Azure Estates; see the sidebar "Adam Zaius on Business Planning and Startup Costs") estimates that, at current land prices, it should take a new business owner about 10 months to make back the initial investment. Alliez Mysterio agrees, though she thinks that it could take someone a full year to recoup their investment. "After that," Adam explains, "you have a much healthier margin for a business to live on."

■ WHAT LAND COSTS AND HOW TO GET IT

To have a home or to set up a business in *Second Life*, the first requirement is land. Residents who want to leave things set up—a furnished home, a store with merchandise, even that half-built project—need enough land to support the number of prims in the objects. Only avatars with Premium accounts (US$9.95/month or $72/year) can buy land on the mainland. This is one reason why the land business does well—any avatar, even those with a free Basic account, can rent or buy island property from a land developer. Keep in mind that your customers will face the same restrictions, so only those with Premium accounts will be able to purchase mainland plots from you. (Anyone can rent properties on the mainland, however.)

Buying whole islands (even several of them) from Linden Lab, on the other hand, doesn't require a Premium membership. Those who don't need much land or who don't want to pay maintenance costs for a whole island can acquire subdivided plots of island property from land businesses.

NOTE

Avatars who don't own land can go to public Sandboxes to practice building or to pull things out of Inventory. For new avatars, Sandboxes are good places to check out the contents of their Inventory Library folder. Rules at Sandboxes vary, but most do not allow weapons or selling. Visit several until you find one you like. Sandboxes are traditionally cleared of all content daily.

CHAPTER 5

WHAT IS THE
SECOND LIFE
LAND
BUSINESS?

THE
FINANCIAL
SIDE OF THE
LAND
BUSINESS

PLANNING:
TO SELL
OR RENT?

THE
REQUIRED
SKILLS

SETTING
UP SHOP

THE BEST
LAND FOR
YOUR
BUSINESS—
HOW TO
CHOOSE?

COMPETING
IN THE LAND
BUSINESS

WEATHERING
THE LAND
BOOMS AND
BUSTS

Once you actually possess land, monthly land-use fees (known as *tier fees*), are assessed according to how much land you have. It may be dawning on you how Linden Lab makes money off a product that is "free." Figuring out how much your monthly tier fees are and how much the land itself costs can seem like it requires a calculus expert. In reality, it's not all that complicated, it just takes a little getting used to. For starters, it's worth noting that *Second Life* land, particularly on the mainland, is a commodity whose cost varies according to market conditions. Those who have been in the land business for some time all point to the boom-and-bust cycles that the market goes through. For anyone serious about starting a new *Second Life* land business, it's important to pay close attention to market conditions.

As with many things, determining the pricing of *Second Life* land depends on whether you're talking about mainland property or islands, and who you're buying the land from. Land in *Second Life* is available from three sources: individual residents, Linden Lab (`http://secondlife.com/auctions/`), and real-estate developers. Here's how each scenario works.

BUYING LAND FROM LINDEN LAB

When you're deciding whether to buy an island or mainland property from Linden Lab, islands are probably the easier case to understand. Buying mainland property directly from Linden Lab is a tad more complicated. (For more on the mainland vs. island debate, see the section "The Best Land for Your Business—How to Choose?" later in this chapter.)

ISLANDS

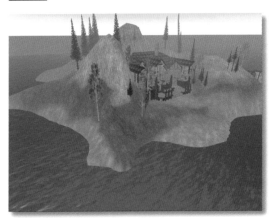

Figure 5.4: There are thousands of islands in Second Life, and anyone can buy a new one if they're willing to pay the purchase price.

Islands are sold through Linden Lab's Land Store; they have set pricing and tier fees. There can be delays in delivery, so don't wait until the last minute to order needed land. Linden Lab allows you to select the specific placement of your island on the existing land grid (`http://secondlife.com/apps/mapapps/buy/`). If you already own one or more islands, you may want to locate any new ones you buy near those you have already. As of this writing, an island sim like the one in Figure 5.4, which is 65,536 square meters of land, costs US$1,675 plus a US$295 monthly fee. Educators and certified nonprofits can buy islands at half price and pay a lower monthly fee. As with any valuable commodity, the price for islands goes up from time to time. Again, it's essential to pay attention to pricing and plan accordingly. (See the sidebar "Tier Fees for *Second Life* Land, by Size.")

CHAPTER 1
CHAPTER 2
CHAPTER 3
CHAPTER 4
CHAPTER 5

CHAPTER 6
CHAPTER 7
CHAPTER 8
CHAPTER 9
CHAPTER 10
CHAPTER 11
APPENDICES
INDEX

MORE INFO

TIER FEES FOR *SECOND LIFE* LAND, BY SIZE

On the mainland, tier fees (all in **US** dollars) are as follows:

- An entire sim: $195/month
- 1/2 sim, $125/month
- 1/4 sim, $75/month
- 1/8 sim, $40/month
- 1/16 sim, $25/month
- 1/32 sim, $15/month
- 1/64 sim, $8/month
- 1/128 sim, $5/month

MAINLAND

The most straightforward way to buy land is through Linden Lab's official auction system. This system is for newly created land that the company adds to the grid from time to time or land that was abandoned by users. For example, as of this writing there were 22 different mainland plots available, ranging in size from 768 square meters to 5,120 square meters and jumping up to a full sim. The prices ranged from US$70 to US$3,251. As with real-life real estate, the main issue is to think about what your customers need and how you can satisfy that need.

BUYING LAND FROM A PRIVATE PARTY

Figure 5.5: There are many ways to find land for sale in Second Life. *One is fly around and find "for sale" signs.*

It's possible to buy islands and mainland plots secondhand. The price is set by the market and comes with a US$100 transfer fee to be paid by the seller. These sales occur outside the official auspices of *Second Life* and Linden Lab and are often conducted through the many community forums. There are two easy ways to find such land for sale. First, you can look at *Second Life*'s in-world map, on which any available resident-owned plots are clearly marked as such (Figure 5.5).

Second, if you're in *Second Life*, you can click on the Search button and choose the Land Sales tab. At any given time, there are dozens of plots for sale, from tiny 16-square-meter plots to entire sims, and the prices vary wildly, depending in large part on the demand for the location.

NOTE

Don't worry that land is up for sale because it's flawed. There are many reasons why someone would sell their land, including pure speculation. Some people no longer want to do whatever it is they originally set out to do on an island, others can no longer afford their parcel, and others have decided to own land in another area. (Do look for potential problems before you buy, though.)

It is also possible to buy developed land directly from one of the many *Second Life* land businesses. These outfits are in it for the money, however, so the prices they charge are very likely to be too high to constitute a profitable investment.

RESIDENTS SPEAK

ADAM ZAIUS ON STARTUP COSTS

Adam Zaius, co-owner of Azure Estates, is one of the most successful land developers in Second Life. He shares his thoughts about how much money it might cost to get into Second Life businesses of different sizes.

STARTUP COSTS FOR A SMALL ESTATE (ABOUT 10 SIMS)

- **Land: 10 regions at US$1,675 = US$16,950**

- **Design: Negligible because you will want to do it yourself**

- **Support: Negligible because you will want to do it yourself**

- **Miscellaneous costs (including island maintenance, tier fees while designing regions, item and system purchases, and miscellaneous contractors and consultants): US$4,000**

- **Total initial investment: About US$21,000**

A small estate is about the average size of estates in Second Life, Adam points out. Most fall between 5 and 20 sims each. These are not large enough operations to justify paying for help on design or support, so they will require a fair amount of work to get things going and to keep your customers happy.

STARTUP COSTS FOR A MEDIUM ESTATE (ABOUT 40 SIMS)

- **Land: 40 regions at US$1,675 = US$67,800**

- **Design contractors: US$10,000**

CHAPTER 1
CHAPTER 2
CHAPTER 3
CHAPTER 4
CHAPTER 5

CHAPTER 6
CHAPTER 7
CHAPTER 8
CHAPTER 9
CHAPTER 10
CHAPTER 11
APPENDICES
INDEX

- Support contractors: One or two people, about US$1,500 per month

- Miscellaneous costs (as spelled out above): US$8,000

- Total initial investment: About US$90,000

Adam says that a medium-sized estate should, if managed correctly, give a return on investment of about the same as an average full-time job, with the equivalent amount of work. That means about US$48,000 a year.

STARTUP COSTS FOR A LARGE ESTATE (150 OR MORE SIMS)

- Land: 150 regions at US$1,675 = US$254,250

- Design contractors: US$20,000

- Support contractors: Several people, about US$3,000 per month

- Miscellaneous costs (as spelled out above): US$25,000

- Total initial investment: About US$300,000

Although few people could muster up the capital to start this large a business, Adam says that doing so could, after a year or so, to make back the investment and earn you a good living. Managing the business would be a full-time job, and you'd have to ensure that you had support staff spanning many time zones. That's because support and professionalism are absolute requirements for a large estate. It's a seven-day-a-week job.

PLANNING: TO SELL OR TO RENT?

In the land-development market, there are two main business models: selling land and renting it. Each model works differently, and each has its advantages. They do have one thing in common, though. In each case, the business provides the paying customer with a piece of *Second Life* land that they can use without having to deal with some of the complexities that come with buying such land directly from Linden Lab or from individuals selling their personal land—often undeveloped mainland properties without covenants.

SUMMARY

Most people don't like rules that much. We are no exception. Therefore, the OTHERLAND COVENANT isn't much more than common sense put in words plus some rules that should make sure that the general character of the land is preserved. You came here, because you liked the land and the neighborhood. Let's try to keep it like that.

0. No Ban Lines!

1. Build your house such that it could fit (with a grain of salt) into a residential area in RL!
2. Preserve some vegetation and keep it with the style of the sim you are living in!
3. Preserve the general style of the landscape when terraforming!
4. Respect your fellow residents privacy!
5. Don't raise your own fences (prims, bans or aggressive scripts) too high!
6. Use the resources of your sim in a fair way (watch the lag you might be causing)!
7. Be nice to your neighbours! Remember: you want them to be nice to you, too!

Figure 5.6: A covenant is the set of guidelines that estate owners can impose on their land to make it more attractive to residents and would-be residents.

Developers typically set rules, known as *covenants* (Figure 5.6), for the land they sell, often because such agreements offer assurance to land buyers that their neighbors have agreed to rules governing behavior, zoning, aesthetics, and more, often in a large, themed, master-planned region.

SELLING LAND

Selling *Second Life* land as a developer is not quite the same thing as putting it up for grabs at auction or exchanging cash for a tennis racket on Craigslist. Rather, the development businesses that sell *Second Life* land do so on what amounts to a management basis. That is, the business buys the land, develops it according to whatever theme it specializes in, takes care of many of the practical complexities that come with land ownership—such as terraforming, prim management, liaisons with Linden Lab, fitting the land into a larger managed region, and more—and then offers it for sale to the *Second Life* community.

Figure 5.7: Most successful Second Life real-estate developers maintain websites like this one with listings of their available properties.

Most of these outfits maintain websites on which they list their available properties, general information about the themes they focus on, their prices, their covenants—the terms and conditions of buying property on a seller's estate—and more (Figure 5.7). Sellers often cater to their customers' needs. If someone wants to buy 512 square meters of managed land—the smallest parcel one can own in *Second Life*—someone will sell it. Just because whole-island sims are all the rage right now doesn't mean you shouldn't try to sell smaller plots. As you might predict, selling plots of all sizes is the way to attract the most diverse range of customers.

SPOTLIGHT ON ADAM ZAIUS AND NEXUS NASH OF AZURE ISLANDS

Nexus Nash (shown here) and Adam Zaius own Azure Islands, one of the largest land-management organizations in *Second Life*. When I first talked to them, about two years after they opened up their business, they had grown from a single sim to more than 150 sims and more than a thousand residents. But how did they do that?

Zaius recalls that the two started in March 2005, taking their initial investment of L$200,000—around US$800 at the time—with a mainland sim called Meins, and a month later moved to their first island.

Although many people want small parcels of land, the Azure Island founders felt that a minimum of around 4,000 square meters was the right amount of space to live in. So they don't cater to those who seek the small plots. Says Adam, "It's possible to make smaller parcels, sure, but people don't tend to want to keep them for very long."

Another signature element of Azure Islands was their commitment to selling parcels of land that fit their regions rather than forcing everyone to buy square grids. The result? "We've got a waiting list," says Adam. "We tend to sell out within 24 hours of putting a new region up."

Azure Islands has grown, in part, because Adam and Nexus have been willing to put most of their profit back into the business. Doing so has allowed them to expand at a natural rate and not to have to dip into their pockets to go beyond their initial investment.

"We've been growing fairly organically," said Adam. "One sim has funded the next, and so on. [Our growth rate has been] around 40 percent growth every three months, although that's increased dramatically [recently] and become exponential rather than linear due to the general influx of new residents."

■ RENTING LAND

If you are a land developer, you can make money by renting it instead of selling it. In many ways, the two business models are similar. However, with rental property you maintain ownership of the land and continue to hold the asset. If tenants stop paying the rent, you're still responsible for paying the tier costs, but the land is yours and you can find a new renter. If you develop your mainland properties with an eye to the value you add with covenants, themes, landscaping, and the like, and you want to make sure that atmosphere is maintained, you may prefer to rent the land, keeping control of each aspect of the estate and the type of community you've planned.

When renting out land, you will have to take the land you buy and fold it into your larger holdings. That means terraforming, managing prims, dealing with Linden Lab, and many of the other responsibilities that sellers have. Additionally, you will have to manage your tenants' needs. In exchange you get rent and you continue to own the land. Landlords, like sellers, cater to their customers' needs, often making plots of all sizes available.

On an island, when you "buy" a plot, you are contracting with the sim owner and not Linden Lab. As far as Linden Lab is concerned, the sim owner continues to own the whole island because the sim owner is who pays the US$295 per month. The plot "owner" pays tier to the sim owner, not Linden Lab.

Renters can decide to move on, so from time to time you will need to locate tenants. However, if you're a good land manager and have created desirable regions with attractive landscaping, low-impact tenants, and decent pricing, you should have little trouble finding replacements.

MORE INFO

Spotlight on Alliez Mysterio of d'Alliez Estates

Alliez Mysterio is well known in *Second Life* as one of the most successful landlords, and one who produces beautiful, well-thought-out land for rent. Recently, she added land sales to her portfolio, but for years she only rented.

In April 2004, Alliez met a *Second Life* newbie and soon found herself helping him out

CHAPTER 1
CHAPTER 2
CHAPTER 3
CHAPTER 4
CHAPTER 5

CHAPTER 6
CHAPTER 7
CHAPTER 8
CHAPTER 9
CHAPTER 10
CHAPTER 11
APPENDICES
INDEX

as he bought a lot of land, built a newbie center, apartments, a club, and a shopping center. Eventually, he handed over management of the land to her. In return for managing his property, he gave Alliez a piece of land to build on—and she turned to famed *Second Life* builder Versu Richelieu, who completed Rue d'Alliez, a French-themed shopping area.

Alliez and her former business partner, Tony Beckett, put US$500 into the project—and d'Alliez Estates was off and running.

Alliez says she knew that she wanted to be in the real-estate business because she had a lot of experience working with people of all kinds and because she enjoyed taking nothing—say, an empty piece of *Second Life* land—and turning it into something. "I felt that the people of the [*Second Life*] community needed a place to call home," Alliez says. "*Second Life* gives all a chance to have whatever they want."

Like Azure Islands, d'Alliez Estates is always sold out and has a waiting list. And in part that's because Alliez makes customer service her number-one priority. It's easy to say that, of course, but Alliez is adamant about running her business based on a philosophy that the customer is always right and should always be able to get the help they need. As a result, Alliez and Tony took that one sim that Versu built for them and turned it into a mini empire that now numbers more than 50 full sims—and is still growing.

THE REQUIRED SKILLS

In the land business, there are two different kinds of skills. One is the business and marketing you need to do to develop and maintain your clientele. This includes any community development you do, from setting up covenants to creating open community lands such as parks. The other is the technical side of things. In this case, that mostly means subdividing and beautifying the land that you will be making available, either for rent or for sale, to your customers.

■ SUBDIVIDING YOUR LAND

Dividing sims can play an important part in your business success. Linden Lab provides estate (land management) tools that are fairly simple to use. To begin, click on the land you want to manipulate, and then select Edit Terrain from the pie menu. This opens up a set of menu choices that will allow you to do a number of things with your land, such as subdivide it. (Simply select the land with your mouse, drag to select a rectangle of the size you want the new parcel of land to be, then click the Subdivide button.)

NOTE

Parcels that are sharing prims between them do not have to be adjacent to each other but they do need to be in the same estate.

It's very important to note that when you combine prims among multiple parcels in a single estate, it's possible to suddenly "blow out" or lose parts of a build because you've exceeded the prim limits. This can happen if you sell land where you've used this prim trick, when the new owner finds they suddenly do not have enough prims to continue to display the build.

The same terrain-editing tool also lets you determine how many prims to allot to each parcel. Because the *Second Life* tools allow you to distribute the prims of unused land plots to plots on the same sim, you can determine whether keeping some of the land empty—or covered in water, like d'Alliez Estates does—might be a good way of increasing the prim limits for your customers on populated land.

Of course, not every land business is going to want to follow d'Alliez's example, given that the model requires giving up about half of the usable land—an expensive luxury, especially for a new business trying to make back its investment. However, you still need to understand how to divide the land you have unless you're going to be selling or renting only full sims. If you're new to this business, that's pretty unlikely.

MORE INFO

UNDERSTANDING THE ESTATE TOOLS

Some land-management tools are available only to landowners with island estates and to their designated helpers. Estate tools include the ability to change the look of the terrain by editing the ground texture. This makes it easy to swap snow for a field of grass, for instance, just by changing the texture applied to the land.

Because these tools are grayed out in the *Second Life* user interface for everyone else, few have yet mastered use of them. Mainland properties do not offer the same levels of control.

Each sim has 15,000 available prims, but you don't have to be locked into those numbers. (See Table 3.1 in Chapter 3 for details on the prim limit per land parcel.) To increase the object bonus, go to the World menu, then click Region/Estate and change the object bonus to 2.000 or a more appropriate ratio.

CHAPTER 1
CHAPTER 2
CHAPTER 3
CHAPTER 4
CHAPTER 5

CHAPTER 6
CHAPTER 7
CHAPTER 8
CHAPTER 9
CHAPTER 10
CHAPTER 11
APPENDICES
INDEX

WARNING

In the Second Life Knowledge Base, Linden Lab cautions against using the object bonus haphazardly: "In order to allow that parcel to be double primmed it would be sensible to set aside an equivalent sized parcel that has no prims on it to balance this out," the site says (http://secondlife.com/knowledgebase/article.php?id=097). Bear in mind that using the object bonus does not increase the total number of prims available for a whole sim.

Remember that land can hold a given number of prims, but that setting is overridden by your prim limit total. That's useful, since you can actually use your entire allotment of prims when building on a plot that's technically too small.

MORE INFO

THE D'ALLIEZ ESTATES APPROACH TO SUBDIVIDING LAND AND INCREASING PRIM LIMITS

d'Alliez Estates is famous for giving customers privacy—and the maximum number of usable prims—by reserving around half the sim for water.

Using water on the interior of a sim, between parcels of land, enhances privacy for each. Using water as an interior boundary also has the benefit of giving each customer waterfront property.

To increase prim limits on its parcels, d'Alliez halves the amount of usable land and then increases the number of prims that can be placed in a given parcel of land using an object bonus. The idea here is that a multiplier ratio can be set, increasing the number of prims available to each parcel on a sim *if and only if* the amount of usable land is halved. By keeping that ratio intact, d'Alliez makes their parcels more valuable.

■ TERRAFORMING

When you receive a sim from Linden Lab, there are six default islands to choose from. For your own custom island, you can either use a RAW terrain file or *Second Life*'s terrain-editing tools to modify the features of any land you own. On a basic level, the tool offers basic abilities to reshape land—for instance, lowering or raising it (simply select a plot of land, click on it, and choose Select Land). Once you're done, you can click on Apply to Selection to have it take effect.

You can terraform with a lot of detail if you choose very small pieces of the land at a time and change them each separately. But that gets you only as far as changing the features of the land itself. You'll probably also want to add landscape features such as rivers, waterfalls, trees, grass, and so on. One method is to choose Edit Terrain tool and click the Create button. Two rows of buttons will appear; the second from the right is for trees and the rightmost is for grass. To insert a grass or tree texture, select the corresponding button and then click the magic wand that appears on the location where you want the grass or tree to appear.

TIP

Each time you click the land with the Edit Terrain wand when you have Grass or Tree selected, SL will insert a different, random plant. But if you check Keep Tool Selected, it will insert the same kind of greenery each time. If you want multiples of the same plant, select it and then hold down Shift and use one of the drag handles that appear to duplicate the object.

Alternatively, in every *Second Life* resident's Inventory are many useful default objects, including the same trees and grass also available via the Edit Terrain tool. You can find the individual item you want—say, an aspen tree—and drag and drop as many copies as you want from the Inventory Library.

Water features—like rivers or ponds—are often a nice addition to your land. There are several methods of incorporating these elements. If your land is at sea level and you dig a trench using the terraforming tools, it will fill in with water, creating in effect a river or pond. You also can use animated water to fill streambeds, ponds, swimming pools, or hot tubs. Home and garden stores offer a selection of water features that are easy to set up, even in skyboxes or mountaintop land high above the water table. You also can add many features to your land by applying more-complex texture maps, as detailed in the next section. It's even possible to buy scripts that enable avatars to swim in all this water!

CHAPTER 1
CHAPTER 2
CHAPTER 3
CHAPTER 4
CHAPTER 5

CHAPTER 6
CHAPTER 7
CHAPTER 8
CHAPTER 9
CHAPTER 10
CHAPTER 11
APPENDICES
INDEX

USING 3D TOOLS TO CREATE TERRAFORM TEXTURES

For making changes to existing land, use Linden Lab's terraforming tools. If you have a lot of land to terraform and you want to have it all look a specific way, it is possible to use a drawing program like Photoshop to create a RAW file that essentially replicates the design of a sim and allows you to import it into *Second Life* to use automatically in your terraforming activities. "Say we bought six sims," says Alliez Mysterio. "We could bring that RAW file in and, poof, have a sim that looks just like our other ones. Fast. It saves a lot of time." RAW files also can be used when ordering new islands, to get exactly the desired terrain.

SETTING UP SHOP

Although Anshe Chung dominates the land business, there's no doubt there is room for others, just as smart entrepreneurs in real life can make money in the same business as Donald Trump. *Second Life* is growing every day, adding new land and growing at an explosive rate.

Much of the land rush stems from the thousands of people who are signing up and swelling the ranks of the *Second Life* community. It took *Second Life* more than three years to reach a million registered accounts (though that number does not correspond to individual users because a single user can have multiple accounts), but only eight weeks for the next million. That means that for an individual or small team with a clear plan, some capital to invest, and some patience, *Second Life* land offers an opportunity to make some money in that most solid of markets: real estate, even if it is all digital.

RESIDENTS SPEAK

ANSHE CHUNG ON STARTING A BUSINESS IN *SECOND LIFE*

This interview is adapted with permission from a CNET News.com article by Daniel Terdiman, "Virtual Magnate Shares Secrets of Success," December 21, 2006 (http://news.com.com/Virtual+magnate+shares+secrets+of+success/2008-1043_3-6144967.html).

Q: What challenges do you think someone would face in trying to start a business in *Second Life* today?

AC: I think one challenge I faced when starting—and that people face now when starting—is to discover one niche that offers a good

(Continued)

CHAPTER 5

WHAT IS THE
SECOND LIFE
LAND
BUSINESS?

THE
FINANCIAL
SIDE OF THE
LAND
BUSINESS

PLANNING:
TO SELL
OR RENT?

THE
REQUIRED
SKILLS

SETTING
UP SHOP

THE BEST
LAND FOR
YOUR
BUSINESS—
HOW TO
CHOOSE?

COMPETING
IN THE LAND
BUSINESS

WEATHERING
THE LAND
BOOMS AND
BUSTS

opportunity . . . I think the recent surge in population offers many opportunities in niche markets and products that were not viable when the number of potential customers was smaller. Ask yourself, "How can I make people happy?" Once you make people happy, it is not so hard to actually also profit from it.

Q: What other advice would you give someone starting a *Second Life* business today?

AC: I would suggest careful optimism and avoiding the blindness of the hype about *Second Life*. It has very strong and solid growth, but I still think that people who invest $200,000 of their real-life savings now are risking too much. The first step to succeeding in a virtual world is not to invest huge sums of money but instead to become a resident of the world, learn how to live here, play in it, use it, and do what everybody else does and more. You don't go to Indonesia and say, "Here, I have a million dollars," and blindly invest.

Q: Once you got going with your business, what set you apart from your competitors?

AC: I generally did not set my pricing model at "How much can I make people pay?" I kept it at cost plus (a small) margin. And I always tried to scale up, to increase the volume of business with lower margins.

IDENTIFYING YOUR CUSTOMER

As you might expect, there are some similarities between running a *Second Life* land business and running any other kind of *Second Life* business. One of the most important is that you decide precisely what niche you are going to cater to. Although it's certainly possible to serve the population at large, you'll be competing with some of the most-established names in the business. Therefore, it's probably best when you're getting started to think about one niche in which you can be a leader.

One great thing about *Second Life* is that there are so many distinct communities, each of which can support a wide variety of businesses. Some examples of specific niches you can market to include Furries (Figure 5.8), newbies, cyberpunks, club areas, non-English-speaking communities, and those focusing on either businesses or residential communities. Often, products or services created for those communities can fetch a premium over normal prices because members are willing to pay more for specialization.

Figure 5.8: Lusk—a sim catering to the Furry community

That's why Adam Zaius points out that marketing land development to specific communities—castles to vampires, forests to elves, etc.—is a good way to deal with the fact that tier pricing is going up and will likely continue to do so for some time. Of course, you don't want to pick a community you know nothing about, so it is important that you choose something you know you could learn. Otherwise, your work won't feel authentic and you will have trouble making sales.

USING A COVENANT ON YOUR ESTATE

*Figure 5.9: Ban lines are the red borders that you see when you try to enter a **Second Life** property that is closed to public access.*

When trying to create a land estate that has a distinctive set of characteristics, you'll need to define a set of behavioral guidelines (called a *covenant*) that those who buy land on the estate must follow.

Often, people don't like rules, but your selling point can be that you've created a unique environment based on common principles and that things will stay the way that they were when the customer bought the land. As the manager of the estate, you get to set the specifications of the covenants—everything from the way prims are used to whether residents can put up *ban lines*

(Figure 5.9), to the style of buildings they can erect. It's up to you, and your customer base will evolve based in part on what that covenant is.

Covenants are not technical specifications. They are more like community standards, and you need to be willing to enforce them to make them effective. Otherwise, some of your customers will ignore them, which can quickly lead to a collapse of the overall cohesiveness of your estate. However, if you are consistent about enforcing the covenants, are fair about how you apply them, and communicate your intentions well, the customers who want to live in such a place will be grateful and will refer their friends.

That's Dana Bergson's strategy with the Otherland Group (see the sidebar, "An Example Covenant: The Otherland Group"). "We carefully design the land, design it so that every parcel is beautiful in itself . . . and we have a covenant which restricts building within some sensible limits, and contrary to other real-estate firms, we actually make sure that the covenant is upheld. It costs us a few customers, but makes the others happy."

MORE INFO

AN EXAMPLE COVENANT: THE OTHERLAND GROUP

The Otherland Group, one of the largest managed estates in *Second Life*, prides itself on being a collection of real estate that *Second Life* residents choose for its beauty and its neighborliness. In part, that's possible because Otherland has set forth a series of rules—its covenant—that govern the behavior of those who have land in its "archipelago." This is the summary of the covenant, as prescribed on Otherland's website (www.otherland-group.com/rules/covenant.html):

"Most people don't like rules that much. We are no exception. Therefore, the Otherland covenant isn't much more than common sense put in words plus some rules that should make sure that the general character of the land is preserved. You came here because you liked the land and the neighborhood. Let's try to keep it like that:

- No ban lines!

- Build your house such that it could fit (with a grain of salt) into a residential area [in real life]!

- Preserve some vegetation and keep it with the style of the sim you are living in!

- Preserve the general style of the landscape when terraforming!

- Respect your fellow residents' privacy!

- Don't raise your own fences (prims, bans, or aggressive scripts) too high!

- Use the resources of your sim in a fair way (watch the lag you might be causing)!

CHAPTER 1
CHAPTER 2
CHAPTER 3
CHAPTER 4
CHAPTER 5

CHAPTER 6
CHAPTER 7
CHAPTER 8
CHAPTER 9
CHAPTER 10
CHAPTER 11
APPENDICES
INDEX

🔶 Be nice to your neighbors! Remember: you want them to be nice to you, too!

Otherland enforces its covenant by being friendly and polite, by sending reminder instant messages when needed, and by having patient discussions with people when it's clear that a customer doesn't understand the covenant's standards.

◼ CHOOSING THE RIGHT TEAM

If you think that an outfit like Azure Islands, which manages an estate of more than 150 sims, can get by with just its two owners doing all the work, you may not fully understand how much work there is in this business. (See the sidebar "Adam Zaius's Advice for a Newcomers to the *Second Life* Land Business.")

In fact, owners Adam Zaius and Nexus Nash employ eight people to help them with the various jobs that are required to run a business that covers so many sims and hundreds of customers. A few of them work full-time hours, while others work part time. The goal of having the team is to ensure that Azure has people working during business hours for any time zone where it has customers.

RESIDENTS SPEAK

ADAM ZAIUS'S ADVICE FOR NEWCOMERS TO THE *SECOND LIFE* LAND BUSINESS

🔶 Look for niche markets—such as those that cater to *Second Life* subcommunities like Furries, elves, or vampires—where you can charge premium fees that will help cover higher tier costs.

🔶 Make sure you are teamed up with at least one other person. Having a business partner can be invaluable because he can fill in when you are unable to focus on the business and because together you can cover a large number of time zones.

🔶 Adding value to your land is important and is becoming the chief differentiator in the land business as *Second Life* goes through its exponential growth period. This is vital, as you will be competing with others on features, not price.

(Continued)

- **Be prepared to work insane hours.** This means being around after grid updates to make sure that your content is still intact, as well as being sure you or someone from your outfit is available as often as possible to tend to customers' needs.

- **Be prepared to stick it out in the business through both the boom *and* the bust times.** *Second Life*'s economy is cyclical and, despite its well-publicized growth, will no doubt go through peaks and valleys in the future. You absolutely have to stick with it if you want to see a return on your investment.

- **Don't neglect to learn the market first.** If you just entered *Second Life* two days ago, don't expect to be a millionaire tomorrow. Spend three months finding out how things work, who does what, who can help, etc.

- **Don't kill the goose that lays the golden egg by doing something greedy in the short term.** Your reputation is golden. You will have to aim longer term to succeed.

- **Don't try to work on higher costs—in other words, don't rent sims.** It's not a smart move if you are trying to succeed in the longer term. The added costs will decimate any potential margin you want to make.

- **Don't quit.** A lot of businesses find it's too much work and sell whenever the market takes a downturn, often for far less than they are worth. If you are going to sell out your business, do it at a fair rate that includes the work and goodwill you have bought up, not just the value of your assets.

You need to be smart about how many people you're going to bring on board to help. You don't want employees' wages to take too much of your budget. Instead, make sure they're contributing to the bottom line. *Second Life* contractors can easily earn US$15 and up per hour. You have to look at your accounting and decide if paying someone that much is going to be worth it. Particularly when you're getting started, it will be worthwhile to see if you can take on a new task yourself rather than hiring someone. However, when it's crucial that someone else do the work, you have to be willing to pay for it.

CHAPTER 1
CHAPTER 2
CHAPTER 3
CHAPTER 4
CHAPTER 5

CHAPTER 6
CHAPTER 7
CHAPTER 8
CHAPTER 9
CHAPTER 10
CHAPTER 11
APPENDICES
INDEX

As you look for employees, you have to be sure that they're going to be able to do what you want them to do: If they are there to provide customer service, make sure they're good at dealing with people. If they are good builders, can they deliver on time? The *Second Life* community is full of people with talent—but talent is not the same thing as the ability to get the job done right, the first time, and *on time*. As Adam puts it, "Bad help is worse than no help. If you have someone who continually creates work rather than solves it and can't be proactive about getting things done, then you will end up spending more time managing them, rather than the problem. Good help is necessary to survive, but do be discriminating in who[m] you pick."

With a virtual world like *Second Life*, how do you find the right people to work for you? It's an important dynamic to consider, given that the talented people who want to work in *Second Life* are from all over the world and have all kinds of work styles. (And who you choose might dramatically impact the success of your enterprise.) Traditionally, face-to-face meetings might be a good way to meet potential employees, but that's hardly true to the spirit of *Second Life*! (Besides, it's highly implausible that in-person meetings would be convenient or economical.) Fortunately, you can easily conduct interviews in-world. Of course, the broader Internet offers countless other options for getting to know people; teams working together remotely often use TeamSpeak or Skype for hands-free chat. And the new built-in *Second Life* voice client adds to that toolset.

TIP

Dana Bergson of the Otherland Group suggests starting prospective employees out as contractors so you can work with them for some time before hiring them outright. That's because it's important for you to get to know them before you entrust too much of your business to them.

But *Second Life* is a unique environment—and if you're going to operate in it, it's vital to understand that people have different work needs and expectations than in real-world businesses. Be prepared to deal with your employees as their *Second Life* personas and respect their need for privacy. "It's all about trust," says Dana. "Trust builds slowly [and] it can never be replaced by contracts alone. So my payroll grows slowly, and I put a lot of emphasis on talk, talk, talk." Communicating with your employees is the way to learn whether you can trust them. In the end, whether you succeed or fail in this business will depend in part on who you hire to help you out. So, before you bring someone on board, do your best to be sure that they can do what you want them to do: Look at their previous work. Talk to them about the things that are important to you. And use your instincts. This is your business, after all!

CHAPTER 5

WHAT IS THE
SECOND LIFE
LAND
BUSINESS?

THE
FINANCIAL
SIDE OF THE
LAND
BUSINESS

PLANNING:
TO SELL
OR RENT?

THE
REQUIRED
SKILLS

SETTING
UP SHOP

THE BEST
LAND FOR
YOUR
BUSINESS—
HOW TO
CHOOSE?

COMPETING
IN THE LAND
BUSINESS

WEATHERING
THE LAND
BOOMS AND
BUSTS

THE BEST LAND FOR YOUR BUSINESS—HOW TO CHOOSE?

When you're trying to decide whether to specialize in offering mainland or island properties, three things will likely sway your decision: price, traffic, and control. Ultimately, you have to decide what you want to specialize in. If your land business succeeds, you can diversify later, but in the early days you'll most likely want to choose one or the other.

PRICE

The law of simple supply and demand means the mainland costs less than islands do. There are always a lot of mainland parcels available, though entire sims may be harder to come by. For someone wanting to get a foothold in the land market, the mainland is a more economical place to start. There are, of course, exceptions to the price rule: waterfront property will likely be expensive. Desirable spots near well-regarded stores or other locations often fetch a premium price.

TRAFFIC

Mainland plots offer a higher degree of random walk-through traffic than islands do. Whether that's a good or a bad thing depends entirely on who you think your clientele will be. If you'll try to lure shops, clubs, or other venues that rely on heavy traffic for their business, then foot traffic is something to play up. Conversely, if you're aiming at a more residential market where people want privacy, low lag, and more control over their borders, then you probably want to stay away from areas with high foot traffic.

CONTROL

One of the biggest differences between the mainland and islands is that the mainland tends to be more democratic: even if what you're trying to build is a nice pastoral garden or beach, your neighbors are going to be building whatever they feel like. What they build might fit your theme, but more likely it won't. On the mainland, there's also less control over issues such as people putting up scripts and other things that cause lag. Those issues are easier to deal with on islands. Islands tend to develop on themes, and owners develop agreements on things like lag, building styles, and even whether land is zoned commercial or residential.

Islands also tend to have a specific look, so if what you want to offer is tropical desert islands, romantic cliffs in a medieval landscape, or the plains of Mars, you can buy an island and set it up to your specifications. On the mainland, you couldn't do something like change the textures of the ground to be a flower-strewn field or the electronic circuitry of a cyberpunk village. You don't have the same range of controls via a covenant that you have on an island.

CHAPTER 1
CHAPTER 2
CHAPTER 3
CHAPTER 4
CHAPTER 5

CHAPTER 6
CHAPTER 7
CHAPTER 8
CHAPTER 9
CHAPTER 10
CHAPTER 11
APPENDICES
INDEX

COMPETING IN THE LAND BUSINESS

You've figured out the technical side of things, and you've decided whether to sell or rent and whether to focus on islands or the mainland. But competition is heavy in this business; Anshe Chung, her million dollars, and her picture on the cover of *Business Week* have ensured that.

So how will you set your business apart from the crowd? Will it be through superior customer service? Unmatched attention to detail and quality? Or maybe with the little extras you'll build into the land you offer? The special elements you offer are known as your *value add*. Whatever it is (and you can expect it will take more than one of these to compete successfully), don't make it an afterthought. Make it an integral part of your business and build your reputation on it. The following sections provide some examples of value-adding strategies.

COMMUNITY

Adding value to the land you rent or sell fits in with one of the most important lessons you can learn as a *Second Life* businessperson: succeeding means making a contribution to the larger community. It's not enough to offer a product. Prokofy Neva is one of the most controversial figures in *Second Life*—thought by some to be a naysayer, he writes his own blog, Second Thoughts (http://secondthoughts.typepad.com/), about problems related to the virtual world or its management. Prokofy is also the successful owner and manager of Ravenglass, a midsize land business (Figure 5.10). As someone with a keen eye on the health of the *Second Life* economy and on in-world trends, he has some pretty strong opinions about what it takes to make a go of things in the land business.

Prokofy says one thing that draws his customers is a focus on building neighborhoods and community. He says he has learned a valuable lesson from Anshe Chung. "Most people

Figure 5.10: Prokofy Neva of Ravenglass

in the land business want to scorch and burn, make a killing and never look back at the people who bought from them," he says. "Anshe figured out that it is not a land business. It's a customer-service business and a development business. The Lindens also drive you to that conclusion. Philip [Rosedale, CEO of Linden Lab] rewards and fetes those who put 'value add' on land. He hates arbitrage. So if I make interesting buildings, events, activities, zoning, and relationships, I have value add. So it's about community building, not real estate."

DESIGN AND AESTHETICS

Figure 5.11: The Otherland Group tries to set itself apart from other Second Life real-estate businesses by creating land that is beautiful and attractive to prospective customers and existing residents.

For Dana Bergson, the value add is beauty (Figure 5.11). What she calls Otherland's *unique selling proposition* is taking plots of land that start out bland and boring and making them look good. Though some buyers just want plots of land with large footprints or big prim limits, she says, "We don't cater to that market, because it is just boring and you are easily undercut. It's just a matter of price: Buy a sim, make it flat, add a sand terrain. Voilà! Islands in the sand. But that is boring. And ugly six weeks later."

Instead, she says, Otherland carefully designs its parcels to be detailed, beautiful, and unique, and they focus on the 4,000- to 8,000-square-meter size range. They also develop and enforce the Otherland covenant (mentioned earlier in this chapter) in such a way that it restricts building, meaning that property in Otherland's estate will likely be more peaceful and less cluttered than land on many other estates.

CHAPTER 1
CHAPTER 2
CHAPTER 3
CHAPTER 4
CHAPTER 5

CHAPTER 6
CHAPTER 7
CHAPTER 8
CHAPTER 9
CHAPTER 10
CHAPTER 11
APPENDICES
INDEX

Alliez Mysterio also tries to distinguish d'Alliez Estates properties from the rest of the market through careful, considered design. As discussed earlier, she creates islands that offer her customers privacy and water frontage by dividing the sims so that half the land is covered in water and each parcel is an "island" of its own.

Azure Islands—Adam Zaius's and Nexus Nash's business—also tries to sell its properties based on the design sensibility rather than just the ability to "slice and dice" a sim. There is a big market for neatly cut up sims, but it's cutthroat and much, much harder to be a go-to seller or renter in that segment of the market. In the end, that's why each of these successful businesses prides itself on offering careful design that will please the customer, even if it costs a little bit more.

CUSTOMER SERVICE

Succeeding in the land business in *Second Life* is very much about the kind of customer service you can provide. Excellent customer service is a surefire way to keep customers happy, which means they'll come back or refer others.

"Customer service has to be number one," says Alliez Mysterio. "We decided if our customer service ever was too much to handle, we would not expand anymore." For Alliez, customer service means many things, but ultimately it's about providing answers to questions, solving problems quickly and efficiently, and offering something extra. Alliez says that she and her team are always available to help customers—something that's possible because d'Alliez has a staff that is on-call around the clock. She even teaches free classes on various aspects related to *Second Life* land, like how to terraform, twice a day to cover different time zones.

Being responsive also means knowing how to handle just about anything that comes up. There's no point in being available to answer a question if you don't know the answer, after all. You must stay abreast of the latest issues, and reading the various *Second Life* blogs and forums is a good way to do that.

Offering good customer service is even more important now than it was in the earlier days of *Second Life* because the in-world population has changed. "When we started . . . customers usually were some four or five months old [in *Second Life* experience]," says Dana Bergson. "Nowadays we get customers who can barely walk, and who want to buy 8,000 square meters of land. [That] takes a lot more hand holding."

In general, Dana says, providing good customer service is hard work. Her team consists of just four people, and they make a point of being quick and responsive to questions and calls for help. "Instant message and email helps a lot," she says. "I am available some 16 hours per day. Thank God for BlackBerries."

RESIDENTS SPEAK

DANA BERGSON ON AVOIDING LAND-BUSINESS PITFALLS

There are pitfalls in any business. Dana Bergson thinks some can be avoided. Here the principal owner of the Otherland Group shares her advice.

- Don't try to compete on prices alone, because there is always one guy who will do it even cheaper.

- Don't avoid bookkeeping, because only the books will tell you where you make money and where you don't.

- Never assume, "Just build it and they will come."

- Don't enter bidding wars on the land market, either in the open market or at the auctions, because there is always that idiot who won't do his homework. If you get in a competitive frenzy, you pay more than it's worth.

- Never insult your customers. People can be incredibly stupid, naive, angry, and insulting. But no matter what *they* do, you keep cool. Because this business, at least our segment, is all about return business and referrals. Most of our customers buy at least the same amount of land after they have bought their first parcel. So you'd better not piss them off.

Of course, there is no end to the number of ways you could make your land offerings unique. Just use your imagination, talk to others in the business, ask potential customers what they want, and follow your instinct.

WEATHERING THE LAND BOOMS AND BUSTS

As with any developing economic system, *Second Life* has a complex cycle—particularly on the land side of things. Throughout the history of *Second Life*, says Adam Zaius, land prices have traditionally gone in three- to six-month boom-and-bust cycles. As of this writing, there is an extended boom because the number of new residents continues to climb briskly, creating high demand for land.

Of course, there's no way to know if that pattern will continue. After all, *Second Life*'s growth since fall 2006 has been astronomical because media attention on it has been remarkable. It shows no immediate signs of slowing down, but eventually the growth will—at the very least—level off. When that happens, demand for land will slacken.

Part of the reason for cycles is pure land speculation, says Adam Zaius. "During the cycle, higher influxes of new users create a tremendous demand on land in *Second Life*," he explains, "because land is released on the mainland—which sets the cycle for everywhere—via auction. Auction prices dictate the cycle. Loads of new residents result in people bidding based on predicted values of what the market will be like in three to five weeks. More and more people try to make a dollar speculating on the ever-increasing land prices."

Assuming the growth rate does slacken, the next phase of the cycle will come shortly afterward. "Eventually, there are so many people buying land via auctions that the market is satiated," says Adam. "The new resident flood slows down . . . and people are left with regions they are trying to sell. Each undercuts the other, trying to cut their losses, and the land price crashes."

The ranges of the cycle, Adam says, go from land at around L$3–4 per square meter to around L$14–20. It's not just the mainland that is affected by these booms and busts. Adam points out that land prices on the open market are set comparatively, meaning that as mainland prices grow, so do island prices. "If land pricing is above around L$6.50–7 per square meter, islands can be bought and sold instantly, with no time to recoup the initial investment. If land is below that price, island growth slows down."

WARNING

A particularly buggy Second Life version release can lead to a mass exodus, with some selling their land at artificially low prices.

If you want to be in the *Second Life* real-estate business for the long haul, you have to avoid running from the busts. To date, *Second Life* land has always regained its value. If you're willing to stick it out, odds are you will likely be able to recoup any losses that occur during a downturn. However, if you run when prices are low, you could lose everything.

CHAPTER 1
CHAPTER 2
CHAPTER 3
CHAPTER 4
CHAPTER 5

CHAPTER 6
CHAPTER 7
CHAPTER 8
CHAPTER 9
CHAPTER 10
CHAPTER 11
APPENDICES
INDEX

CHAPTER 6

CONSTRUCTION PROJECTS BIG AND SMALL

By the time you're reading these words, there will likely be more than 10 million registered *Second Life* accounts. Even accounting for the many people who register but never engage with *Second Life*, we're still talking about hundreds of thousands or even more than a million real people deeply involved in this vibrant virtual world. Many of them will want a dwelling, store, tower, museum, tree house, office space, or one of the many types of buildings found in-world.

Some will figure out how to build what they want on their own or with friends, but many more will need to hire someone to do it for them. And that's just the existing *Second Life* residents. The people and businesses on the outside that are clamoring to come in want projects done as well, often big ones calling for substantial budgets.

This chapter explains how to pursue this particular line of *Second Life* work as a money-making venture, either as a full-time profession, as a growing number of people have done, or as a way to supplement your bottom line.

CONTENTS

THE BASICS OF BUILDING

One of the most impressive things about *Second Life*, particularly to newcomers, is that wherever you go, you're almost certain to be surrounded by an incredible array of creative, imaginative, and fantastic buildings. They could be towers or domes or castles. They could have long connecting bridges or all-glass atriums or wonderful sky-high dance floors.

Naturally, plenty of what you see is either uninteresting or downright unattractive. But as you start to explore the many popular locations in *Second Life*, you'll begin to look beyond the dull building structures and see stunning examples of Japanese architectural design, post-modern mansions straight out of *Entourage*, or a real-world technology magazine's headquarters made to look like a building-sized video card. For many people, *Second Life* is a creative wonderland, and they enjoy nothing more than buying or renting a small piece of land and playing around with the building tools until they have designed their dream house, or at least a reasonable facsimile of it. However, there are countless others who don't have the skills or the time to create their own structures. Armed with some tips and tricks to cater to that market, you'll find a booming business in designing, creating, and selling the buildings for others to install on their little—or not so little—pieces of virtual paradise.

A TERMINOLOGY PRIMER

There are various kinds of "building" in *Second Life*—everything from crafting chairs or cars to constructing futuristic skyscrapers. That's because all content creation starts with prim "building blocks." For the purposes of this chapter, however, I'm going to restrict "building" to the creation of structures—houses, towers, theaters—all the way up to full sims. Hopefully, that helps to avoid any semantic confusion as you read and as you talk to *Second Life* residents and others interested in this business.

WHAT'S OUT THERE?

What's out there? Everything. There's a reproduction of New York's Times Square, complete with ever-changing neon signs, and a subway station, complete with a subway train itself. There's Nakama (Figure 6.1), an anime-themed city whose features include a giant destructive robot and the office buildings it flattened, as well as more lighthearted fare like a rainbow on which a couple of cartoon cats are sitting.

You'll also find sim after sim full of smaller buildings, little houses, mountain chalets, glass-walled stores, and so much more. To get a real sense of the variety, there's nothing like simply going in-world and exploring. Go to an island and walk or fly around. Note what you

Figure 6.1: Nakama is a full-sim design by well-known builder Neil Protagonist that's based on a Japanese anime theme.

see. Meet someone and ask what builds they like, or look at the "Picks" listed in an avatar's profile, then go exploring. You'll soon notice that, especially from the air, *Second Life* looks much like any developed area: There are pockets of densely populated land, open areas with sparse construction, tall skyscrapers, long malls, outstanding and wondrous designs, and everything in between. The buildings, like almost everything you see in-world, were created by members of the *Second Life* community, not by the virtual world's publisher. Nearly every structure was conceived of and created by someone acting either for themselves or on behalf of a customer.

WHAT'S POSSIBLE?

As we've discussed in previous chapters, the *Second Life* economy is a mature, developed mechanism that is supporting millions of US dollars' worth of regular transactions and created assets. The building and construction business is a substantial part of that economy. For those who are working in it—at least those with the skills and the commitment to succeed—it can be a lucrative undertaking.

I won't pretend that anyone who wants to create a building business is going to be able to quickly quit their day job. Success doesn't come overnight, and there are no guarantees. However, it can be done. After all, there is no shortage of people who have managed to make building in *Second Life* their full-time job, and many more who earn enough doing it to make it worth the investment of time. You can expect to earn between US$15 and US$65 an hour, depending on your skills and how well-known you are for the work. Given that you can do the work from just about anywhere, the job can offer a significant level of flexibility. But you will need to be serious about it.

WHO'S BUILDING?

Second Life builders are an eclectic bunch. They come from all walks of life and have had all kinds of experience. This chapter shares business tips and lessons learned from Foolish Frost, Aimee Weber, Kim Anubis, Insky Jedburgh, and Neil Protagonist. Of course, there are many other star builders, but these five represent a spectrum of the *Second Life* community and some of the cream of the crop of builders. For those who know the virtual world, their work is often quite familiar and is among the best quality that exists there. In real life, they come from all over the globe, but they share a passion for realizing visions of fantastical structures in the virtual world.

Figure 6.2: Foolish Frost, a well-known builder, in front of his Free Tibet build

Foolish Frost (Figure 6.2), who is known for his full-sim builds, took about two months to learn how to sell his builds in *Second Life*. He had a lot of experience working in 3D graphics programs and had a lot of texturing skills. All told, he had a background of more than 20 years as a professional programmer.

Insky Jedburgh is known as the creator of highly detailed Gothic castles. Since he was a child, Insky had been touring castles in real life, and he and his ex-wife used to visit castles in her native Romania.

One of the first professional builders in *Second Life*, Kim Anubis actually worked in-house at There.com, another 3D social virtual world, before becoming immersed in *Second Life*. She'd been involved in online community management since the 1980s, and after she left There.com, she joined *Second Life* because she wanted to own land.

"My first client was a friend who wanted a waterfall," Kim remembers. "I stayed up for an entire night working on it, because I really wanted the Linden dollars right away to buy boots for my avatar."

A history in game development led Neil Protagonist to *Second Life*. A former visual effects artist at Microsoft Game Studios who was working on an Xbox title, Neil found that the game development skills he'd learned over the years were invaluable in creating vibrant interactive user experiences in the virtual world.

Figure 6.3: Aimee Weber created a Second Life store for American Apparel, one of the first big companies to show up in the virtual world.

"Working in console and PC game development, you have to learn how games work, why you have the limitations you have, and how to work with and around them," Neil says. "The important bit . . . is to [suggest that builders] read up on game engines and developing art for games."

For her part, Aimee Weber started working in the texture-based rendering program Bryce 3D more than five years ago and became one of the best-known builders and designers in *Second Life*. Her projects have included Midnight City, a sort of faux New York, as well as the *Second Life* presences of American Apparel (Figure 6.3) and the American Cancer Society's Relay for Life.

MORE INFO

WORKING WITH A TEAM OR GOING SOLO?

If you're a builder in *Second Life* you can either work alone or be part of a team. Each has its advantages, and its limitations.

For Insky Jedburgh, working alone is his key to getting done what he wants to. "Creative control," he says, when asked why. "It's hard enough for me to build around a client's wishes. But I move pretty fast when I am just thinking about what I need to do, and then doing it."

On the other hand, he acknowledges that he doesn't have all the skills that a team could provide. So he knows that he either needs to consult with someone else when presented with a problem he doesn't have the answer to or when it may not even occur to him that there could be a solution.

"So I am limited, perhaps, in the number of options I can offer," Insky says. "I have no doubt that when I have certain problems to solve, there are ideas I simply didn't think of."

One solution, he says, is to just buy things that he needs and doesn't have the time or the skills to build, such as a special door or maybe a good fire script. He also says he uses scripted tools created by others to make complex objects.

For someone starting out in the business who doesn't have all the skills but who wants to work alone, this may be the best answer, though you would have to be careful not to spend so much on additional components that you lose your profit margin.

The flip side of things is Kim Anubis's method. As a leader of The Magicians, she has a dedicated team of people working for her, each of whom is free to concentrate solely on the jobs they're good at. It may be a good approach for a small team of people, each of whom possesses discrete skills but who, combined, cover a wide range of abilities and handle complex builds. But for Kim, working with a team in *Second Life* can be hard and time-consuming—and managing her team takes time away from doing the building that she loves.

The message is this: Be careful which direction you go in, and do it intentionally. If you're smart about it, you can succeed.

UNDERSTANDING YOUR CUSTOMERS

Obviously *Second Life* is not like the usual working environment. After all, how many other jobs let you teleport to client meetings? There are some substantial cultural differences between the *Second Life* community (and the clients it represents) and the real world. *Second Life* residents are all too willing to express themselves in ways they rarely would in real life. Someone who in her real-life job dresses in a conservative suit and does her best to fit in might well be the leader of a subcommunity of Furries in *Second Life*. She might run around as a sexy fox avatar, looking to spend her time hanging out with raccoons, tigers, and ferrets in Luskwood, a prime spot for residents with such proclivities.

If you want to go into business in *Second Life* selling big building projects, you should be prepared to accept the residents as they are and cater to their needs. If you're working for real-world clients wanting a presence in the virtual world, you'll need to help them understand who they're going to be dealing with, as well. Says Foolish Frost, "You run into a lot of things here that you normally would not. I have done work for both masters and slaves from Gor, and Furries who need a home. I've built a temple for the Queen of the Damned. You have to learn to deal with all of these people. Not only deal with them, but do so without judgment or contempt."

IDENTIFYING YOUR TARGET MARKET

Although *Second Life* is unique, to be successful you need to know who you're selling to, just like in the real world. Marketing is discussed in Chapter 3, but it's worth noting here that you need to be crystal clear about what design style suits your interests, talents, and skills. You can cater to more than one segment of the *Second Life* population and be successful, but you must be deliberate about what you do. You'll want to spend a substantial amount of time in-world exploring and talking to people, seeing what you like and don't like, figuring out what styles you understand, and then narrowing in on your niche.

Whether it's modern designs, Gothic castles, cyberpunk cities, seaside manors, or whatever, be sure of what you're going to sell before you start. Residents of each community know their style and are not likely to buy something that doesn't match it. If it's not authentic or true to a style, it won't be accepted. A proper aesthetic is a crucial design element for anyone hoping to draw in visitors or customers. As the builder, it's your job to make sure they get what they want. Otherwise, residents will look elsewhere for their building needs.

THE DIFFERENCE BETWEEN RESIDENT AND OUTSIDE CLIENTS

CHAPTER 1
CHAPTER 2
CHAPTER 3
CHAPTER 4
CHAPTER 5
CHAPTER 6

CHAPTER 7
CHAPTER 8
CHAPTER 9
CHAPTER 10
CHAPTER 11
APPENDICES
INDEX

As a builder, you will be dealing with two broad categories of clients. In the first category are the thousands of *Second Life* residents who are already familiar with the virtual world, its mores, its styles, its communities, and such. Dealing with them as clients means one thing and requires one set of skills. The second category includes the outside clients who hire builders to create something for them in *Second Life*, but who themselves may not be familiar with what goes on in-world. Such clients probably need a fair bit of education before they're ready to set up shop, and it's up to you to provide that education, if for no other reason than that if your clients are successful, your chances for repeat business are better.

SELLING TO *SECOND LIFE* RESIDENTS

One of the things that Linden Lab is most adamant about in its virtual world is that it's not a game. After all, it doesn't have a goal. However, residents of *Second Life* are accustomed to treating its economy as, if not a game, somewhat less realistic than that of the real world.

It's not that residents don't value their money—otherwise, you wouldn't have people sweating over whether they can afford an L$300 piece of clothing—a US$1.11 purchase. Rather, when they're in-world or considering in-world purchases, they often don't want to think about how little they're actually paying for things.

"I think most *Second Life* residents come with the idea that (it) is a game," says Aimee Weber. "They will pay you at Linden dollar scale, maybe L$20,000 for a build, which is a lot of *Second Life* money, but very little real-life money."

As a builder, it may be hard to accept L$20,000—about US$74—for a build that may have taken you a couple of weeks to create. But when selling to that community, you have to remember a couple of things. First, that's the scale of the economy you're working in. Second, as you build your skills and reputation you may be able to ask for higher fees. At the same time, Aimee says, there's another side to the coin. *Second Life* residents may not want to pay much for what they buy, but they are also more likely to be calm about some of the things that real-life clients are most uptight about. "They won't have big commitments riding on you," says Aimee. "If you don't make a deadline . . . it's not a big deal."

For Kim Anubis of The Magicians (one of the longest-running building businesses in *Second Life*), dealing with residents is much more about understanding their specific needs and quirks. In other words, it's essential that you accept them as they are and be willing to handle some of the more unusual requests or situations you can think of. "You will do better and enjoy it a lot more if you are accepting of people's inner selves or fantasies or roleplaying, and go along with it whenever it seems like fun to you" says Kim. "I have had to evict a squatter from a client's build who said he was there hiding from an enemy army. I think he was elvish. I went along. If he is an elf in this world, then that's who I am talking to, and I discussed with him better places to hide out and avoid the bad guys."

If you're selling prefabs, the money you'll make will come from repeated sales. A few dollars for something you spent a couple weeks building may not seem like much, but since there is no additional cost to you for making—and selling—the second, third, and fourth copies of it (and so on), your money will add up as your sales increase.

SELLING TO OUTSIDE CLIENTS

Figure 6.4: During the playoffs after its 2006–2007 season, the National Basketball Association (NBA) launched a multi-sim basketball fan's paradise. Built by The Electric Sheep Company, the project includes courts where avatars can pick up a game.

For *Second Life*, 2006 and 2007 were the years when the outside world started to show up in force. One after another, big companies and institutions like Pontiac's Motorati, CNET, the NBA (Figure 6.4), Reebok, IBM, Coke, and many others came in-world, often launching major builds that cost more than US$100,000 to develop. For the most part, those giant builds are being handled by third-party contracting firms like The Electric Sheep Company, Rivers Run Red, or Millions of Us. These companies employ some of the top builders, scripters, and texture artists in *Second Life*. Working for companies like these may be one career path for those who have well developed skills.

However, outside clients are also turning to individual builders or small teams. If you're considering catering to that market, you should understand a little bit about how to help those potential clients make themselves welcome in *Second Life*.

HELPING OUTSIDE CUSTOMERS UNDERSTAND WHAT *SECOND LIFE* IS ABOUT

Clients who are newcomers "have to be willing to spend a good amount of time learning [these] cultures," says Foolish Frost, who works for many outside clients. "They have to be *carefully* brought in. They have world views that don't include what can be seen here, and [their] initial response can be explosive. For example, Foolish recalls when one outside female client came into *Second Life* and happened upon a Gorean slave girl. "It was not pretty," Foolish says of the client's reaction to seeing a female avatar in a slave-like situation. "But the fact is, if she was warned and educated about the fact that *nobody* in *Second Life* can really be forced to do anything, the situation might have been avoided. It sounds simple, but how to even broach the subject can be awkward."

Yet, as the contractor, it falls upon you to make sure that your outside clients are properly informed about the realities of *Second Life* so that they are not surprised by situations like the one Foolish recalled. It means talking with your clients honestly about what goes on in *Second Life*. If you're not entirely sure what that entails, then you probably need to spend a little more time in-world, exploring and getting used to the notion that although plenty of residents would seem "normal" in the real world, many others are using the virtual world as a place to express sides of themselves that they can't in real life. You'll need to help your clients understand that *Second Life* has very visible subcommunities whose members walk around chained to each other or dressed like dragons or who may be having sex in a public place. Avatars may look like mermaids, tiny ponies, grungy hoboes, or couture-wearing fashionistas. It might not be normal from their real-world perspective, but in *Second Life*, it's what people do. It may make them a bit uncomfortable at first, but your outside clients will need to deal with these facts if they want to be part of *Second Life* and if they want to be well-received by its community.

RESIDENTS SPEAK

FOOLISH FROST'S ADVICE ON PURSUING A BUILDING BUSINESS

To those who know Second Life *and its impressive building projects, Foolish Frost is a name to be reckoned with. He has been around longer than most and is known for his attention to detail and for his unfailing honesty. Here, Foolish shares his ideas about how to make it in the building business in* Second Life.

- Be knowledgeable about your products.

- Be knowledgeable about your clientele.

- You never know it all.

- Never treat people as lesser. You *never* know who they are and what they know.

- Do what you enjoy.

- Ego and drama are *not* your friends. If you're having a bad day, then shut up and log off.

- Treat everyone with respect in the way they want. They want to joke with you? Joke. They want to call themselves "this girl?" Let them and deal with it.

- You are not always right. Other people are often smarter. Learn from them. If they are not smarter, learn from their failings.

CHAPTER 1
CHAPTER 2
CHAPTER 3
CHAPTER 4
CHAPTER 5
CHAPTER 6
CHAPTER 7
CHAPTER 8
CHAPTER 9
CHAPTER 10
CHAPTER 11
APPENDICES
INDEX

(Continued)

> 🔹 Avoid judging others by what you see. That furry sex machine that you are laughing at may be an EMT who saves people's lives. You know nothing about them. Again, it's about respect.
>
> 🔹 Don't just come here for business, or you will fail. Join the community. Make friends. Help new people coming in. It takes time, but you get remembered more for that than for any build.

THE SKILLS FOR BUILDING IN *SECOND LIFE*

Building in *Second Life* is not the easiest thing in the world. It's not the hardest, either, but you're going to need some specific skills in order to do well. Regardless of how well you know your software and your tools, you need to have a good sense of architectural design or at least an innate sense of what works when it comes to building in *Second Life*. This section is a primer on the technical skills you'll need. Once you have a good understanding of those needs, spend the time making sure you are good enough to utilize them at a professional or at least a semiprofessional level. Be prepared for that process to take weeks or even months.

Figure 6.5: **Second Life's Object Editor**

▪ THE OBJECT EDITOR

The Object Editor (Figure 6.5) is the tool that comes up when you click on the Build button at the bottom of the *Second Life* interface. It is used to create and modify objects. Additionally, you use the Object Editor to place things where you want them in-world and to adjust things that are attached to your avatar.

Linden Lab offers a short object editor tutorial (http://secondlife.com/knowledgebase/article.php?id=164) that covers editing prims—moving, resizing, rotating, linking, and more.

RESIDENTS SPEAK

CHAPTER 1
CHAPTER 2
CHAPTER 3
CHAPTER 4
CHAPTER 5
CHAPTER 6

CHAPTER 7
CHAPTER 8
CHAPTER 9
CHAPTER 10
CHAPTER 11
APPENDICES
INDEX

AIMEE WEBER ON THE SKILLS NEEDED TO BE A SUCCESSFUL BUILDER

For Aimee Weber, one of the best-known builders in Second Life, *the Object Editor is just one piece of an overall, broad set of skills that you need to have to build for money in* Second Life. *They're just guidelines, but together they provide a glimpse at what you need to know to succeed.*

- **Architecture. This is pretty challenging, because most people don't have an architectural background. But you have to be familiar with real-life architecture so your builds feel legit.**

- **Drawing applications. Photoshop is the most popular, but you could use GIMP or a few others. Learning Photoshop alone opens career doors for you. In** *Second Life*, **you need it as just one of many applications.**

- **Scripting. Most programming languages are basically the same. I'm sure a programmer would yell at me for saying that. But you have conditionals, tests, and loops, and all kinds of basic logic structures. You need to learn them. Often the jobs of scripter and builder are done by different people, but there is enough overlap that one should be familiar with the other. (Linden Scripting Language, or LSL, is the** *Second Life* **scripting language.)**

- **Personal creativity. It's one thing to know Photoshop, and another to create textures that look nice in** *Second Life*.

2D AND 3D SOFTWARE

If you're building to sell in *Second Life*, then you'll need to know some third-party software. You'll probably need to know at least a 2D drawing package, but you may find it useful to add some 3D modeling skills to your repertoire to give your builds more realistic lighting and shadow effects.

2D SOFTWARE: PHOTOSHOP AND BEYOND

For personal builds and the general in-world market, builders often use purchased textures, widely available in-world. For custom build projects, custom textures are preferred and may even be required by customers. One thing everyone agrees on is that you'll need to know some kind of 2D drawing program to create custom textures that you will apply to the surfaces of your objects. The most common 2D software used by *Second Life* builders—and those in other *Second Life* businesses, like fashion—is Photoshop. This is a full-featured software package from Adobe that gives users the ability to create and manipulate textures at a high level. Another option is GIMP (http://www.gimp.org/), the GNU Image Manipulation Program, a free software package that offers some of Photoshop's features without its hefty price tag.

Regardless of which 2D software you use, you'll want to become fairly proficient at it. Then, once you've learned how to create the kinds of textures you want, you will need to import them into *Second Life* and apply them to your builds. It is possible to simply take a high-resolution photograph of a texture you like—perhaps a piece of wood—and use it, but you would likely still want to manipulate it in a software program like Photoshop to sharpen it, adjust the colors, focus it better, crop out parts you don't like, adjust it so that it tiles well (since you'd likely use many of them side-by-side in a grid, and you don't want visible seams) and make sure it's in the right file format (.tga or .jpg). Then in *Second Life,* you upload the file, through the File: Upload menu. You are charged L$10 for every image you upload.

Once the texture image is uploaded, it will be in the Texture folder inside your Inventory, and you can apply it to a single side of an object by selecting the object and applying it to that face, to all sides at once, or you can select a set of objects and apply the texture to all. To do this, you can use the Object Editor or options under *Second Life*'s Edit menu. When you're very proficient with the Edit tools, and can use all the options in the Edit windows rather than having to do everything manually, you can work more quickly and accurately. So, it's worth spending some time studying the various options in the Edit window and seeing what works for you.

Ultimately, if you're good enough at Photoshop or one of the other 2D drawing programs, you can create shading and other elements of your textures that make it look like it's 3D. Working in these graphics programs will let you add the detail work that will sell your builds.

3D SOFTWARE: ADDING HIGH-QUALITY LIGHTING EFFECTS

If you really want your textures to look like they have 3D lighting effects, you'll need to paint them in with a 2D program like Photoshop or use a 3D modeling package. There are several to choose from, but among the most popular are Maya, 3ds Max, and LightWave. The first two are very expensive, however, so unless you already have a copy or are certain that you want to spend between US$2,000 to $3,500, you may not want to go that direction. LightWave is much cheaper, at just under US$800 for a full version, and may offer you what you need. There's also Blender (http://www.blender.org/), a free, open-source 3D modeling package used by many for creating textures.

Neil Protagonist recommends LightWave because it's a good general package suitable for beginners that has lots of available tutorials and a strong and active community of users. It's also designed for a single developer, while Maya is aimed at a studio environment.

Figure 6.6: By using 3D modeling software, builders can create realistic shadow and lighting effects, as Aimee Weber did in this build.

On its own, the *Second Life* client actually streams the world to your computer, without requiring you to download DVDs full of images. The virtual world is not currently designed to support 3D effects because doing so would put too much strain on the servers. But by using a 3D modeling package, it is possible to create a model for a house, say, that makes lighting and shadow effects that look much more realistic than with 2D software (Figure 6.6).

MANAGING PRIMS

For *Second Life* builders, everything comes down to primitives, or *prims*, as they're known. These are the basic building blocks of *Second Life*, the cubes and other shapes that builders use as the main elements of nearly everything they create. Look at any building and what you're seeing is really a collection of prims that have been manipulated into the shape of a structure. But prims are a scarce commodity. As detailed in Chapter 3, "Walking the Runway: Fashion in *Second Life*," *Second Life* limits the number of prims that can be used in a region. That's why Foolish Frost says, in all seriousness, "Prims are the real currency of *Second Life*."

For any builder worth their salt, prim management is one of the most important skills to have. It's something you're going to need to learn over time, after playing around at building and figuring out how things are built. "Learn by playing with the [building] tools," says Neil. "Try building random things, play with all the values and buttons and get a good feeling for how they all look and what they all do. Then you really know what is and is not possible."

The fastest, and most accurate, builders become power users, working by typing in numbers and using keyboard commands. For a large build or precision custom work, or when your work must match up with that of the rest of a team—accurate measurement and placement can have a big impact on how fast you can complete the project.

TIP

The Second Life *building-tips forums* (http://forums.secondlife.com/ forumdisplay.php?f=8) *are a good place to learn from community members.*

For Insky Jedburgh, managing prim counts is like managing any kind of commodity. "A sim has a 15,000 prim cap, no matter how rich you are," says Insky. "So it forces conservation." One of Insky's favorite ways to conserve is to learn how to use textures on prims rather than to employ more prims to add detail. Even if you're not particularly good at designing prim-conserving textures, there are plenty of people in *Second Life* who sell them, and for a small investment you can save a lot of prims.

Another of Insky's favorite exercises for someone wanting to learn how to manage prims is to challenge yourself to make a house with a roof, door, and window with less than 10 prims. The idea is that if you can successfully make the house in that number of prims, it will give you a sense of how to build without wasteful use of prims and will begin to lead you down the road to efficient prim management. That skill will no doubt make your builds more attractive to customers who themselves are looking for ways to cut down on prim usage.

One technique Insky recommends for cutting down on prim usage is to install ramps in your buildings instead of stairs. Though it's a well-known trick among builders, it's not something you would normally think of, in part, perhaps, because ramps don't look very realistic in places where a real-world building would have stairs. But Insky points out that ramps offer two big advantages, even if he himself has to constantly convince his clients that it's the better way to go: First, they use fewer prims than stairs do, and anything that offers such savings is worthwhile. Second, stairs are not easy for avatars to go up and down.

TIP

You can design ramps with textures that look like stairs from a distance. The illusion won't hold up close in, but from afar it can trick the eye into believing there are stairs.

■ USING HUGE PRIMS

Using *huge prims* (Figure 6.7) for things like paving spaces or putting the tops on mountains is a good way to conserve prims. There is some uncertainty about whether huge prims are allowed in *Second Life*, particularly on the mainland. It is generally accepted that they're here to stay, but that using too many in one build can be bad for the stability of the sim.

Figure 6.7: Using huge prims is a good way to create a large floor or wall without needing many prims.

CHAPTER 1
CHAPTER 2
CHAPTER 3
CHAPTER 4
CHAPTER 5

CHAPTER 6
CHAPTER 7
CHAPTER 8
CHAPTER 9
CHAPTER 10
CHAPTER 11
APPENDICES
INDEX

But if you use them properly, they can be a terrific way to cover large amounts of space with one or a small number of prims, and you can easily cover them with textures to make a nice floor or wall. Huge prims are available for sale on SL Exchange (www.slexchange. com) or OnRez, (http://shop.onrez.com/), 2D web shopping sites for *Second Life* merchandise. These sites are popular with shoppers who are browsing or who can't log into *Second Life* from work locations or during updates, for instance. The popular Heart Gardens landscaping store sells a variety of huge-prim–based trees. Such uses can help cut down on overall prim count even for nicely landscaped builds.

RESIDENTS SPEAK

FOOLISH FROST ON SPATIAL ARRANGEMENT FOR REALISM IN BUILDS

One skill that, properly employed, can make for much more realistic builds is good use of spatial arrangements. Although it's not possible to cover every instance where this can come into play, here are a few examples, courtesy of Foolish Frost.

- Doors and ceilings need to be higher in *Second Life* than in real life, because your eyes—the normal view you see when in-world—are about three to six meters above your shoulder and behind you.

- You can't put furnishings next to walls normally, because the camera jumps through the wall.

- You have to make rooms a minimum of 10 meters wide if you want people to be able to turn around properly.

CONSIDERING THE THREE BUILD TYPES

What kinds of buildings are there in *Second Life*? We've talked already about some of the varieties: castles, modern houses, towers. One thing that nearly any *Second Life* entrepreneur talks about when discussing how to be successful is to look for a new niche, as it's the best way to avoid competition. If you have a good idea for a building style that no one has done in *Second Life* before, and you can carry it out well, you are likely to be successful. That's why Insky Jedburgh has been able to earn a full-time income: he discovered and filled an untapped desire in the community for Gothic castles. He took a chance, and it worked.

Let's say you'd rather go for something a little less risky. There's no reason you can't make money selling beach houses—recent trends are moving away from Bali-style thatched huts to luxurious beach homes you might expect to find in the southern Thai islands like Phuket. As long as your building skills are impressive, and matched with marketing acumen and an ability to please your customers, your business can succeed.

In your travels around *Second Life*, you will encounter three general kinds of building projects, and you'll need to decide which of them you want to offer prospective clients. Broadly speaking, there are prefabs, custom builds, and full-sim builds. Each has its own design, marketing, pricing, and technical issues that you'll want to become proficient in before you set up shop, as well as challenges that you'll want to think about before you pursue them. Your experience level is one consideration. Another is your desire to work with outside clients, or perhaps a preference to work solo. Also consider how much freedom you want or need—are you willing to build to a specification, with a team, on schedule, and on budget? Or do you prefer to wait for inspiration, then build as the muse suggests?

The following is a discussion of the three build types. I'll go into detail about the pros and cons of each, as well as the skills necessary to create them later in the chapter.

PREFABS

In *Second Life*, prefab buildings are just what they sound like: structures that residents can buy directly from a seller. Prefabs are sold ready to be installed on someone's land with little or no fuss. They allow a resident to shop for a house as they would a sofa, browsing sellers' stores to look for what they want or what they can afford. The options are nearly endless. There are small prefab skyboxes that sell for L$999, big, fancy modern houses that sell for L$4,499, Gothic castles that go for up to L$14,000, and everything in between.

Clearly, the amount of money you can make with prefabs is limited only by how many you can sell. The lower the price, the more you have to sell to have it add up to real money. With the exchange rate at around L$270 to US$1, that means that even an L$14,000 castle (which is a lot of money for a *Second Life* item) is selling for only around US$51.

Figure 6.8: Insky Jedburgh sells highly sought-after prefab castles. This sign gives a glimpse of one.

Yet, for Insky Jedburgh (Figure 6.8), who specializes in selling prefab castles, even items at that price let him make a full-time income in *SL*. "I was working this miserable sales job," Insky recalls of his early days in the castle business, "and thinking that I almost could make *Second Life* work as a job, but I still didn't believe it. [A month later] I earned more than [I did at] my full-time real-life job."

How did that come to pass? Well, Insky has such a distinct style and his castles are known to be of such good quality—he bases his designs on real-world castles he has visited—that the sale of one leads directly to many more. "Each prefab acts like an advertisement," Insky says. "People see a friend's prefab and instant-message me out of the blue."

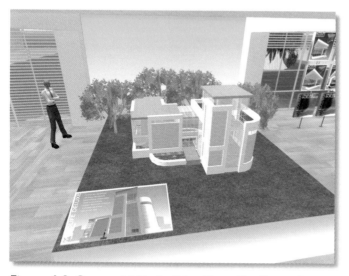

Figure 6.9: *Second Life* builder Rem Koolhaas (not the real-life Rem Koolhaas) sells modern-style prefab houses.

Like Insky, many prefab builders try to establish an easily identifiable style so that well-informed residents can recognize their work wherever it is. One such builder is Rem Koolhaas (Figure 6.9), whose ModLife store features several of his build designs, which according to the information he provides, have a "signature style" that speaks of "clean lines and modern expression. The uniqueness lies in the use of texture and form with minimal prim count to derive bright white spaces that seem bigger than they are."

Many builders are likely to start by designing prefabs because they don't require a commission. Commissioned work follows from being well-enough known to warrant being hired to build. For some builders, doing prefabs offers a nice balance between earning potential and freedom. "You can build whatever you like at your own pace with prefabs," says Aimee Weber. "It's more relaxing.

She explained that you are likely to get paid a substantial amount more to do a custom job than you would ever be able to sell a single prefab for. "Custom work normally pays more [in the] short term," Aimee says, "and often pays enough where a prefab will never make as much. [However], prefabs may pay more in the long run."

If you create a prefab that a lot of people want, the small amounts you earn on each individual sale can quickly add. Prefabs can also act as an advertisement for your business. Doing prefabs also means you don't have to worry about someone else's special requirements. If they don't want what you have to sell, they don't buy. "If [builders] just want to build what they want," says Kim Anubis, "[if] they want to put a minimal amount of effort into dealing with clients and their wants and needs, then they should do prefabs."

Neil Protagonist agrees. Prefabs give people "something that they can do out of their own heads that doesn't require dealing with anyone else," Neil says. "I prefer doing work for myself than for other people. I'm always easier to deal with because I can read my own mind."

RESIDENTS SPEAK

 ### KIM ANUBIS ON DECIDING WHAT KIND OF PREFABS TO BUILD

For Kim Anubis, if you want to build prefabs and don't know exactly what kind to build, there are several ways to figure it out.

"I would employ some traditional market research techniques," she says.

- **Give a gift to people who fill out a questionnaire about what sort of prefab they would want.**

- **Start a thread about it on a message board or forum, or more than one.**

- **Talk to lots of people about it.**

- **Put a number of things on sale and see what sells, and what doesn't."**

In the *Second Life* freebie stores that cater to new residents, like YadNi's Junkyard, the GNUbie Store, and New Citizens Plaza, one thing you can expect to find are free prefabs, made by some of the best names in the business. Checking out these buildings by unpacking them in a Sandbox area is one great way to learn about building, and you'll notice when you follow up with visits to the stores of these builders, their work keeps getting better. Making prefabs is a great way to practice your building skills and learn about what will sell. If the day comes that your prefab store starts doing well, you can donate a few of your popular models to the stores that cater to newbies. Not only does this help get your name out, you're also giving back to the community and making *Second Life* a bit easier for new avatars.

However, selling prefabs is a business that requires good customer service skills, since your customer base will include newer avatars who don't have advanced skills. You may need to help them understand how many prims their land can hold, how to flatten, or terraform, their land enough to place a prefab, how to unpack a boxed home, and how to work in Edit mode without breaking things.

Unless you sell a lot of prefabs, the work doesn't pay that much. We're talking about items that, for the most part, cost customers less than US$10. That's worth considering if you want to do prefabs: can you sell enough of them to make it worth your while? On top of that, can prefabs sustain your interest, since your business will be built around selling many of the same items? On the other hand, making prefabs is a good way to make some money on projects you build when you're trying out a new style, for instance. Popular prefab builders do a steady stream of business, as customers can afford to purchase a new building each time they'd like to change the style of their home—an option that illustrates one of the many reasons why so many enjoy having a residence in *Second Life*. Back on Earth, replacing your whole house would be prohibitively slow, expensive, and difficult, but in *Second Life*, it's relatively quick, cheap, and easy.

CUSTOM BUILDS

The flip side of the prefab building business is custom building, in which builders work with clients to create exactly what they want. For the builder, this means working on someone else's schedule and following their direction. However, if you have drive and don't mind working to someone else's specifications on deadline, says Aimee Weber, one of *Second Life*'s best-known and most accomplished builders, you can make more money than you can as a prefab builder, since custom builds can command US$65 an hour or more.

The economics of doing custom builds is different. Whereas prefabs are sold automatically through vendors for *Second Life* prices, custom building is often done at hourly rates that approximate what skilled designers in other fields can get paid. That's because custom builds are often commissioned by real-world clients who want to bring a real-world brand or company into *Second Life* and want to hire someone to build their presence for them. Other times existing *Second Life* residents will ask builders to design something custom for them, and in those cases, you'll most likely need to charge more-reasonable Linden-dollar rates.

CHAPTER 1
CHAPTER 2
CHAPTER 3
CHAPTER 4
CHAPTER 5
CHAPTER 6

CHAPTER 7
CHAPTER 8
CHAPTER 9
CHAPTER 10
CHAPTER 11
APPENDICES
INDEX

For Kim Anubis, the best thing about doing custom work is that it's always different. "I try not to do the same thing twice, or anything someone else has done," she says.

First, there's a good chance that when you do a custom build, it's going to be an interesting challenge. After all, if someone wanted something not all that challenging, they'd probably just buy a prefab. Why pay custom prices when you can buy something from a store for much less? There's a good chance you'll find your interest constantly piqued doing custom work, and isn't that something we all strive for? But one downside about custom work for some builders, says Foolish Frost, is that they don't like turning their work over to clients with full permissions, as custom builds often require. It means giving up all control over what you've created and, for some, that is hard to do.

FULL-SIM BUILDS

In some cases, clients want someone to do full-sim builds for them. This means that the client has bought or rented an entire sim and wants it built up.

This is a substantial task—and not something that a newcomer to the business is likely to be ready for because it entails a high degree of skill and talent and a commitment of dozens of hours. But once you've reached a certain level of expertise doing smaller prefab or custom builds, you may move on to full-sim builds because they can be quite lucrative and interesting.

Figure 6.10: A full-sim tree house build, with a library, birdhouses, hidden hot springs, and much more, made for the worldwide marketing agency Leo Burnett.

It's hard to estimate how much you can charge for doing a full-sim build, but if it took 80 hours to complete the work and you charged US$50 an hour for it, that would total US$4,000. For a high-quality build, that's probably on the low end of what you can earn doing this kind of work. And that most likely doesn't include the cost of ongoing maintenance, such as cleanup, repairs, and upgrades. When a whole sim is used by a single client (Figure 6.10), you'll often need to design the entire sim with a unified theme. Popular full-sim builds include The Lost Gardens of Apollo, Midnight City, Luskwood, Dublin, and The Pot Healer Adventure—Numbukulla Island Project.

Also, because owners of full sims control the environment on their land, the builder needs to have highly developed knowledge of how to use *Second Life*'s estate-management tools. Essentially, the estate-management tools allow the builder or the owner to set various environmental parameters for the sim. These include everything from the textures used for the ground, the time of day for the sim (for those who don't use the default four-hour day of *Second Life*), the sun or moon position, and even who is allowed to enter the sim.

Additionally, designing full-sim builds requires being able to add what designer Foolish Frost, who is often hired for full-sim builds, calls "gadgeteering" touches. "You have to not only create the sim," Foolish says, "but any effects used. Fog? That's a gadget. Fire? Lava? Building a sim is about creating an *experience*. Not a single building. It's about making things that are single devices. A ring that helps you to fly higher. A device that rezzes a glass plane that falls and shatters. A taxi that automatically takes people around a sim. Teleporters, particle effects, etc."

TIP

Because of the various skills required for full-sim builds, working with a team is beneficial. You don't need to have all the skills yourself, so long as the people on your team combine to have all the necessary skills.

To be frank, full-sim builds are not something most people are going to do. The work requires a great deal of skill and experience, and in many respects is just like doing smaller custom builds, only writ large. Thus, one of the pros is that the work pays a lot. If you're doing full-sim builds, you are likely getting paid more than $50 an hour or, in some cases, a fixed fee for the sim, for work that will probably take weeks to finish. With the creative rewards comes the responsibility to clients who are paying more and demanding more than someone buying something smaller. The point is, when you're ready to think about going into the business of doing full-sim builds, you should consider whether the payoff is worth the headaches. Chances are, if you've got the skills it probably is. Just be sure you're aware of what it really means before you take on the task.

DEVELOPING YOUR BUILDING BUSINESS

We've discussed what building in the virtual world means, what kind of builds there are, how much you can make doing this, who your potential customers are and how to work with them, and the skills you'll need to proceed. We've also talked about the pros and cons of the different options, and who some of the famous builders are—and what kinds of backgrounds they have. Now, it's time for you to join them.

CHAPTER 1
CHAPTER 2
CHAPTER 3
CHAPTER 4
CHAPTER 5
CHAPTER 6

CHAPTER 7
CHAPTER 8
CHAPTER 9
CHAPTER 10
CHAPTER 11
APPENDICES
INDEX

Clearly, you're not going to be able to start selling the minute you decide to go into business, at least not for any amount of money worth working for. It's going to take time, practice, and some intangibles that the experts say are absolutely crucial.

STARTUP COSTS

One of the nice things about the *Second Life* building business is that it doesn't cost much to get going—at least in financial terms. You should be able to get your business going for less than US$100, not counting professional software. The most expensive part is probably going to be the software you need. Photoshop, for example, can cost several hundred dollars, and 3D modeling software—should you decide to go that direction—can be much more. But, as I've discussed, there are also free 2D and 3D programs, and so you may not even need to invest in those. Or, you might already have them, depending on what you've been doing for work already.

Other costs include an optional Premium *Second Life* account—$9.95 a month—and at least a small plot of land. Builders may want to have a store, and they also may want enough land to build projects in privacy, away from the busy, public Sandboxes. Indeed, many builders prefer to work uninterrupted in a private sky-box, if the size of the project allows for it, when they're focusing on their work.

> **NOTE**
>
> *Kim Anubis started with US$5 worth of Linden dollars, and a 512-square-meter plot of land on which to build. That much land can be had for next to nothing.*

You'll also want to spend some money on marketing. Kim Anubis says her expenditures there are minimal, just around L$200 a week. That's not to say you'll be able to do the same, since you won't begin with name recognition, but the basic idea is that it doesn't cost much to start your business. As for what you spend later—on a sim, on stores, on buying building elements you don't do yourself—those numbers can add up, but it's hard to quantify them.

BUILDING FOR LOVE

One common sentiment among those who have succeeded at building in *Second Life* is that before you try to make money at it, you should spend some time developing that passion for yourself and the kinds of builds you want to do.

"Build for yourself at first," says Foolish Frost. "Make your own home. Find out what you like." Indeed, one mistake many people wanting to open up a business in *Second Life* make is to try to jump right in without really spending any time learning *Second Life*. And many people feel that approach is patently transparent—and not appreciated.

"Do it because you enjoy doing it, and [for] no other reason, or it won't work," says Neil Protagonist. "You won't know what to create if you don't know the world. I've seen a lot of people come into *Second Life* strictly to make money, and a lot of them aren't here anymore."

Neil added that he thinks there is a clear line separating those who succeed and those who don't. "That line usually came down to attitude toward the world," he says. "Those who saw it as something to milk didn't make it far. Those who really sought to bring something to the world are now some of the top in their respective fields."

CHAPTER 1
CHAPTER 2
CHAPTER 3
CHAPTER 4
CHAPTER 5
CHAPTER 6

CHAPTER 7
CHAPTER 8
CHAPTER 9
CHAPTER 10
CHAPTER 11
APPENDICES
INDEX

■ HOW LONG WILL IT TAKE YOU?

One of the first questions I get asked when I talk to people about making money in *Second Life* is how long it takes to ramp up. In the building business, it's hard to say. It definitely depends on your skill level when it comes to the *Second Life* building tools and the outside software. For example, it took Foolish Frost about two months before he was ready to start charging for his work—and he had substantially developed 3D graphics and texturing skills already.

Kim Anubis says that a couple of months is the minimum amount of time you should expect to have to prepare before being ready to make money at building. "I would say that you shouldn't expect to do anything really useful, other than collect information and [get] used to things for a month or two at least," Kim says. "And by that, I mean logging in every day and practicing. You are not going to become a novelist in a month. You are not going to become a rock star in two months. And you are not going to become a top *Second Life* builder in a month or two unless you come up with an incredible idea, or you come in with some skills already."

RESIDENTS SPEAK

KIM ANUBIS'S ADVICE ON PURSUING YOUR BUILDING BUSINESS

Kim Anubis of The Magicians has been building for money longer than most people in Second Life. Her wisdom, developed over several years and countless builds, is priceless. Here, she shares her ideas about how to make it in the building business in Second Life.

- 🔹 **Spend as much time as you can afford in-world learning your way around before making important—and costly—business decisions.**

- 🔹 **Don't do it unless you would be doing it for fun and for free anyway.**

- 🔹 **The quality of what you're selling is paramount. Don't rush your work. Take your time.**

(Continued)

CHAPTER 6

THE BASICS
OF BUILDING

UNDERSTAND-
ING YOUR
CUSTOMERS

THE SKILLS
FOR BUILDING
IN SECOND
LIFE

MANAGING
PRIMS

CONSIDERING
THE THREE
BUILD TYPES

DEVELOPING
YOUR
BUILDING
BUSINESS

MARKETING
YOUR
BUILDING
BUSINESS

- Try something new.

- Keep in mind that this is a social environment, and that most people are here to have fun.

- Don't forget to have someone test your objects, scripts, and permissions before you sell something.

- Don't let your inventory become a horrible, chaotic mess.

- Don't forget to make backup copies of things you're in the middle of building.

- Don't let your business avatar do anything you wouldn't want your grandma to hear about—or see a screenshot of.

- Don't forget the value of a Linden dollar. Even if it says 10,000 in front of it, in Linden dollars, it still isn't so much.

MARKETING YOUR BUILDING BUSINESS

In Chapter 11, "The Future of *Second Life* Entrepreneurship," I'll discuss a wide range of general *SL* business marketing topics. But as with any individual area of business, there are some marketing specifics to consider, and I'll cover some of those for the building business here.

YOUR CUSTOMER BASE

Get to know the blogs, websites, unofficial forums, and in-world publications. You can learn a great deal about your customers from them, and you can advertise in them. There is no single form of media that most in *Second Life* will see, which does make it more of a challenge to market your work. "So what do you have left?" Foolish asks. "Your customer base."

He says the best way to market your building business is to start small, rent a store, and "build for the crowd that frequents it." That means talking to the people who come through the shop and observing them—seeing what they want and like. "If you see a lot of leather-thonged girls go by with fangs and male slaves on chains," Foolish says, "don't make colorful chairs with puppy-dog images. Wander with them," Foolish says. "Let them take you touring. Have them show you the places that they love."

Opening multiple stores is also a good idea, though not in the same sim. Some think that putting your store in a high-traffic area is generally a good idea. One of the most powerful marketing tools is word of mouth and making friends. Consider going to events, meeting people there, and talking about what they are interested in. Additionally, Foolish advises people to think about building their avatar's Profile and putting something on the Web tab of the Profile. "Don't count on people to click to launch their outside browser," he says, "especially if you are selling to people in-world."

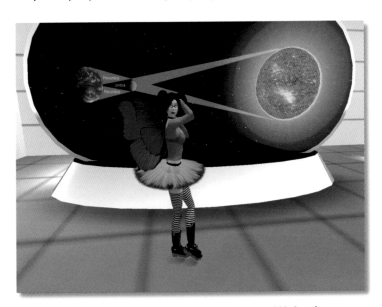

Figure 6.11: The distinctive look of Aimee Weber's avatar makes it a walking advertisement.

Make sure to include your store in your Avatar's Picks (in the Profile) and take out a Classified ad (also from the Profile), so residents can search for keywords related to your business (this helps if you're making something distinctive that people might search for, like Quonset hut prefabs). Kim points to Aimee Weber—and the fact that Aimee's avatar is very recognizable (Figure 6.11)—as an example of using your avatar as a walking advertisement. However, she cautions that if you're going to do that, you should be careful about the avatar name you choose and about protecting your avatar's image. She suggests having two avatars—one for business and one for play.

CHAPTER 1
CHAPTER 2
CHAPTER 3
CHAPTER 4
CHAPTER 5
CHAPTER 6

CHAPTER 7
CHAPTER 8
CHAPTER 9
CHAPTER 10
CHAPTER 11
APPENDICES
INDEX

CHAPTER 7

MAKING MONEY IN THE *SECOND LIFE* SEX TRADE

From animations and furniture to sex toys and escorting, the sex trade is alive and well in *Second Life*. This chapter discusses the different options for creating a profitable adult-oriented business, covering financial investment, preparation time, how much someone can make in the industry, some of the skills and knowledge required, and marketing tips.

   As this chapter is a discussion of sex-industry opportunities, it is not for the faint of heart. If you're likely to be offended or otherwise unhappy with such a discussion, please skip these pages. Otherwise, please read on.

CONTENTS

WHAT IS THE *SL* SEX TRADE?

If ever a phrase was a truism, it's "sex sells." It's true in magazines, movies, music, books, and particularly on the Web. It's definitely true in *Second Life*, whose tools, social mores, and large and growing population make it the ideal playground for the sexually curious and adventurous. Despite *Second Life*'s high media profile, Linden Lab has largely decided to leave residents alone when it comes to sexual behavior.

There are some exceptions, of course. One relates to what is known as "age play," defined somewhat broadly as sexual behavior between two or more residents in which at least one is using what appears to be a child avatar and the other is using an adult avatar. Because of the obvious allusions to child pornography—despite the fact that the residents behind such behavior are very likely to all be adults—Linden Lab does not tolerate such behavior in any public places and will ban anyone found engaging in it.

Beyond that, adult or sexual content and behavior is restricted to specific zones. Some areas of the virtual world are reserved for what is called PG, or "non-mature" content, while other areas are rated M, or "mature." All sexual behavior is officially relegated to the Mature areas.

The official *Second Life* community standards (http://secondlife.com/corporate/cs.php) state that "*Second Life* is an adult community, but Mature material is not necessarily appropriate in all areas.... Content, communication, or behavior which involves intense language or expletives, nudity or sexual content, the depiction of sex or violence, or anything else broadly offensive must be contained within private land in areas rated Mature (M)."

It may be odd to designate some areas as PG when no one under 18 is allowed in the main *Second Life* grid in the first place: Teens between 13 and 17 have their own grid, the *Teen Second Life* (see Chapter 10, "Running a Business in *Teen Second Life*"). But clearly, many *Second Life* residents don't want to be subjected to adult or sexual content. Also, although minors are not allowed in the main grid, there will always be some who make it in. It's in Linden Lab's legal interest to create an additional layer of formal separation between adult content and that meant for the general public. Even so, there's no shortage of Mature areas, and adult-oriented content of all kinds is easily found. For those interested in engaging with that content or selling it, *Second Life* is a wonderland of opportunity that caters to just about every desire and taste.

HOW MUCH SEXUAL CONTENT IS THERE?

CHAPTER 1
CHAPTER 2
CHAPTER 3
CHAPTER 4
CHAPTER 5
CHAPTER 6
CHAPTER 7
CHAPTER 8
CHAPTER 9
CHAPTER 10
CHAPTER 11
APPENDICES
INDEX

There is no way to measure it accurately, but it's estimated that approximately 30 percent of the economic activity in *Second Life* is related to sex or adult content or behavior. However, well-known *New World Notes* blogger Wagner James Au and others dispute the 30 percent figure.

In an entry he wrote in February 2007 (`http://nwn.blogs.com/nwn/2007/02/ a _ census _ of _ sec.html`), Au questioned the amount of sex-related content on display even in one of the most sexually charged clubs in *Second Life*, concluding that at most, 10 percent was directly related to sex. Au writes in the entry, "If it's just 10 percent *here*, how much smaller is it across the wide swath of the grid?" Perhaps we can assume that it's less than 30 percent and more than 10 percent. Either way, though, it's clear that it's a big number representing a lot of profit potential.

And why is there so much sexual activity? "We didn't plan it that way at all," Linden Lab programmer Phoenix Linden told Wired News for a 2006 article (`http://www.wired. com/culture/lifestyle/news/2006/06/71135`). "But people love the novelty of it. You can be whatever you want—a dragon or a fox or a dominatrix. There's no formula and the possibilities are endless."

WHAT KIND OF SEX-RELATED GOODS ARE FOR SALE?

Like many other industries in *Second Life*—fashion, building, toys, etc.—the availability of adult and sexually oriented items, content, and experiences is about as broad as the real-life human experience. That is, if you can imagine it, it probably exists. If it doesn't, then you might just have happened on a valuable new business idea.

Where to start? The *Second Life* sex industry consists of the following categories: fashion, accessories, genitals, clubs, escorts, toys, furniture, and animations. An explanation of each follows.

FASHION

For the most part, it's hard to specifically distinguish between normal fashion and sex-related fashion. After all, they're practically the same thing: clothing, skins, and the like. However, a significant subset of the fashion industry is dedicated to creating sexy items, and there's a lot of opportunity here. You can create gorgeous, lacy lingerie, suitable for the most exquisite and naughty bride; make a skimpy French maid's uniform; or check out a selection of several designers' interpretations of Leeloo's costume from the film *The Fifth Element*. Similarly, a lot of people will buy highly detailed skins because they provide residents with more-realistic bodies—for example, with more well-defined breasts for female avatars or with more muscular chests for males—than come with the standard avatars that everyone gets when they join *Second Life*.

CHAPTER 7

● WHAT IS
  THE *SL* SEX
  TRADE?

● UNDERSTAND-
  ING THE
  FINANCIAL
  ASPECT

● GETTING UP
  AND RUNNING

● SCRIPTING
  FOR SUCCESS

● COMPETING
  IN THE SEX
  INDUSTRY

● THE
  CHALLENGES
  OF THE SEX
  INDUSTRY

Ultimately, sexual fashion is really any kind of thing a resident might think is sexy to dress up in. In general, fashion items will run L$1,000 or less, depending on the item. A good set of "Sexy Nurse" lingerie from BabyDoll LaFontaine's store, BabyDoll's, costs L$400, for example (Figure 7.1).

Figure 7.1: Sexy nurse sign from BabyDoll's; sexy lingerie could be considered a product in the sex industry.

ACCESSORIES

Accessories can be the platform shoes, the stethoscope in the naughty nurse's outfit, and the gold coin bangles on your pirate or harem outfit. One sexy pirate outfit from Rebel Hope Designs (Figure 7.2) comes with a scripted cutlass so that the lady pirate is ready for battle.

You might also consider accessories such as sound-effects packages sold by places like Xcite (http://www.getxcite.com/) (Figure 7.3). Sound effects might include a range of sexual expressions, from a pleased murmur to a full-throated X-rated dialogue.

Essentially, adult accessories are the details that add veracity to the fantasy. Since the variety is so broad, it's hard to pinpoint what they may cost. For example, you might pay L$300 for a package of sexual sound effects or a set of sexy bath accessories, or up to L$1,000 for one of Strokerz Toyz's strap-ons.

Figure 7.2: Rebel Hope Designs' Lady Pirate Anne outfit includes a cutlass so that the buyer is ready for battle.

*Figure 7.3: Xcite is one of the most popular sex emporiums in **Second Life** and specializes in products that are part of its interoperable "system."*

Genitals

Genitals are the sex organs that *Second Life* users add to their avatars' skins to give a more realistic human (or animal, if that's their style) definition. *Second Life* avatars don't come with genitals—and as a result there is a huge business in these add-ons. People can buy a wide range of penises and vaginas in various sizes and levels of functionality and complexity to fulfill different kinds of fantasies. One of the things they do is offer feedback to sexual partners about the wearer's presumed level of interest.

Genitals also can have sophisticated scripts added, depicting everything from increased arousal and even male climax, to the much more complex. Andrea Faulkner, who was once a leading *Second Life* escort and who now sells adult toys for Strokerz Toyz, described a particular female genitalia product the store sells as "the very first [vagina] in *SL* that I'd ever really use, and that's because it creates a private room and sex poses on demand, on the spot."

Genitals also provide a visual element to sex that isn't possible with stock avatars, allowing partners to simulate penetration or other sex acts dependent on genitalia for visual veracity. Because *Second Life* is not limited to strictly human behavior, there is also a market for parts that would have pleased Catherine the Great (i.e., animal penises) and for special scripts, like those that residents can use to simulate graphic sex poses.

Genitals can run in the L$400 to L$750 range, regardless of whether they're male or female. As always, there are items for less and more, but that's a good range of prices to shoot for.

Clubs

Clubs in *Second Life* include venues that cater to all manner of sexual activity, either by being tolerant to residents having sex there or by inviting residents who want that kind of atmosphere. Clubs are often among the more crowded places in *Second Life*, particularly in the evening. Because the *Second Life* population is worldwide, it is usually night for a substantial number of residents.

The advantages of sex clubs are that like-minded people can gather together "behind closed doors," and seekers of sexual activity can find what they're looking for or discover something new. You can find clubs with topless dancers, a simulated tropical beach for gay men, a fully BDSM (bondage & discipline/domination & submission/sadism & masochism) Goth dungeon, and everything in between.

If you search in the *Second Life* Places category, many of the top hits are going to be X-rated clubs. A lot of those clubs are open to anybody, and you'll find strippers, dancers, and girls hanging out to be chatted up. There's usually music, drinking, and dancing. Club owners are often trying to create an attractive front-of-the-house atmosphere and sexy back-room environments. Some of those front-room areas also are screening rooms. They have to

CHAPTER 1
CHAPTER 2
CHAPTER 3
CHAPTER 4
CHAPTER 5
CHAPTER 6
CHAPTER 7

CHAPTER 8
CHAPTER 9
CHAPTER 10
CHAPTER 11
APPENDICES
INDEX

CHAPTER 7

WHAT IS
THE *SL* SEX
TRADE?

UNDERSTAND-
ING THE
FINANCIAL
ASPECT

GETTING UP
AND RUNNING

SCRIPTING
FOR SUCCESS

COMPETING
IN THE SEX
INDUSTRY

THE
CHALLENGES
OF THE SEX
INDUSTRY

inform the curious and the genuinely interested about what's available and about the rules. The people in action areas in X-rated venues must accept whatever rules and boundaries have been set up and understand what the areas are for. Many clubs are free for patrons to visit, and some charge nominal entrance fees. The money for the club owners is in charging a commission to the DJs, dancers, and escorts who work there. Often the club gets a 20 percent cut of any money that people who work there earn. And that can add up quickly in popular venues with in-demand dancers, escorts, and others.

ESCORT SERVICES

Escorts are effectively *Second Life* residents who hire themselves out to perform sexually for clients. They work as freelancers, prowling the streets of areas like Amsterdam, or they work in clubs, giving a percentage of their earnings to the venue owners. There are people whose job it is to manage the escorts, though many escorts work on their own.

The level of service escorts provide depends on their own personal experience and desire, as well as what they charge. Clients can pay moderate amounts for inexperienced escorts who will do some small number of things, while more expensive escorts will offer a wide variety of services.

In general, female escorts will make much more, though there is certainly no shortage of males in the business. Escorts generally earn anywhere from L$200 to L$4,000 an hour, depending on their experience, skill, wardrobe, and other factors.

No wonder, says Genvieve Hutchence, who owns the Supreme Fetishist BDSM club and who has experience with what escorting entails. "If I was giving [oral sex to a *Second Life* client], I would describe it in intense minute detail," Genvieve says, "get [the client] so hot [he] would stop what [he] was doing and *have* to [have an orgasm]."

For many, this can be one of the most lucrative professions in *Second Life*, which probably isn't a surprise, since it is, after all, the "oldest profession in the world." In fact, Andrea Faulkner says that when Linden Lab recently changed its policies and began allowing new users to join without credit cards, it caused a flood of new people, many of whom quickly migrated to escorting. "Frankly," Andrea says, "escorting freelance is the easiest way to make money for a new person. To a newbie, L$200 an hour is a lot of money."

CHAPTER 1
CHAPTER 2
CHAPTER 3
CHAPTER 4
CHAPTER 5
CHAPTER 6
CHAPTER 7

CHAPTER 8
CHAPTER 9
CHAPTER 10
CHAPTER 11
APPENDICES
INDEX

RESIDENTS SPEAK

ANDREA FAULKNER ON ESCORTING

For a long time, Andrea Faulkner was a successful escort in Second Life, *bringing experience as a real-life escort with her into the virtual world. She's no longer doing it, having moved on to helping to manage the Strokerz Toyz empire, but she is still brimming with knowledge about what it takes to succeed at providing personal sexual services in the virtual world.*

- **Invest in your body: The best hair, skin, eyes, shape, animation overrides, poses, and costumes.**

- **Set a realistic price for yourself until you build a stable of regulars.**

- **Avoid pimps and escort services who demand a cut of your money.**

- **Don't get into a relationship. It's going to be drama eventually, no matter what he says. No one wants to date a hooker.**

- **Finally, don't be afraid to say no to a request. If you start degrading yourself and hating the job, you'll burn out.**

TOYS

Figure 7.4: Toys like this tickler/duster are a big part of what a sex emporium like Xcite sells.

Toys seem to be generating a very significant portion of the *Second Life* economy. A smart entrepreneur with a humorous and generous attitude could choose to go into a business that supplies customized toys, including items like handcuffs and whips, dildos, scripted wings, and tails that can be stroked and actually interact with genitalia to provide excitement to the wearer. In addition to overtly sexual items, there are also more subtle products, including some that are designed to set the scene, as it were. Examples include an absinthe set, a bong, various scripted alcohol sets, and cigarettes with tools that let users choose from an elegant variety of smoke rings.

A tickler and duster set (Figure 7.4) can sell for L$150, blindfolds for L$200, vibrators for L$175, paddles for L$150, and strap-ons for L$400 and up. As always, there are many more examples of items with lower and higher prices.

CHAPTER 7

WHAT IS
THE *SL* SEX
TRADE?

UNDERSTAND-
ING THE
FINANCIAL
ASPECT

GETTING UP
AND RUNNING

SCRIPTING
FOR SUCCESS

COMPETING
IN THE SEX
INDUSTRY

THE
CHALLENGES
OF THE SEX
INDUSTRY

ANIMATIONS

A skilled animator can make a very good living in *Second Life*. When it comes to in-world sex, animations are a crucial ingredient because any kind of visual depiction of sex acts requires a custom animation. Three basic kinds of animations are sold: still poses, animation loops for an individual avatar, and group animations.

Indeed, animations have helped *Second Life* grow as fast as it has, given that they allow avatars to do just about anything someone can imagine—and script (dancing being a common example). In the sex trade, some animators sell individual animations or bundles of many to other entrepreneurs who make sex toys and furniture or who run clubs. If you're making a dance pole, buy animations that make grinding, sexy dances. If you're building a sex club, you can buy from a good animator the animations that avatars can use to put their bodies together and go through the motions of sex. It's the difference between talking about it and seeing it. Similarly, a homeowner could buy an animation to put in a private skybox allowing avatars to engage in sexual behavior there. During a visit to any good sex emporium, you'll almost always find couples trying out various sexual animations in one corner or another. Beds and rugs, too, are common places for adding erotic animations, as they are obvious places to engage in sexual activity.

One popular form of erotic animation is that which allows couples to simulate engaging in sex. Such animations can run between L$250 and L$500, depending on their complexity.

FURNITURE

Figure 7.5: A SexGen bed, one of the most popular pieces of furniture in the Second Life sex industry.

Furniture in *Second Life* can be scripted, so anything someone would want to do probably is being sold as a script. You can buy a scripted shower set up for three avatars to take a very naughty, long time in, or a dance pole that includes 20 or 30 different animations that become a complex show when an avatar plays on it. A furniture maker might buy the animations that go in a sexy bed, making it into an interactive sex bed. There are lap-dance sofas where one avatar sits while the other avatar dances in front of them. There are beds that can come with dozens of sexual animations, like a top-of-the-line SexGen bed from Strokerz Toyz (Figure 7.5), which goes for L$12,000. The bed could be scripted for two residents, or for many. Simple beds start around L$500.

CHAPTER 1
CHAPTER 2
CHAPTER 3
CHAPTER 4
CHAPTER 5
CHAPTER 6
CHAPTER 7

CHAPTER 8
CHAPTER 9
CHAPTER 10
CHAPTER 11
APPENDICES
INDEX

Figure 7.6: A St. Andrew's Cross lets residents tie each other up for imaginative sex play.

Popular furniture also includes things like the scripted sofa on which several couples and a few individuals can sit, presumably in the corner of a nightclub, and each set of couples would have a different animated make-out scene. There's also the iconic desk setup for a scene between the "boss" and the "secretary." The St. Andrew's Cross (Figure 7.6), which sells for L$250, is a contraption where one avatar gets strapped in and the other gets to choose from a variety of whips and tickling devices. There's also a picnic blanket with make-out scripts included that, upon closer examination, reveals a more explicit Red Riding Hood/Big Bad Wolf scenario.

Other items include statues for L$400 and even slave crates, which cater to a very specific niche market, for L$150. Generally, the prices are going to be under L$1,000, although specialty items can run much higher than that.

MORE INFO

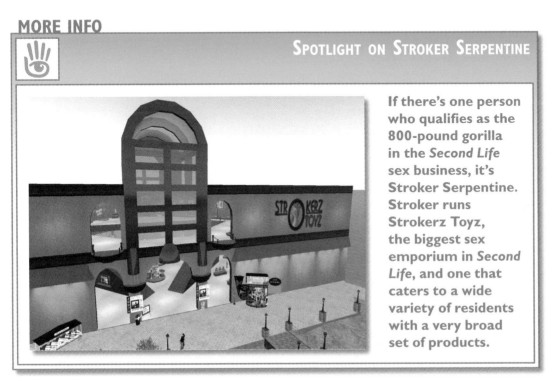

SPOTLIGHT ON STROKER SERPENTINE

If there's one person who qualifies as the 800-pound gorilla in the *Second Life* sex business, it's Stroker Serpentine. Stroker runs Strokerz Toyz, the biggest sex emporium in *Second Life*, and one that caters to a wide variety of residents with a very broad set of products.

(Continued)

These days, he's probably better known for the US$50,000 he got for his adult-themed sim, Amsterdam (shown here), a sort of mall based on the Dutch city's Red Light District, where residents can buy all kinds of sexy outfits, watch porn films, meet escorts, dance for hours with scantily clad performers, and much more.

But Stroker would be the first to tell you that he—and his partners—are much more than that. First, he prides himself on the entire "empire" he has built, which includes Strokerz Toyz and Eros, a community of residents built around erotic exploration and mutual interest.

Stroker came into *Second Life* in late 2003, not long after the virtual world launched. He had been running what he calls a "thriving business" in SeduCity, a 2D adult-oriented virtual world. But he left that environment for *Second Life*'s user-created content and its opportunities.

Today, Strokerz Toyz is an erotic retail powerhouse that employs 14 people who are paid full-time, real-world salaries, as well as many others who help out in specific roles. But regardless of the fact that he has many partners in his ventures, he is without a doubt the Strokerz Toyz figurehead and spiritual leader—and as such, he sets its vision. Stroker seems to be on the cutting edge of much of what develops in *Second Life*. He claims, for example, to have been involved in the creation of the "poseball," the nearly ubiquitous item that contains custom animations often used to depict sexual actions or other provocative behavior. Its creation, he says, was a reaction to something he and his partners saw as missing in the virtual world.

Similarly, he stakes his claim to having created the first "sex bed," a bed with built-in sexual animations. "There were no custom animations" in *Second Life* at the time, he says. "So we did a down and dirty hack of some of the proprietary Linden animations, looping them, starting and stopping them, to give the appearance of sexual motions."

These days, Stroker is the biggest name in one of the biggest segments of the *Second Life* economy, but he's happy to share his wisdom with those who are just getting started. Among the most important things to remember, he says, are to look for ways to innovate and to be sure to both be willing to accept help and support from others, and to do the same for those who come after you.

CHAPTER 1
CHAPTER 2
CHAPTER 3
CHAPTER 4
CHAPTER 5
CHAPTER 6
CHAPTER 7

CHAPTER 8
CHAPTER 9
CHAPTER 10
CHAPTER 11
APPENDICES
INDEX

Plus, he says, try hard to overcome what he sees as the biggest challenge to opening up a business in *Second Life*: finding balance between your real life and your new endeavor. "Never forget that there is a real life behind your chair," he cautions. "I see a lot of people get burnt out and leave *Second Life* because they dive in with no moderation, thinking that they must spend 16–18 hours a day in front of their PC to be a success. Sure, we've all done it. But a real-life respite goes a long way to stimulating the creative juices. Look to your real life for ideas. Don't get tunnel vision."

RESIDENTS SPEAK

STROKER SERPENTINE'S ADVICE FOR NEWCOMERS TO THE INDUSTRY

- Innovate and update. Listen to your customers and put your products in their faces. Use creative marketing and don't let your competitors dictate your business.

- Read the forums religiously. Be willing to be teachable.

- Don't beat yourself up if your new line of genitals doesn't fly off the shelves. Move on to something new.

UNDERSTANDING THE FINANCIAL ASPECT

If you are willing to put in the time to learn the skills and develop your operation, you can make a good deal of money. Of course, not everyone is going to be Stroker Serpentine, and even earning a full-time living is probably out of the reach of most. However, industry experts believe there's still a tremendous amount of opportunity open to newcomers.

The good thing is that the sex trade is not a capital-intensive business. In fact, almost anyone could scrape together the cash to start an operation in the *Second Life* sex economy. As in many *Second Life* industries, the real capital that must be invested into the sex trade is time and effort, not money. As long as you have the time and the commitment, you won't have to dip too far into your bank account to get things started. The costs vary from segment to segment, but are relatively similar whether you're going to be designing sex beds, custom animations, erotic toys, or anything where you'll be selling your products out of a store. The exceptions are sex clubs and escort businesses, but we'll get to those in a bit.

■ STOREFRONT BUSINESSES

The industry subsets of fashion, accessories, genitals, toys, furniture, and animations all share at least one common element: they are best sold from an in-world store. When you're starting out, the cost of getting the land and the building is going to be one of the biggest investments. You'll need to decide whether to open up shop on the mainland or on an island—I'll cover that later in the chapter. Either way, the cost of your initial plot of land is likely to be less than US$100. That's because you almost certainly will be able to get going on a 512-square-meter plot, which can be had almost anywhere for US$20 or less. Even if you decide to go a little bigger, you're still not talking about spending more than US$50 or so.

Once you have a successful business and a substantial cash flow, you'll want to consider your own sim—a US$1,675 initial investment and US$295 monthly tier payment if you buy an island. But that's a long way off if you're just starting out.

"If you want to start a business, you just need some land for a shop, some time to build the items, and voilà, you are a *Second Life* business," says Nyteshade Vesperia (Figure 7.7), the owner of Xcite, one of the biggest *Second Life* sex businesses.

Figure 7.7: Nyteshade Vesperia owns Xcite, a popular sex store.

Of course, there's a lot more to creating a successful business, including thinking about finances, land, and marketing. Nyteshade says that you'll need to invest in the land, pay for some marketing, and buy some software such as Photoshop (see the section "The Skills to Succeed" later in the chapter). Marketing includes placing Classified ads in *SL* or ads on *Second Life*–related websites and blogs. You also could sponsor some events. "It's not terribly much in the way of cash outlay," Nyteshade says, "but enough to separate the people who are serious from those who aren't." Unless you need to buy Photoshop or some form of 3D modeling software, which can cost several hundred dollars, you can get started for about US$200.

■ ESCORT SERVICES

If you're looking for a good return on investment and you don't have many qualms about what it takes to get it, then being an escort in *Second Life*—especially if you have a female avatar—may well be your best bet. Escorting is no simple task—it requires knowing how to give clients sexual satisfaction without ever touching them. However, because much of that comes from the things you communicate to them, either verbally, through a spoken voice mechanism (such as *Second Life*'s built-in tool or Skype), or via text chat, the required monetary investment is low.

According to Andrea Faulkner, the total outlay of necessary equipment, even for someone wanting to shoot for the high end of the business, would be about US$75. She says that the keys are to make sure to choose the right equipment and make your avatar—again, most likely a female—look as sexy as possible. There's no shortage of potential customers, and it's common for *Second Life* newbies to go straight into escorting because they've heard that it's a good way to make some money. While lamenting that it can hurt the market for established escorts, Andrea also recognizes the profit potential, even on the low end. "Your basic escort will go find a decent skin, hair, shoes, bikini, and some attachments, like a [vagina], or nipple rings," and go to work, Andrea says. "I took great pride in my appearance, and in my acting and writing abilities, so I went further. I found the best skin, the best hair, the best eyes, best clothes, best animation overrides, better breast shading, the best sex poses, etc."

CHAPTER 1
CHAPTER 2
CHAPTER 3
CHAPTER 4
CHAPTER 5
CHAPTER 6
CHAPTER 7

CHAPTER 8
CHAPTER 9
CHAPTER 10
CHAPTER 11
APPENDICES
INDEX

NOTE

> *Breast shading is a texture you can buy that gives the illusion of making an avatar's breasts bigger, an effective marketing trick. Other tricks include making an avatar's body look oiled, another attraction for some would-be clients.*

All told, it would probably take about L$10,000 to outfit an avatar to look and move like Andrea. You'd also need to get a small plot of land and a sex bed. Andrea explains, "Most escorts in *Second Life* get a SexGen bed because it takes very few prims and gives them the best versatility in having any pose the client might want to use."

■ SEX CLUBS

Sex clubs are another potentially lucrative business in *Second Life*. Residents can go with a partner to play sexually in a private, themed space, or possibly to find someone new to play with, all while listening to music from DJs, Internet radio, or live musicians. The financial upside is substantial, but the required investment and ongoing costs are also significant.

Figure 7.8: The Supreme Fetishist is Genvieve Hutchence's BDSM-themed sex club.

A sex club generally takes up a larger amount of space than a store, especially a newcomer's store, so the club owner's largest expense is likely to be land. You probably won't need an entire sim for a club, but you probably do want a plot bigger than the standard 512 square meters because you'll want your prim limits high enough to accommodate everything that you'll need to start. Genvieve Hutchence of the Supreme Fetishist (Figure 7.8)—which uses approximately 5,000 prims—says that a new sex club would need a minimum of around 2,000 prims. Let's say that you could get by with 1,875 prims. That would mean you could start with an eighth of a sim, or between 4,609 and 8,704 square meters.

As of this writing, that much land would come with a US$40 monthly tier fee. You could also rent that much space for not much more. In Genvieve's case, the Supreme Fetishist is on 21,000 square meters, or half a sim, which comes with a US$125 monthly tier fee.

NOTE

Please refer to Table 3.1 in Chapter 3 for details on prim limits per land parcel.

However, land is not the only expense. To begin with, you'll need to hire DJs, escorts, and dancers to entertain guests, and the talent will, of course, need to be paid. Genvieve says that a common way to handle paying these people is to give them a major cut of whatever they bring in—in the case of the Supreme Fetishist, that works out to about 80 percent of their take. It might not seem like much, but the 20 percent the club keeps is a major part of its income, since most clubs don't charge a cover. Additionally, you'll need partners or several employees. Among the roles that need to be filled are shift manager, who makes sure that your stage is staffed with dancers; security manager; and event manager. "A large club needs a large staff," says Genvieve.

In general, you could probably buy the land you'd need to get started for around US$200, with monthly tier payments of about US$50 or rent it for approximately US$60.

GETTING UP AND RUNNING

Any new business requires time for learning and ramping up—and a business in *Second Life*, even though it's in a virtual world, is still a business. Even after you've figured out the costs, you're going to have to make a big investment in time and preparation. Before you can get your sex-related business up and running, you'll need to learn about the *Second Life* user interface, its community, and its tools. Although there are many different segments of the *Second Life* sex industry, the basic requirements for getting started don't differ materially from segment to segment, with one or two exceptions. In this section, I'll break down the time required to get a business going.

■ STOREFRONT BUSINESSES

It's actually fairly simple to figure out how much time it will take you to get up to speed in running a storefront *Second Life* sex business. Whether you're selling animations, furniture,

CHAPTER 1
CHAPTER 2
CHAPTER 3
CHAPTER 4
CHAPTER 5
CHAPTER 6
CHAPTER 7

CHAPTER 8
CHAPTER 9
CHAPTER 10
CHAPTER 11
APPENDICES
INDEX

toys, or something else, the ramping up time is really no different than if you were trying to sell tuxedos or prefab castles in-world. Although a lot of *Second Life* business successes will tell you that you need to love doing what you do—and be willing to do it almost for free—before you can be any good or happy making an enterprise out of it, that's not necessarily true. Still, you probably need to at least like *Second Life* before moving forward with a business. It is, after all, a difficult environment with fragile technology that requires patience and understanding.

"In *Second Life*, not liking what you do can certainly shorten your attention span," says Nyteshade Vesperia. "I see lots of businesses disappear voluntarily because it becomes too much hassle for what a lot of people still look at as a 'hobby' or a 'game.'"

Assuming you're still interested, you're almost certainly looking at several months of ramp-up.

"Learning to use the *Second Life* tools takes some time, and doing some market research takes some time," says Nyteshade. "Two to three months would be a very good estimate, I think, with six to eight months representing what I would call 'perfecting time.'"

Figure 7.9: Amethyst Rosencrans runs the Dungeon Online mall and sells the Amethyst line and the Sensations line of adult-oriented products.

Amethyst Rosencrans, who runs the Dungeon Online mall and who co-creates the Sensations brand of *Second Life* sex products (Figure 7.9), has a slightly different take on this, particularly for someone wanting to start a business but who has no skills whatsoever. She says that for someone starting from scratch, it takes six months to a year to really get going. If someone does possess some technical skill, a shorter period of time is probably enough. "It was probably four to six months before I started selling anything," Amethyst says.

Ultimately, Amethyst thinks that the key to making a business work is commitment. "I think anyone can be at least moderately successful if they apply enough time and energy," she says.

■ ESCORT SERVICES

Escorts are a unique breed among *Second Life* businesspeople. To hear Andrea Faulkner tell it, someone could join *Second Life* and be out on the streets of the virtual world making money as an escort almost right away. Such is the power of the sexy female body. But that kind of nearly instant business startup corresponds to the low end of the escort pay scale.

WHAT IS
the *SL* SEX
TRADE?

UNDERSTAND-
ING THE
FINANCIAL
ASPECT

GETTING UP
AND RUNNING

SCRIPTING
FOR SUCCESS

COMPETING
IN THE SEX
INDUSTRY

THE
CHALLENGES
OF THE SEX
INDUSTRY

To get to the point where you're making the L$1,000 or L$2,000 per 30 minutes that Andrea says she earned … well, that's a different thing. In that case, we're talking about a learning curve of several months. "It's something you gain with experience," she says. "You have to be willing to take criticism and learn from your mistakes … I spent time in chat rooms … and learned about cybersex and roleplaying. It translates really well here."

■ SEX CLUBS

Sex clubs, like escort services, require you to put in a significant amount of learning time before you're ready to make money on your own. For one, it's because you need to learn the tips and tricks of the trade. The best way to learn, suggests Genvieve Hutchence, is to work in others' clubs for awhile, soaking in experience and seeing what works and what doesn't. Indeed, Genvieve says she had worked for at least six different clubs before finally getting her own place, the Supreme Fetishist, off the ground. At first, she says, she danced as a stripper and worked as an escort for three different clubs, learning how those elements worked. Then she managed three other sex clubs, seeing first-hand what it takes to keep such a venue up and running. In the end, it took Genvieve several months before she was ready to make a go of her own club and handle the substantial tier fees, employee pay, and commissions to the dancers, escorts, and DJs.

MORE INFO

SPOTLIGHT ON PROFESSOR SADOVNYCHA

In November 2006, Professor Sadovnycha became a *Second Life* resident. At first, the account lay fallow, with no interest, and not even a departure from Orientation Island. But in February 2007, after talking with friends and studying what was going in the *Second Life* economy, Professor decided to go in-world, move beyond the welcome area, and embark on a very ambitious endeavor. The project? Professor had challenged himself to go from knowing nothing about *Second Life* to running a profitable business in three months.

Fortunately, he knew what he wanted to do. His concept was the Princess Reform School, a place with products and classes designed around helping couples learn how to get pleasure and excitement from mutually agreed-upon sexual domination.

Professor purchased a 512-square-meter plot on the mainland and began studying the *Second Life* building tools. He was intent on doing everything himself on his road to (hopeful) profitability.

"The first thing was to understand what my product really was," he says. "To teach somebody how to dominate or be dominated. In *Second Life*, that means animations, animation overrides, poseballs, scripts, furniture, etc."

He went in search of the tools he needed, and found Avimator (http://www.avimator.com/), a free animation editor. He then studied up on building and the Linden Scripting Language—the fundamental *Second Life* scripting language—and got to work "building things that would make [his] students do what [he] was telling them to do."

If you wander into Princess Reform School, you'll find three rooms filled with all kinds of toys, furniture, and accessories designed to let couples learn how to enjoy domination. In addition to selling more than 50 different products, Professor teaches several weekly classes, most of which are free. The idea, he says, is to get the students interested enough in what they're learning to buy his products. And increasingly, it's happening just as planned.

"It feels so cool to see the window drop down with that cha-ching [indicating a sale] during class," Professor says, "when somebody buys something I just demonstrated."

Professor says he came into *Second Life* with a rudimentary understanding of scripting. With that, he was able to figure out how to take advantage of one of the most ubiquitous things in the virtual world.

"I found out scripts drive most devices in *Second Life*," he says. "I started ripping open freebies for open-source scripts I could look at. I'd Google codes and look at tutorial sites. Once I understood the basic concepts, I could just open an item, see the sounds and animations the script was playing, delete them, and put in my own."

It didn't take him long to start to get close to his goal. In part that's because his classes are the best form of advertising he could have. The classes "make money because folks drunk on sex tip well," he says, "and I sell a lot of products after class."

Professor says it took him about a month to learn the basic *Second Life* navigation, building, and commerce skills he needed to move Princess

(Continued)

CHAPTER 7

WHAT IS
THE *SL* SEX
TRADE?

UNDERSTAND-
ING THE
FINANCIAL
ASPECT

GETTING UP
AND RUNNING

SCRIPTING
FOR SUCCESS

COMPETING
IN THE SEX
INDUSTRY

THE
CHALLENGES
OF THE SEX
INDUSTRY

Reform School ahead. At six weeks, he was making enough to pay for his initial 512-square-meter plot. Within a couple of months, he outgrew his original plot and grew to 2,048 square meters. At three months, he'd built the business to the point where he was earning enough pay for the larger plot, with a little left over. His success is partly due to one of the great things about *Second Life* business: the products you create can become perpetual revenue-generation machines.

"What's so great about a *Second Life* business is the infinite and instant scalability," he says. "What I build now will make money forever, with no inputs. And I can supply as many customers as I have."

Professor still has a lot to learn, but he's figured out how to leverage websites like SL Exchange and OnRez to sell products, and he gives free classes to female avatars who are willing to run around public areas with Princess Reform School signs.

Ultimately, he looks primed for success because he did the one thing that nearly every *Second Life* business success recommends: find and fill a niche. Of course, Princess Reform School is only slightly profitable. Professor still has to work his day job. But he says he can see beyond that. "If I [do] a publicity ramp-up as aggressively as my product build-out," he says, "I could probably quit my job."

RESIDENTS SPEAK

PROFESSOR SADOVNYCHA'S ADVICE FOR A SEX-BUSINESS STARTUP

- Gather freebies [free products from stores] like a filter-feeder. Then harvest useful scripts.

- Before you pay for anything, search in-world and on the Web for a freebie version.

- Mind your permissions. Make sure you're not giving away a factory when you think you're selling an item.

- Put your landmark in everything you make. It's like a homing beacon for the truly curious.

- Be generous with giving away freebies. The word of mouth you'll get from sending somebody away loaded down with free stuff will be worth it.

CHAPTER 1
CHAPTER 2
CHAPTER 3
CHAPTER 4
CHAPTER 5
CHAPTER 6
CHAPTER 7

CHAPTER 8
CHAPTER 9
CHAPTER 10
CHAPTER 11
APPENDICES
INDEX

SCRIPTING FOR SUCCESS

You've got your concept. You know what you want your business to be. You know who your customer is, and how to reach him or her. However, adult-oriented products are frequently very script-heavy, so you'll also need some scripting skills and the ability to use 2D programs like Photoshop or 3D modeling programs like 3ds Max.

What you need to know when it comes to those software packages is very similar to the knowledge required in other areas of *Second Life* business. For details on the technical skills involved in running your enterprise, please refer to Chapter 4, "Walking the Runway—Fashion in *Second Life*" and Chapter 6, "Construction Projects Big and Small." Between those two chapters, you should find enough instruction and direction on learning and using 2D and 3D software to get going.

To Nyteshade Vesperia, the technical skill you most need when trying to launch a *Second Life* sex business is scripting. "Programming and scripting are almost necessities," Nyteshade says. "Everything runs on scripts, so being able to script and script well—there are a lot of bad scripters out there—can make a real difference." That means learning the Linden Scripting Language. If you're already a programmer, or at least familiar with programming or scripting languages, you probably won't have too much trouble. But if you need to learn, there are good tutorials online. For example, Linden Lab has a wide variety of information on its LSL Portal (http://wiki.secondlife.com/wiki/LSL _ Portal).

One good way to see how LSL works is to look at the script on an existing object. You also can take scripts that you find in some objects and use them as the base for your own objects. That's one of the ways Professor Sadovnycha learned to script his own items. "I scavenged a lot of open-source scripts for my objects," Professor says, "I know enough about scripting to repurpose some." For example, he says he took a script he found in a riding crop and first used it to make a whip. Later, he took the same script and used it to make what he calls a TickleBug, which makes an avatar curl up as if in a fit of laughing at being tickled.

Scripting is at the heart of much of what sells in this industry: animations are based on scripts that are attached to items like poseballs, genitalia, furniture, or other things. There's almost no way that you can hope to sell any actual products in the *Second Life* sex industry if you don't learn scripting, unless you strictly use other people's scripts.

There are several ways you can use others' scripts. The first would be to partner with or hire someone who does your scripting for you. In fact, this is a common arrangement because it allows different members of a team to focus on different things. The other is Professor's method: taking existing and freely available open-source scripts and using them for your own purposes. Many are available, and scripting is available on sites like the one posted above and others that make it possible for a non-scripter to learn how to build a scripted item.

COMPETING IN THE SEX INDUSTRY

You should know one thing if you plan to enter the *Second Life* sex industry: It's a crowded field. So how can you set yourself apart and do the kind of business that will reward the long hours you'll need to put in?

There are two kinds of competition that you can't worry about. On one hand, you have ultra-successful outfits like Strokerz Toyz and Xcite, which you'll never be able to knock off their perches. On the other, there are the fly-by-night operations that have so little integrity and business sense that you should have little problem surpassing them. It's the vast middle that is more challenging: the competent businesses with innovative products and owners who care what they're doing. It's not so much that you should try to beat them, but you should think about ways to be competitive.

To Xcite's Nyteshade Vesperia, the best qualities your business can have to succeed are innovation, integrity, perseverance, and concern for your customers, as well as a thick skin. "Lead your market," Nyteshade says. "Don't simply strive to copy what others do, and people will see you as a leader, even if you aren't (yet) monetarily." Also, she says, being innovative means that you need to be constantly keeping your product line fresh so that your customers have reason to come back again and again.

Integrity is a more ephemeral quality, but one that your customers and the *Second Life* community can smell from a mile away—especially if you don't have it. "If all you do is copy other people's ideas or repackage their items, you will get a reputation for just being an also-ran, which is not good for business," Nyteshade says.

Stroker Serpentine agrees. "I am of the opinion that only innovation succeeds," Stroker says. "You can make a sex bed prettier, more complex, and chock-full of animations, but at the end of the day, you just have a sex bed. *Second Life* is the ideal environment to develop brands and models previously nonexistent. I challenge my team to be innovative, not clones. . . . The true path to profitability is in creating something that has never existed before."

Being committed to innovation can be exhausting. That's why Nyteshade insists that perseverance is necessary to succeed. "There are a lot of hurdles in *Second Life*, and in business in general," she says. "You will not make a success overnight. You need to stick with it if you want to grow."

CREATING A NICHE

CHAPTER 1
CHAPTER 2
CHAPTER 3
CHAPTER 4
CHAPTER 5
CHAPTER 6
CHAPTER 7

CHAPTER 8
CHAPTER 9
CHAPTER 10
CHAPTER 11
APPENDICES
INDEX

Though he has yet to create the kind of profit powerhouse that Stroker and Nyteshade have, Professor Sadovnycha has done one thing that many say is vital to succeeding—he identified and filled a niche. Princess Reform School is a new take on the BDSM market. There are other *Second Life* BDSM businesses, but few if any approached it the way he did. He created classes and products with an emphasis on giving the person being dominated a way to pleasurably interact while it's happening. And that's why a visit to his store, even though it's small and he hasn't been able to afford to buy a highly placed Classified ad, usually results in running into very curious potential customers.

"Find a subject that is not well covered and focus on that," says Amethyst Rosencrans of Sensations. "And listen to the consumers. Hear what they want. They are the ones that make your business successful. So make sure you keep them happy."

To be sure, identifying and knowing how to fill a niche isn't easy. But Stroker is right: if all you do is create a new kind of sex bed, you're just one more entrant in the vast sex-bed market, and you'll find it that much harder to set yourself apart. The key is to spend the time to look around *Second Life* and see what's out there. You can't possibly know what's a niche or what's innovative unless you've taken the time to investigate. Talk to people. Ask them what they like, and what they *would* like. Ask what's missing. And see what might suit your interests to create.

WORKING WITH "SYSTEMS"

One of the things that has made Xcite such a success is that it has developed a very popular "system" of sex products—body parts, accessories, and the like—that work together. For instance, if both members of a couple are using products from the system when they're having sex in *Second Life*, their avatars can express pleasure or excitement when they touch each other or when the two products touch.

What has helped Xcite even more is that, while the system is proprietary, it allows other businesses to create products that interact with the system. If you, for example, create a collection of products that work within the Xcite system, you have a huge potential market open to you. "Someone building an item that complements our line would certainly be wise to make themselves compatible with other established systems," says Nyteshade. "It adds value to their items to do so."

But Xcite chooses only partners that it considers complementary, and never chooses competitive products to interact with its system. That's why, if you see a hole in someone else's system, you might do well to create your own. "If they are building something from scratch to solve what they see as flaws in the existing offerings," says Nyteshade of newcomers to the business, "or have a totally radical new way to do something, then building their own system is smart, especially if it truly is an improvement and will revolutionize their particular market."

Ultimately, the point of creating a system, or working with someone else's, is that it creates a broader market: It means that users can buy several different products and have them all work together, giving the user a more complex sexual experience—and giving you more potential sales.

THE CHALLENGES OF THE SEX INDUSTRY

Before you jump into business in the *Second Life* sex industry, you should be aware that there are a few unique challenges involved. Some revolve around tricky moral and social issues. Others have to do with how people perceive you. Regardless, these are not things that should deter you, but it's worth being aware of them before you embark, so you're not surprised.

Seen as a social ill: Although many *Second Life* users appreciate and participate in the virtual world's vibrant sex industry, many others simply can't stand it. If you start a business in the industry, you should be prepared to be the target of derisive remarks that are perhaps intended to encourage you to leave. Others will write in the forums or on blogs or will simply talk about you in-world as examples of "what's wrong with *Second Life* today," says Nyteshade Vesperia, often because they just don't agree with what you're doing, or the adult industry in general, on moral grounds.

"In this industry, you have to be willing and able to ignore these sorts of things," says Nyteshade, "take satisfaction from your own accomplishments, and enjoy that private little giggle when that fundamentalist fanatic that just slammed you and your business all over the forums turns out to be a customer of yours."

Assumptions about you: Amethyst Rosencrans notes that *Second Life* residents often make assumptions about her strictly based on her business. It's not that she minds so much, but it is something she has to deal with. "Because I [sell] obedience collars, cuffs, and whips," Amethyst says, "people assume that I am a [dominatrix]. And because I make hermaphrodite parts, that I am into that. . . . You need a thick skin. You have to expect to get some strange requests and that people will make assumptions about your sex life."

Legal issues: Although there are currently no crackdowns on the *Second Life* sex industry, that doesn't mean it won't happen. "Adult businesses in the real world are always at risk of running afoul of a variety of hazards, including local laws that target adult industries, individuals who take issue with anything adult-related, and international/ cultural concerns," says Nyteshade. "Linden Lab does not help this situation much given that it is neither clear nor consistent with its own policies or the interpretation of real-world laws. In this industry, you just have to get used to the idea that at any moment, your entire enterprise may be deemed illegal, and have an exit strategy on hand."

Age verification: Linden Lab recently announced plans to implement an age-verification system that would give those who operate Mature regions the ability to restrict admission to anyone who hasn't been certified as over the age of 18. Certainly, there are going to be minors who make it through the filter, but many in the *Second Life* adult industry are breathing a sigh of relief that such a system is on its way. That's because the system means that they can be reasonably sure that those who enter their establishments are of legal age. (This might also offer them legal protection.)

"If I lose sales because minors can't purchase items or people are upset with Linden Lab for forcing them to verify their identity," says Amethyst, "then that is fine with me."

RESIDENTS SPEAK

NYTESHADE VESPERIA'S ADVICE ON MAKING IT IN THE SEX INDUSTRY

As co-owner of Xcite, Nyteshade is one of the biggest experts on what it takes to make it in the Second Life sex business. Here she shares five suggestions a newcomer to the industry should be sure to follow.

- **Innovate and stay active. Too many businesses grow stagnant in *Second Life*, and that means people lose interest and move on to the next new guy on the block.**

- **Have a plan. Don't just decide to sell toys one day. Plan your strategy, have goals, think ahead of time what some of your hurdles will be.**

- **Assume the worst, both from *Second Life* and from other people. Don't be blindsided when someone decides to take public issue with you. Also be prepared for each new patch to bring your business to a grinding halt.**

- **Take the high road. Maintain your integrity and don't give people a chance to drag your name through the dirt. Preserve your reputation. A good perception of your brand name is gold.**

- **Do your homework. Find out about your customers. Find out what they like and don't like. Listen to suggestions. Ask questions. Customers *love* to talk, and you can learn a lot from them. No matter how smart you may be, you don't know everything. You *need* to learn from what the market tells you.**

CHAPTER 1
CHAPTER 2
CHAPTER 3
CHAPTER 4
CHAPTER 5
CHAPTER 6
CHAPTER 7

CHAPTER 8
CHAPTER 9
CHAPTER 10
CHAPTER 11
APPENDICES
INDEX

CHAPTER 8

SELLING OBJECTS, FROM TOYS TO WEAPONS

Second Life is an environment where a countless number of fertile minds have created an almost infinite number of toys and gadgets for residents to play with in any combinations they choose. From an entrepreneurial perspective, this is a good thing because it means that there is almost no limit to the kinds of objects you can make and sell. If you can imagine it and you have the skills to create it, there's a pretty good chance that you can also sell it. This chapter explores the ins and outs of the objects business.

CONTENTS

WHAT IS THE *SL* OBJECTS BUSINESS?

It's hard to categorize the many different kinds of objects you can find in *Second Life*, so rather than try to break them down into endless groups, it's probably better to use a smaller list so that you can see what's possible and use existing examples to stoke your imagination of what you might want to offer. The objects business spans the spectrum, from weapons to HUDs; the opportunities are nearly limitless.

TOYS

Let's face it: everyone likes toys. In *Second Life*, they come in all shapes and sizes, and there's most likely something to suit any imagination. But there's also plenty of room for new items—and that's where you come in.

Figure 8.1: Starax's famous magic wand could make cows fall from the sky, tsunamis appear out of nowhere, and much more.

Starax Stotasky's wand (Figure 8.1) is one of the most famous toys in *Second Life* history. The wand was capable of conjuring up some of the coolest things you can imagine: a tidal wave that sweeps across the land; cows falling from the sky; a giant pig you could ride; a glass house with breakable windows; a rocket ship that appears, starts its engines, and then takes off (flames shooting out of its end). Starax is famous for his sculptures, so the objects rezzed by the wand are often silly, but are also works of art.

The magic wand built a huge following, despite a price tag of around US$55. To the sorrow of many, the wand is no longer updated, or even sold. Starax, rumored to be tired of maintaining the scripts to keep working with an ever-changing *Second Life* codebase, seems to have moved on to other things. Even today, though, long after the wand has gone off the market, there are many fans who pine for its return.

Figure 8.2: The author poses wearing both Hiro Pendragon's samurai swords and one of Wynx Whiplash's kittens.

On the other side of the spectrum are the many kinds of objects that, usually, are more aesthetic than anything else. Wynx Whiplash's wearable pets are very popular (Figure 8.2). Residents can wear the little animals (cats, mice, dragons, birds, frogs, pandas, etc.), which really serve no purpose except to be cute or funny. They can be worn on the shoulders, in the arms, on top of the head, and elsewhere. At L$300, they're inexpensive, yet for Wynx they are a money-maker because so many people see them, love them, and buy them.

MORE INFO

SPOTLIGHT ON WYNX WHIPLASH, SECOND LIFE INNOVATOR EXTRAORDINAIRE

Wynx Whiplash (below left) is one of the true innovators of Second Life, having invented what are known as Tinies (an example of which is shown on the right below)—an increasingly popular form of miniature avatar. They can be little animals, such as rabbits or skunks, or small people. In general, they stand no higher than a normal avatar's knee. She's also created a toy that is seen increasingly in Second Life: her wearable pets.

(Continued)

When Wynx Whiplash joined *Second Life*, she knew that she wanted to be a content creator. For six months, Wynx played around, meeting people and thinking about the things she might like to do. She realized that she probably wouldn't be very good at making clothing, but did enjoy a furry avatar that she bought and wore for a few days. That gave her some ideas about what she might want to do as a business. She played around with new design techniques and hired people for a few hundred Linden dollars at a time to make scripts for objects for her. Still, it wasn't what she wanted.

"One day I was cleaning my cat's ears and he had this *look* on his face—so *angry*," Wynx says. "So I made the Mad Cat avatar." That avatar, a sort of wild-eyed cat, became a hit.

On the *Second Life* forums, some people told her that they liked the avatar and said "if that was really small, I'd buy it in a heartbeat." She filed that comment away for later, and it became the impetus for the Tinies. One day, a friend told Wynx that he really liked the Mad Cat design, but wasn't interested in wearing it as a whole avatar.

"He asked if I would make one so it would look like it was falling off his shoulder," Wynx recalls. "That became the [wearable] pets. So I made [a] gray cat and then all the colors. Then I started making mice and whatever came to mind."

If you happen to see someone walking by with a little purring black-and-white kitten or a small dragon on their shoulder that occasionally breathes fire, there's a good chance it's one of Wynx's.

RESIDENTS SPEAK

EXPERT ADVICE FROM WYNX WHIPLASH

💠 Be as original as possible. Redoing an already popular idea isn't going to make a name for you.

💠 Add surprises. Something folks wouldn't expect.

💠 Stay on top of the latest technology: flexiprims, lighting, sculpted prims—whatever is new today.

CHAPTER 1
CHAPTER 2
CHAPTER 3
CHAPTER 4
CHAPTER 5
CHAPTER 6
CHAPTER 7
CHAPTER 8

CHAPTER 9
CHAPTER 10
CHAPTER 11
APPENDICES
INDEX

- The customers make or break you. You're there to help them, no matter what they ask. Even if they ask you for your scripts, animations, or textures. There are polite ways to say no and encourage them to be original.

- Use the forums: Cesspool of discontent on the one hand, invaluable resource on the other. Don't get bogged down in the drama, but read everything you can in the Content Creation area and download all the templates.

- We all start at the bottom. It takes time to be successful.

- Do not steal content or do anything immoral just to start making money. Making an item that looks like someone else's and saying it was "inspired by" is a good way to get a bad name for yourself. Your name is all you have.

- Have patience. Don't give up. If you see that your product isn't doing well, try [something] new.

Figure 8.3: At Alphazero Sugar's Core Chicken and Waffles store, you can buy a chicken grenade gun or a kitten that purrs and follows you around.

Alphazero Sugar's Core Chicken and Waffles store is a testament to the love of toys. This is where he sells his "poultry-based weapons system," like the ChickenGun, which "combines the natural aggression of the modern domesticated chicken with the high acceleration of an electromagnetic rail gun, mixed in with a bit of high explosives to create the deadliest, or perhaps just the most amusing, weapon in *Second Life* today." They may appear to be weapons, but they are simply playful. No actual chickens are harmed in the manifestation of this toy.

But Alphazero also sells less-aggressive toys, like his AstroKitten (Figure 8.3), a little L$100 scripted kitty that will stay, come, and sleep on command—and it purrs, too. He also sells AstroTurkeys (L$175), as well as AstroChickens, AstroRoosters, AstroDucks, and AstroChicks (L$25), which also come in six-packs for L$100.

Essentially, there really isn't a strict definition of toys in *Second Life*—they're objects that can be played with, that likely have some scripting, and that ideally make people laugh.

■ WEAPONS

Although there are a few combat zones in *Second Life*, the virtual world is generally a nonviolent environment. For those who want to play at battles or warfare with others, there's no shortage of appropriate games, such as *World of Warcraft* or *EverQuest*. However, just because you don't have any intention of attacking people in *Second Life* doesn't mean you shouldn't be able to wander around with the latest and greatest samurai swords. And you can: thanks to Hiro Pendragon and several other purveyors of quality Japanese-style blades you can walk the streets looking like a character from a James Clavell novel.

You might say that Alphazero Sugar's aforementioned ChickenGun is a weapon—after all, that's how the item is described at the Core Chicken and Waffles store. However, there are plenty of other objects for which the term "weapon" might better apply, because they can "kill" avatars in one of *Second Life*'s few combat zones. For example, Hiro Pendragon's samurai swords (shown in Figure 8.2) are prim-based reproductions of traditional Japanese swords. They sell for L$300 to L$600 (for a set), and give an avatar an air of dignified menace. Hiro also makes an L$875 pistol, the Colt .45.

Figure 8.4: At Cobra Weapons, **Second Life** *residents can buy all kinds of guns, grenades, flamethrowers, and the like.*

There are plenty of other weapons available in *Second Life*, and even entire weapons emporiums. Cobra Weapons sells a wide variety of handguns (L$599), machine guns (L$1,200 to L$2,000), crossbows (L$400), flamethrowers (L$800), swords (L$800), grenades (L$500), and the like. Visitors to the store frequently encounter loud gunfire as residents try out the various options on a firing range outside (Figure 8.4). It can be a disconcerting experience if you haven't spent much time in such areas, but the store is often crowded, proving that there is a sizable market for these items.

VEHICLES

CHAPTER 1
CHAPTER 2
CHAPTER 3
CHAPTER 4
CHAPTER 5
CHAPTER 6
CHAPTER 7
CHAPTER 8

CHAPTER 9
CHAPTER 10
CHAPTER 11
APPENDICES
INDEX

Figure 8.5: At Sydney Customs, you can choose from several iconic replica cars, including the DeLorean from the Back to the Future *films.*

In a virtual world where almost anything is possible, it should come as no surprise that there are all kinds of fantastical cars and other vehicles. For example, Sydney Customs offers replicas of famous cars like the General Lee from the *Dukes of Hazzard* (L$699) and the DeLorean (L$1,100) from the *Back to the Future* movies (Figure 8.5). The shop also sells the Honda SC2000 sports car (L$1,500) in many different colors, and the tricked-out ambulances (L$1,200) used in the *Ghostbusters* films.

Then there's MH Motors, purveyors of luxury cars like Bentleys (L$2,200), Hummers (L$995), Ferraris (L$1,695), Lamborghinis (L$1,695), and Rolls Royces (L$3,000).

MORE INFO

SPOTLIGHT ON FRANCIS CHUNG AND THE DOMINUS SHADOW

Perhaps the most famous vehicle of all is Francis Chung's Dominus Shadow, which sells for the odd price of L$2,368.

(Continued)

This vehicle, which is designed to look a lot like a 1965 Ford Mustang, is a beautiful manifestation of a car. It has a more refined design than many vehicles you'll see in *Second Life*, plus it has several special features and can be customized in many ways. Not only is it a shiny convertible, but it also has a viewable engine under the hood. It offers a digital speedometer, seven different kinds of high-quality rims that you change on the fly, and an undercarriage that can glow in several colors. On top of all that, you can make the Shadow dance or roll up its wheels and take off, turning into a hover car with a nice animation as it lifts off.

In 2006, Chung donated a special-edition pink Shadow to the American Cancer Society's Relay for Life fundraiser, and it sold for L$600,000 (about US$2,200).

What's the inspiration for all this? Chung is a real-life car lover who wanted to have the best-possible car in *Second Life*. "I love cars. I obsess about them," Chung wrote in *Second Life: The Official Guide* (Wiley, 2006). As a graduate student, she doesn't have the money to own one in real life, being forced to get around largely on the strength of a pair of trusty sneakers and the bus.

"This is where *Second Life* comes in," wrote Chung. "One day I just decided, if I can't have a car in my first life, I'm going to have one in my *Second Life*. I'd live vicariously through *SL* until the day I can have a set of real wheels to call my own. And if I'm going to have a car in my *Second Life*, I'll be damned if I can't have the coolest ride around."

Of course, the vehicle market has much more than cars. You can easily find spaceships for sale. Starbase C3 offers a variety of spacecraft, such as the simple Snub Fighter, which goes for L$1,000. A more complex option, the 1999 Eagle, costs L$2,000. Starbase C3 sells many other ships in the L$1,000 to L$2,200 price range. It also offers *Second Life* versions of military aircraft like the Blackbird SR-71 (L$2,200), moon rockets (L$1,000), and an X-15 Rocketplane for L$1,500.

In-world you'll also find helicopters, a wide range of military jets, hovercraft, motorcycles, a *Second Life* version of the iconic Segway gyro-stabilized scooter, and much more. As always, if you can imagine something new, it's likely you can find a market for it.

◾ MUSICAL INSTRUMENTS

These days, big-name companies or celebrities coming into *Second Life* are nothing to write home about. But in early August 2006, word that recording artist Suzanne Vega would be making an appearance caused quite a stir. Vega was to appear on the BBC's *Infinite Mind* show, which broadcasts from *Second Life*—and designer Robbie Dingo was commissioned to make her a guitar.

CHAPTER 1
CHAPTER 2
CHAPTER 3
CHAPTER 4
CHAPTER 5
CHAPTER 6
CHAPTER 7
CHAPTER 8

CHAPTER 9
CHAPTER 10
CHAPTER 11
APPENDICES
INDEX

Figure 8.6: The guitar that Robbie Dingo made for Suzanne Vega

Robbie is known in-world as the pre-eminent maker of musical instruments, and so it was no surprise that he would be the one to take on such a project. The guitar he made (Figure 8.6) is a lovely acoustic instrument, looking almost as good as it would in real life. Vega had some trouble putting on the guitar during her appearance, but eventually she succeeded. Robbie also created a video showing how he built the guitar, step by step (`http://blip.tv/file/55442/`). It's quite instructive to watch the way someone as skilled as Robbie worked with prims to create something like a guitar.

These days, Robbie is still in the vanguard of the *Second Life* musical-instruments business. At his small store, he sells things like Elven Drums (L$1,500) which can be bought individually or in a set and which contain a number of looped rhythms, "all of which are original and have been created to work in sync with one another to form endless combinations."

Robbie also sells a grand piano (L$650), a Cavatina guitar with case (L$450), bagpipes (L$350), a Fender Deluxe White Stratocaster guitar (L$375), a violin (L$400), a drum and bass set (L$1,250), and many other instruments. All come with pre-recorded sounds that let buyers play music on their own.

Of course, there are plenty of other vendors of musical instruments. Among them are The Piano Man, which sells pianos for between L$600 and L$950. Musician's Paradise offers a vast number of guitars at L$399 each, drum sets for L$199, and pianos for L$199. At AK Creations, you'll find Greek instruments such as a pan flute (Figure 8.7) and a kithara, which sell for L$350 each.

Figure 8.7: A pan flute from AK Creations, a purveyor of Greek-themed goods

NOTE

In general, instruments come with attached sound loops that allow users to play them. They also provide animations so that avatars appear to be playing the instrument.

FURNITURE

Since *Second Life* residents can have houses, towers, offices, and all kinds of other structures and dwellings, it's only natural that they need furniture to make those places more homey or functional. As you might expect, the kind of furniture available runs the gamut, from normal couches, chairs, and tables to more fantastical items like BamBam Sachertorte's flower table and chair sets (L$400; Figure 8.8), a flower lamp (L$400), and a landscape-like field of sunflowers (L$450).

Figure 8.8: BamBam Sachertorte offers flower furniture and dwellings.

Figure 8.9: Glossy Design sells this modern-style curved office desk and matching chairs.

At Homestore, Ingrid Ingersoll sells very straightforward and normal-looking couches, divans, and other pieces that range in price from L$10 to L$245. At Sabrina Doolittle's Chez Petite store—which specializes in low-prim furniture—you can buy a large bed complete with pillows for L$350, a lamp for L$150, a coffee table for L$150, a six-seat dining-room table for L$200 (with matching benches for L$150 each), a patio lounger for L$150, and much more. If more-modern pieces are your style, Glossy Design specializes in just what you need. There's a curved office desk-and-chairs set for L$499 (Figure 8.9), a lounge table with chairs for L$399, and a lounge chair for L$89.

There's also much more theme-oriented furniture available. At Elite Designs, discriminating shoppers can select from among categories like outdoor/patio, bed/bath, living room, baby furniture, Goth/Asian, kitchen/bar, and bridal/garden. In the garden section, for example, you can buy a bed of black roses for L$100 (strictly speaking, you wouldn't call this furniture in the real world, but in *Second Life*, it is), a wooden garden bridge for L$150, or a four-level bursting fountain for L$150. In the baby section—many *Second Lifers* like to play at being parents in-world—a crib goes for L$150, a Superman bunk bed for L$200, a high chair for L$75, and a baby walker for L$50. If you're looking for kitchen furniture, an L-shaped kitchen unit with a fridge, lots of counter space, a sink, and several cabinets goes for L$200 and a U-shaped bar fetches L$100. Over in the Goth/Asian section, a tub costs L$150 and a flame post runs L$50. If you really must have a Goth toilet, they can be had for L$75.

At another store, the Del Sol Open Market, a pool table runs L$400, a chandelier is L$75, a Gothic velvet bed is L$445, and a fireplace is L$100.

All of this illustrates how many different kinds of furniture you can find and what you might expect to pay. It's certainly not an exhaustive list. It also goes to show that there are plenty of similar items available, and if you want to be in the furniture business, you'll need to come up with something that's in limited supply, or a better version of something that's available everywhere.

■ HUDS

An increasingly popular *Second Life* object is the HUD, or *heads-up display*. HUDs are devices that are seen only by the wearer; they provide an easy, automatic way to control several actions or animations.

"HUDs are commonly used to provide status and information," according to the *Second Life* website (http://secondlife.com/app/help/avatar/huds.php), "for example, displaying your velocity and altitude while in a spaceship, recording your high score during a card game, racking up region stats, or even cycling through a photo album."

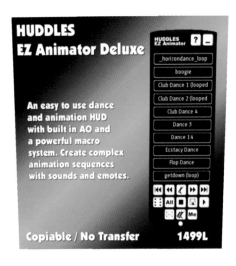

Figure 8.10: You can find the EZ Animator Deluxe HUD at Keiki Lemieux's HUDDLES.

One of the best-known HUD designers is Keiki Lemieux, who sells the devices from her HUDDLES stores. One of her most popular HUDs is the EZ Animator Deluxe (Figure 8.10), which sells for L$1,499. This device provides instant access to several animation and dance commands, allowing users to "create complex animation sequences with sounds and emotes."

Other popular HUDs give the user one-click control over facial expressions or over an inventory of landmarks.

■ ACCESSORIES

For the fashionable *Second Life* resident, there's more to spicing up an avatar than just finding fashionable clothing or sexy skins. Because *Second Life* residents can customize their avatars and add accessories, there's high demand for items that can add some panache or personality. As with many other objects in the virtual world, that means an almost limitless—and sometimes lucrative—opportunity. (You can find scripted pregnancies, umbrellas that rain on the user, scripted knitting needles, roller skates, and many more accessories.) Before you set up shop, you'll want to be clear on what it is you'd like to make and sell, and how you can differentiate your offerings from what others are hawking.

CHAPTER 1
CHAPTER 2
CHAPTER 3
CHAPTER 4
CHAPTER 5
CHAPTER 6
CHAPTER 7
CHAPTER 8

JEWELRY

For female avatars in particular, jewelry is popular way to accessorize—and there is a lot available. Head to Caroline's Jewelry to see a wide variety of pieces, including some that are among the virtual world's most realistic-looking. For example, Caroline sells necklace and earring sets for between L$300 and L$500 that look almost photo-realistic, and which come in various colors and designs.

Figure 8.11: Caroline Apollo's bangles are based on real-life jewelry.

She also sells emerald ring and bracelet sets for L$250, Celtic necklaces for L$300, diamond earrings (L$200), various rings (L$500), and much more. One of the reasons her jewelry often looks realistic is that she uses real-world items as inspiration for her *Second Life* offerings. For example, she saw a set of bangles in a magazine and decided to make a set just like them (Figure 8.11) for her *Second Life* store.

At the Purple Rose Jewelry boutique, a silver ring and bracelet set sells for L$150, and a color-changing necklace brings L$399. Purple Rose also offers "word necklaces," each of which has a stylized word—such as "sexy," "tease," or "brat"—on a chain (L$99 each). You'll also find a wide variety of bracelets and watches for under L$100.

Although there's more jewelry available in *Second Life* for women than for men, the male avatar is not left out of the accessorizing. The Head-Toe boutique features a selection of watches for L$90 each, and chokers and pendants run about L$90. At the Barcelona Marketplace, men's twisted link bracelets sell for L$225, and long gold chain necklaces fetch L$100. The store also sells men's rings in gold and silver, with diamonds and other gems, for L$125.

HANDBAGS AND PURSES

Purses and handbags are another popular way to accessorize. Caroline Apollo sells both at Caroline's Jewelry and Lo Lo Accessories. For example, she sells a purse and a satchel that are much more than attractive accessories. In fact, the two items do something quite odd and fun: they randomly drop things like kitchen sinks, bricks, paper airplanes, and more as their owner walks around the virtual world. The satchel, aimed at men, costs L$100, as does the women's purse. Caroline also sells a selection of other purses that don't drop random things, with prices from L$50 to L$75.

Figure 8.12: The Voodoo Lunchbox, from the Accessory Arsenal, comes in open and closed models for L$350.

At the Accessory Arsenal, you can buy things like lunchboxes, hiker's bags, book bags, camouflage backpacks, and more. The Voodoo Lunchbox (Figure 8.12), which costs L$350, comes in open and closed versions, and the open version has a heart and a drink bottle inside. The store also sells a birdwatcher set (L$350) that includes binoculars, a birding book, and a bird animation; an explorer's lunchbox (L$350) that comes with maps and a compass; and a Soviet book bag (L$900).

THE FINANCIAL SIDE OF THE OBJECTS BUSINESS

One of the nice things about building a business selling objects in *Second Life* is that the financial investment required to get started is small, and the potential upside is far bigger than the downside. Of course, you'll need to put some money into your new venture. However, objects are orders of magnitude less expensive than real estate business, where you might need to put in tens of thousands of US dollars to have a fighting chance of success.

HOW MUCH TO INVEST?

For the most part, your investment to get an object business going is minimal, but it's not zero. There are some things you will need to spend money on to get started.

SOFTWARE

Some say that you need to spend the most money on software—something like Photoshop so you can create textures and manipulate images. To be sure, many *Second Life*

Figure 8.13: Caroline Apollo is the owner of Caroline's Jewelry and Lo Lo Accessories.

CHAPTER 1
CHAPTER 2
CHAPTER 3
CHAPTER 4
CHAPTER 5
CHAPTER 6
CHAPTER 7
CHAPTER 8

CHAPTER 9
CHAPTER 10
CHAPTER 11
APPENDICES
INDEX

content creators use Photoshop, which costs a few hundred dollars. But Caroline Apollo (Figure 8.13) believes that you don't really have to spend money on expensive software if you don't want to. Free versions of 2D painting programs, like the GNU Image Manipulation Program (www.gimp.org/), offer many of the same features as Photoshop.

Keiki Lemieux, who is a leading creator of HUDs, agrees. "The financial investment is almost nothing," says Keiki, "which is what makes *Second Life* so great. If you already have a computer and [Internet service], that's all you need."

Wynx Whiplash suggests going to the Content Creation section of the *Second Life* forums (http://forums.secondlife.com/forumdisplay.php?f=294), which lists free software that is available (and how to use it in *Second Life*), free scripts, and free templates.

A PLACE FOR CUSTOMERS TO GO

According to Keiki, you'll need a plot of land. She says it doesn't matter whether you buy the land or rent it, but you have to have a place to set up a store. For someone starting up a business, land is a fairly cheap investment. There are no set prices for a small plot—say, 512 square meters—but you can probably buy such a parcel for less than US$20, with a monthly maintenance (tier) fee of less than US$6. Renting it would cost no more than US$10 to US$15 per month.

As your business grows, you'll probably need to expand the amount of space you have, if only to increase the number of prims you can have (see the note box).

NOTE

Linden Lab has set limits on the number of prims—the basic building blocks of Second Life—that can be used in any particular space. The total prim limit is set by the size of the land parcel in question. For details on the different sizes of land and the maximum number of prims that are allowed for each size, please see Table 3.1, "Prim Limits," in Chapter 3.

Eventually, if you are doing very well, you may want to purchase your own sim. If so, an island would cost you $1,675 (as of this writing) with $295 in monthly tier fees. Generally, though, a 512-square-meter plot should be fine for someone who is just starting out, says Keiki. "Bare Rose started as a 512 store, and that place was packed because the designs were so good," Keiki says. "She now has one of the biggest and most successful clothing stores."

Wynx Whiplash agrees that it's not necessary to start out with a lot of land. "My first shop was on a 1,024 plot, and I shared it with three other folks," Wynx says. "They also bought some land around the sim [in order to add more prims to the group's limit], but none of us was paying over $15 a month for land, even much after."

RESIDENTS SPEAK

KEIKI LEMIEUX'S ADVICE ON SELLING OBJECTS

Keiki Lemieux is leader in the Second Life *animations and HUDs business, so her advice is worth a lot. Here she shares some tips for new businesses.*

- 🔹 **Keep a focused product line. It's better to be known as the best at something than to have 20 mediocre products.**

- 🔹 **Always treat your customers well.**

- 🔹 **Make your documentation as clear, simple, and thorough as possible. Realize that there will be people buying your product who cannot open a box in** *Second Life.* **I'm not exaggerating.**

- 🔹 **Figure out how you are going to send out future updates of your product.**

- 🔹 **Always look for something that makes your product unique and better than other similar ones. Don't just try to make something that is a knock-off of other products.**

- 🔹 **Don't buy more land than you really need.**

- 🔹 **Do not ever use something that is full-permission in your design without talking to the creator first.**

- 🔹 **Don't copy someone else's design. It's one of those easy ways to get lots and lots of people to hate you.**

> 🔹 **Don't go into business with that hottie you met at the virtual strip club.** *Second Life* romances are typically short and often as emotionally upsetting as real ones. So don't go into business with your virtual spouse. When the divorce happens, it's hard to split the business.

CHAPTER 1
CHAPTER 2
CHAPTER 3
CHAPTER 4
CHAPTER 5
CHAPTER 6
CHAPTER 7
CHAPTER 8

CHAPTER 9
CHAPTER 10
CHAPTER 11
APPENDICES
INDEX

CLASSIFIEDS

Another expense, though a potentially minor one, is advertising in the Classifieds. Buying a Classified ad is one of the best ways to generate traffic for your business. Classifieds start at L$50, but the real cost is based on the keywords you want to buy. The more popular the keyword ("sex," for example, can cost more than US$500 to produce first-page search results), the more expensive the ad. Since you're going to be selling objects, you probably won't need to spend that much. More likely, your Classifieds costs will be a few US dollars.

TIME INVESTMENT

Although you won't have to put a lot of cold, hard cash into starting your business, there is one thing that you will have to invest a lot of: your time. Like any new medium, *Second Life* is tricky, and learning the ropes can be a long, arduous process. If you are already well versed in how the virtual world works, how its businesses operate, and how its residents want things, then you are probably well prepared to get started. If not, it's going to take you a while to learn those things, particularly if you want to make some real money in *Second Life*. Many businesspeople say that, at a minimum, you should expect to put in two months of learning the ropes before you'll be in a position to succeed.

For Francis Chung, the owner of Dominus Motors and the creator of the Dominus Shadow, the amount of time necessary to become successful depends on one's definition of success. "For a lot of people, success is running a business that can pay for their *Second Life*–related hobbies," Francis says. But, to make money (for example, at least US$100 a month on top of any *Second Life*–related costs), she agrees that several months is probably a good start. "I think [a] two- to six-month guideline is about right," Francis says.

Keiki Lemieux agrees. "I believe strongly that, to be successful in *Second Life*, you must be someone who uses and explores and plays in *Second Life*," she says. "That is how you figure out what people want and need. So I . . . would say to someone starting out, 'play' *Second Life* for a while, meet people, have fun exploring the building tools, and don't rush into a business. I hear stories of people coming into *Second Life* and immediately buying [whole] sims and trying to set up businesses. I think they are foolish. Even the big dogs like [real-estate baron] Anshe Chung started by being a player and learning what other players wanted."

RESIDENTS SPEAK

FRANCIS CHUNG ON BUILDING A SUCCESSFUL BUSINESS

Francis Chung's Dominus Shadow is one of the most-recognizable vehicles in Second Life. Here she shares some advice on building a successful business, as she did with cars, her first true love.

- **Find something you love.**

- **Build it better than anyone else.**

- **Don't slack and be lazy anywhere.**

- **Provide everyone with uniformly high-quality service.**

- **Get your friends involved whenever possible.**

As for how long it can take to be ready, she says, "It depends on [someone's] business and their skills. But many things just take time.... It took me six months before I started to see any real money coming in and perhaps a year before I started to see enough money that I could live off it."

HOW MUCH CAN YOU MAKE?

It is like pulling teeth to get people to talk about exactly how much money they make with their businesses. In a lot of ways, it is considered bad taste. However, people will open up about general earning power, and you can get a sense of what is possible. To begin with, it is essential to understand that Second Life is a volume business. That is, you'll have to sell a lot of product before the money starts to add up at all. This principle applies even more if you want it to become a substantial or primary source of income.

It is certainly possible to make a full-time living in Second Life, assuming you are a leader in your particular field. However, doing so requires a huge amount of time to create and maintain the business. More likely, if you create a strong business that develops loyal customers, you'll make less than a full-time income, but still be doing pretty well.

Caroline Apollo earns enough with her business to pay for an entire island (which would cost you $1,675 to start and $295 a month in maintenance fees) and still makes substantial money after that. She still has a day job, but notes, "I could make Second Life a full-time income if I wanted."

Ultimately, how much money you make depends on your skills, your talent, your commitment, your marketing savvy, and your ability to keep your customers happy. If you do well in all of these categories, you should be able to make a minimum of US$100 a month on top of your costs—and possibly much more.

CHAPTER 1
CHAPTER 2
CHAPTER 3
CHAPTER 4
CHAPTER 5
CHAPTER 6
CHAPTER 7
CHAPTER 8
CHAPTER 9
CHAPTER 10
CHAPTER 11
APPENDICES
INDEX

THE REQUIRED SKILLS

Before you can earn any real money with a *Second Life* business, you'll need to gain some proficiency in several specific skills. After all, this is a specialized economy that requires knowing how to manipulate different kinds of software, technical tools, and more, long before you're ready to go into business.

SOFTWARE

Figure 8.14: An aerial view (in Edit mode) of the tall flowers outside BamBam's flower shop shows their prim structure.

Perhaps the most important skill set a *Second Life* content creator needs is being able to use a program like Adobe Photoshop. For someone like BamBam Sachertorte, who specializes in making high-quality flowers (Figure 8.14), Photoshop or a similar program (like GIMP), is essential for manipulating textures, something almost any businessperson will have to know how to do if they want to give their products some graphical and aesthetic nuance. BamBam, whose flowers have many spirals and twisted shapes, says he also likes to use Adobe's Fireworks vector-graphics editing software because it mixes vector and bitmap elements better than Photoshop and GIMP. However, most people won't need that level of complexity.

If you want to create animations, says Francis Chung, you'll probably want to learn how to use a 3D figure-design package like Poser (www.e-frontier.com/go/poser). Francis says that for building sounds into a product, the free, open-source sound editing package Audacity (http://audacity.sourceforge.net/) is useful.

MORE INFO

TAKING ADVANTAGE OF SOFTWARE TUTORIALS

Using software like Photoshop to create textures and upload them into *Second Life* involves complex procedures that require more explanation than we can provide here. However, there are plenty of good, free tutorials available online to help you learn what you need to know. A couple of good sources are Robin Wood's tutorials (www.robinwood.com/Catalog/Technical/SL-Tuts/SLTutSet.html) and the *Second Life* wiki list of texturing tutorials (https://wiki.secondlife.com/wiki/Texture_Tools#Texture_tutorials).

SCRIPTING

It's important to know the Linden Scripting Language (LSL). This is especially true if you want your products to have any kind of interactivity, such as Keiki Lemieux's HUDs or BamBam Sachertorte's opening and closing flowers. LSL is the tool that lets *Second Life* content creators give life to their objects and make them dynamic. Although it's common to hire someone to create scripts for you (as Wynx Whiplash says she does when designing her toys and wearable pets), you can save some money by learning how to use LSL yourself. The scripting language is a programming language, though, so it can take some time to pick it up. BamBam notes that having a programming background makes it easier to pick up LSL quickly. (Learning LSL can be rewarding; if your scripts are good, you can sell them for profit.)

RESIDENTS SPEAK

BAMBAM SACHERTORTE ON RUNNING AN OBJECTS BUSINESS

BamBam Sachertorte is considered one of the leading flower designers in Second Life. *He makes everything from small plants to huge flower rooms with petals that open and close when you touch them. Here he shares his business advice.*

CHAPTER 1
CHAPTER 2
CHAPTER 3
CHAPTER 4
CHAPTER 5
CHAPTER 6
CHAPTER 7
CHAPTER 8
CHAPTER 9
CHAPTER 10
CHAPTER 11
APPENDICES
INDEX

- Make an alt (another *Second Life* account and avatar) to test your products. You need to make sure that next-owner permissions don't break your product. You also need to make sure that they aren't too lax and give your work away.

- Use vendors that track all of your sales. That way you can identify your customers and support them. A grid update [once] broke all of my Lotus Houses. I figured out a fix and sent updated Lotuses to all of my customers on record.

- Always have a customer focus. Never be dismissive or hostile to people who have bought things from you. That may seem obvious, but some people are very rude to their customers.

- Make sure that building is disabled in your store, not just auto-return. You have to disable foreign object entry and creation. Otherwise griefers will mess with your store and hurt your customers.

- Always explore *Second Life* and tinker with new ideas. You never know when inspiration will strike.

Ultimately, scripting can give your products the life they need to stand out. For example, Caroline Apollo says she uses LSL to add sparkle to some of her jewelry and to make her Faberge eggs open and close. LSL is a complex language, but it's not impenetrable. After all, there are countless content creators using it. The best resource for learning the language is the LSL portal (`http://wiki.secondlife.com/wiki/LSL _ Portal`), which offers many resources to help you learn how to use LSL.

MORE INFO

 ### SETTING PERMISSIONS FOR YOUR OBJECTS

Understanding how to use the *Second Life* permissions system is crucial to the integrity of your products. The system allows you to control whether customers can copy, modify, or transfer what they buy from you. The controls on permissions for items that you have rezzed in-world are listed under the Edit menu's General tab. If your item is in your Inventory, then you bring up the Inventory list, right-click on the item, and choose Properties.

(Continued)

> The proper permissions vary greatly depending on the item. If you want to let buyers give the items as gifts, for example, you would allow transferring. But if not, you wouldn't. According to Caroline Apollo, women like to have copy permissions on fashion or accessory items they buy because they want to be able to make copies for different outfits they wear and for which they make different and distinct Inventory folders. There are no hard and fast rules; however, if you are selling an item, you would never want to grant copy and transfer permissions because you would lose all control over distribution of the product.
>
> The *Second Life* Knowledge Base has a series of FAQs and tutorials about how to use permissions (http://secondlife.com/knowledgebase/category.php?id=58).

THE BUILD TOOL AND PRIMS

Primitives, or prims, form the basis of almost any object in *Second Life*. A prim is a modifiable base structure that can be shaped in many ways and, when combined with other prims, makes up the car, backpack, or dragon you want to create and sell. If you want to create objects, you must learn how to work with prims and the *Second Life* Build tools. In some ways, prims are difficult and a burden, because they can be hard to get to do what you want. But they're also satisfying because of the nearly limitless ways they can be shaped.

It is interesting to look at how prims make up *Second Life* objects. For example, the structure of BamBam Sachertorte's flower store shows that it can take a lot of prims to make something attractive. As BamBam puts it, exploring prims can result in discovering how to make some very interesting and useful things. "If you twist a hollow hemisphere [prim]," he says, "you get a shape that is rounded at one end and pointy at the other, perfect for a leaf or a petal."

The process of manipulating prims is known to some *Second Life* builders as "torturing" them. For example, you could rez a sphere prim, dimple it for flatness, and turn it into a box. Ultimately, you'll need to become proficient at using the *Second Life* Build tool and prims in general. Fortunately, there's help. The Building Tools help page (http://secondlife.com/app/help/building/index.php) offers helpful resources for getting started.

CHAPTER 1
CHAPTER 2
CHAPTER 3
CHAPTER 4
CHAPTER 5
CHAPTER 6
CHAPTER 7
CHAPTER 8

MARKETING YOUR OBJECTS

Once you've figured out what your business will be and what technical skills you need to have to create your products, you'll need to think about marketing. Chapter 3, "Developing a Winning Marketing Plan," offers an in-depth discussion of *Second Life* marketing, and many elements of it are the same no matter the segment of the economy. This section offers a quick overview of some of the most important concepts for marketing your objects.

WORD OF MOUTH

There are many different methods of marketing in *Second Life*, but nothing beats word of mouth. Of course, you can't control word of mouth, but if you provide bad customer service or are known to make bad products or rip-offs, you can be sure the talk about you and your business will not be good for your future prospects. Conversely, you'll be on the right path if you provide good customer service and are known in the community for creating unique and innovative products.

Doing those things can lead to very good results, says Wynx Whiplash, recalling that when he was still in *Second Life*, Starax Stotasky, the creator of the magic wand, benefited in a big way from his reputation. "Starax wasn't so much a master of marketing," says Wynx. "I don't think he ever intentionally marketed. People just knew his name and knew if they bought something from him or by him they would not be disappointed."

Some content creators can leverage their reputation so that they don't have to proactively market. "For me, it's all about word of mouth," says Francis Chung, the creator of the Dominus Shadow. "I read something about 'viral marketing' once. Someone was explaining that anything of high quality will be viral. It creates its own buzz. I like to think that's how I get around. That is to say, I like to think that my stuff is high-enough quality that marketing is not a necessary part of the equation."

FORUMS AND FREEBIES

Posting any new products you have in the *Second Life* forums (http://forums.secondlife.com/forumdisplay.php?f=117) is a good way to make sales. That's particularly true because many *Second Life* bloggers read the forums religiously, looking for new items to review. Another way to get bloggers to review your products—though it's not a guarantee that they will—is to give them free copies. Just make sure that the products work and that you're pretty sure they'll like them. "You should never hesitate to give away free product . . . if you think there is a reasonable shot at getting good publicity," says Keiki Lemieux.

Bloggers aren't the only ones to give freebies to, points out Caroline Apollo. She says anyone can help you spread the word about your products. "I give freebies to friends," says Caroline. "If I were talking to a friend and wanted her to see something new I made, I would give it to her. With people that I don't know, I am just being nice."

Classifieds

Using Classifieds is a good way to ensure that the entire *Second Life* community can find you and your store. Although they are generally inexpensive to use, if you don't use them wisely you'll be wasting your money. The way to get the most bang for your buck is to use lots of very specific keywords.

"For instance," Keiki says, "there is someone in *Second Life* who sells a Lindy Hop dance. …If she had a Classified, I would tell her to make sure that she had 'lindy hop' in the keywords, not just 'dance' and 'animation.' You want specific terms, so when someone is looking for my 'crawl' animation and they search the Classifieds for 'crawl,' they find mine."

CHAPTER 9

INTERACTIVE BUSINESS OPPORTUNITIES

Like any large community, *Second Life* offers many different kinds of interactive media and experiences. From bars and nightclubs where residents can dance and socialize, to the DJs who spin the tunes that get those people rocking, to the blogs, magazines, and newspapers that get the word out about what is going on, there are many opportunities to build a business around interacting with the community. This chapter covers what possibilities exist and the skills required to get started.

CONTENTS

● Music:
  DJs,
  Nightclubs,
  and Bars

● News:
  Newspapers,
  Magazines,
  and Blogs

● Games

MUSIC: DJs, NIGHTCLUBS, AND BARS

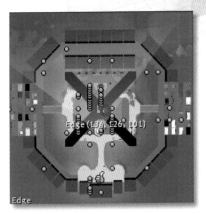

Figure 9.1: When you see large numbers of green dots on the map, you know something is going on there.

In *Second Life*, the "green dot effect" (Figure 9.1) is the phenomenon in which residents looking for things to do use the in-world map to see where people are congregating, and they go where the crowds are. Every person in the grid is represented on the map by a little green dot.

One of the most likely causes of a cluster of green dots is some form of music event. It could be a live band playing a sim launch and piping their music into *Second Life*, or it could be a hot DJ spinning tunes at a bar or a nightclub. If you teleport into the location, say a popular club on a busy night, you're almost certain to find a crowded room with a bunch of residents dancing, chatting, and generally having fun. Chances are good you'll find some good music, too. A lot of the music you'll find in-world isn't making anyone a dime. However, some DJs, bar owners, and club owners have found a way to turn a tidy profit in the *Second Life* music business.

This section looks at successful music-oriented businesses: how they got started, what skills they have, how they persevered, and their suggestions for how someone can follow in their footsteps.

■ THE HOT DJ: NEXEUS FATALE

There are a lot of popular DJs in *Second Life*, but one name that comes up repeatedly is Nexeus Fatale (Figure 9.2), who has been spotted at the launch party for *Popular Science* magazine's in-world presence, parties on the island of the Showtime show *The L Word*, and any number of gigs throughout the virtual world.

Until August 2004, Nexeus had been DJing for an online radio station in the game *Anarchy Online*. But he quickly saw that the virtual world Linden Lab had built offered him a much richer experience.

"When *Second Life* came across my radar as a place to DJ, I was really interested in its possibilities," Nexeus says. "Its interactivity with the crowd: There's no other virtual space

where you can create your own space and have a crowd respond to it. You're also a lot more personal, able to interact with people on a more intimate, one-on-one basis."

He also notes that the *Second Life* community is large enough and diverse enough that almost any kind of music can draw a healthy crowd. "*Second Life* is the only place I've seen," Nexeus says, "where *all* sorts of music do equally well. There's no one particular favorite."

Figure 9.2: Nexeus Fatale DJing a party. (Image courtesy of Nexeus Fatale)

THE FINANCIAL SIDE OF THE DJ BUSINESS

What Nexeus really likes is that there's a booming market for DJs, and one where those who are well-known and well-liked can make a pretty decent amount of money, even as it opens up avenues for new kinds of musical creativity. "Unlike most other [virtual] places, you can profit from [DJing] like one would in the real world," Nexeus says. "It can be a nice business that isn't just Internet radio" or other limited tools.

Nexeus says that DJs committed to their craft have two main sources of money that can add up over time to significant income. "The first is from owners, people who own clubs or land or event organizers who want you to DJ for them," he says. They "ask you to do a show and you tell them what your price is." The second income source comes from tips that DJs receive at events when fans leave behind a few Lindens as a way of showing their gratitude.

Nexeus cautions to be wary of club owners who don't want to pay a flat fee. "A lot of owners feel that tips are the best way for DJs to get paid, as if it is their main source of income," he says, "and it really is not." He charges a minimum of L$1,500 an hour for a gig in which he has complete freedom to do what he wants. But Nexeus also DJs more organized events, like those for Showtime's *The L Word* or the in-world modeling agency ASpiRE!, and for those, his fee ranges from US$35 to US$50 per hour.

However, Nexeus has been around *Second Life* since 2004 and is one of the best DJs around. Not everyone is going to earn what he does. "For someone starting out or not as well known, they get short-changed [on income] because of the tipping perception," he says. That's why he cautions new DJs to be aware that club owners may try to not pay them upfront.

CHAPTER 9

● Music:
  DJs,
  Nightclubs,
  and Bars

● News:
  Newspapers,
  Magazines,
  and Blogs

● Games

As DJs gain experience and visibility, their earning potential will rise dramatically. "I generally feel that L$500 per hour is a good rate for a DJ starting out," Nexeus says, a rate that includes tips. "Will [making good money] happen on day one or in month one? No," he says. "Will it happen somewhere around month six of being consistent, reinventing yourself, and really creating a personality as a DJ? Yes, it is very possible at that point."

In the end, there is plenty of room in *Second Life* for more DJs to come in and make US$100 or more per month after the startup and ongoing costs—approximately US$300 for a high-end media player and some land, and about US$40 or so a month for land and licensing fees. But, as with so many other areas of *Second Life* business, you'll need to be patient.

ROYALTIES

Once you've got your streaming server set up and have mastered your media player (see "The Required Skills"), you are going to need to decide whether to be legal or not. That's because, Nexeus says, as a DJ playing copyrighted music, you have an obligation to pay royalties on the music you play. One alternative to that is to play independent music and work directly with the artists whose songs you spin. More likely, you'll be playing commercial music owned by the artists and controlled by the record companies, and they want to get paid.

As a small, relatively unknown DJ in *Second Life*, you could probably get away with not paying royalties because you almost certainly wouldn't get caught. That's a decision you'll have to make for yourself. On the other hand, if you are popular in-world, you stand a much stronger chance of being found out if you're playing music without paying your fair share.

If you do end up choosing to pay the royalties, there are several ways to go. The easiest, especially for someone just getting started, is probably to use a service like LoudCity (http://www.loudcity.net/), which is designed to give DJs a way to pay for the music they use on Internet radio. LoudCity starts at roughly US$35 per month and the total cost depends on how much music you play, how often, whether you are making money doing it, and other considerations. Alternately, Nexeus says, you can approach the individual organizations that hold music copyrights—Broadcast Music Inc. (BMI); the American Society of Authors, Composers, and Publishers (ASCAP); SESAC (originally the Society of European Stage Authors & Composers but now an international body); and the Recording Industry Association of America (RIAA)—but that is a much more cumbersome process and likely unnecessary because services like LoudCity exist and aren't that expensive.

TIP

One source of information about royalties is a memo written by Washington, D.C. lawyer David Oxenford: http://www.dwt.com/practc/broadcast/bulletins/08-06_InternetRadio.htm.

THE BEST AND WORST TIMES TO DJ

Nexeus Fatale says that almost any kind of music will draw crowds in *Second Life*, but that the genre is not the important element in determining whether you'll be able to pack in the crowds. In fact, he says, the most important thing to think about is the time of day you're going to spin, because there are definitely periods during the week when *Second Life* is much quieter than others and, conversely, times when every popular joint is turning them away. In general, Nexeus says the busiest days of the week are Thursday, Friday, Saturday, and, inexplicably, Tuesday. "Tuesdays, I can't explain why that works," he says. Sunday and Monday are usually quiet, and Wednesdays are unpredictable.

Then, there's the time of day. He says that 4:00 PM to midnight *Second Life*/Pacific time is the sweet spot, since that encompasses the evening in both the east and west coasts of the United States. "You have to factor in that there's a bunch of east coasters, so you always have to think three hours ahead," he says. But trying to arrange a set for Sunday evening is probably not the best idea, he says, as most people are at home preparing to go back to work the next morning and probably not wanting to dance in *Second Life*.

THE REQUIRED SKILLS

To be a successful DJ, you clearly need to have a good taste in music, a well-developed collection of songs, and a sense of how to fit it all together in a nice, tight package. This is not the space to address how to develop those skills and assets. There are plenty of books on how to be a DJ. But DJing in *Second Life* is a different kind of work. First, explains Nexeus, you don't need any expensive DJ equipment. Instead, you need software, and you need to master using it if you want to be recognized as a good DJ.

Nexeus advises that you sign up for an audio-streaming server, such as SHOUTcast (http://shoutcast.com/) or Icecast (http://icecast.org/). These services permit DJs to broadcast audio into *Second Life* and to do so with either live or archived audio. The prices for such services start at around US$25 a month, Nexeus says, with prices rising with usage. He says he spends around US$55 a month. Then, you'd need to choose a media player, the software that lets you control the music you're playing and the mixing of songs across channels. This is, essentially, your digital turntable. A very popular media player is Winamp (www.winamp.com), which is free to use and full of features. Some people, Nexeus says, use SAM Broadcaster (www.spacialaudio.com/products/sambroadcaster/), which is a professional-grade media player that runs US$279.

CHAPTER 9

Music:
DJs,
Nightclubs,
and Bars

News:
Newspapers,
Magazines,
and Blogs

Games

"There is a slight learning curve with Winamp, [but] it's pretty straightforward," says Nexeus. "But with SAM Broadcaster, the learning curve is very steep. It's called the 'Professional broadcasting software,' but you can do most of what you can do in SAM with Winamp. It would take someone just under a month to really be comfortable with SAM Broadcaster, and the same person just under a week to be comfortable with Winamp. If I had to choose between the two, Winamp is the way to go."

Ultimately, Nexeus adds, you should get an iPod on which to store your music and from which to play it. That'll end up being much simpler and easier to organize with than playing CDs.

Setting Up Shop

Figure 9.3: While Nexeus Fatale works many events for other people, he also has his own lounge.

Although many DJs rely on getting hired to do gigs for others, there's also some wisdom in getting yourself a small club so that you can play whenever you want. Nexeus says that you should consider starting out with a 1,024-square-meter space, either rented or bought, because that will allow you some freedom in how you set up the land. A plot of land that size should cost around US$25 to buy and around US$6 a month in fees, while renting will run you somewhere under US$15. You can buy a prefab club or, if you have some building and scripting skills, create it yourself. Nexeus himself runs a lounge called The High (Figure 9.3).

Either way, once you get it started, you'll want to keep an eye on how many people come to dance. More is good, of course, up to a point. Once you hit around 40 people, you'll start to see heavy lag and server load. So, be popular, but not too popular. In any case, Nexeus adds, just because you have your own space and are packing them in, don't let that keep you from talking to lots of other club owners and making contacts because it's those gigs that will likely end up adding up to substantial money.

RESIDENTS SPEAK

NEXEUS FATALE'S TIPS FOR ASPIRING DJS

As one of the leading DJs in Second Life, *Nexeus has a lot of wisdom to share with newcomers. Here, he shares his best ideas of what to do and not to do when trying to make it as a DJ.*

- **Understand what your musical voice is: What music are you comfortable playing? What is your favorite genre? Stick to that sphere. Be comfortable with your music.**

- **Interact with the crowd at your events. Every DJ should make their listeners feel as if they are paying attention and interacting with them. This means talking in between every song or two, not talking over songs. Have a joke or a story ready, and make the crowd know that you are there with them, not just playing music.**

- **Get to know people in** Second Life. **As a DJ, you are a social person. Everyone knows someone else, someone owns a club, and everyone is looking for a DJ.**

- **Be professional and consistent. Make sure that you are always doing a gig on the same night at the same time. And please stay away from singing or talking to the pizza man while the microphone is on. No one needs to hear that. I'm not saying don't be wild and spontaneous. Just know what the line is.**

- **Have a system down. Figure out how you are going to do this equipment-wise (Am I using a microphone or a headset?), software-wise (Winamp or SAM?), server-wise (SHOUTcast or Oddcast), royalty-wise (Am I paying the RIAA or am I just playing independent music?). Whatever your system is, stick to it. It works best for you, and you will be very comfortable DJing.**

- **Take the previous five suggestions, and develop a package, so when they know you're DJing, people can expect what they are going to get.**

- **Unless you're really torturing your fans, I would stay away from playing certain songs or artists such as Aqua, *NSync, "The Electric Slide," "La Macarena." In most cases, bad music *is* bad music.**

(Continued)

> 💬 Don't think that you can DJ immediately and that you're the best DJ known to man on day one.
>
> 💬 Don't make the mistake of not prepping. Take an hour before your gig and get your music together. Know what you are going to do.
>
> 💬 Take your DJing seriously. If you don't have the passion or attentiveness for it, have fun with it, but don't try to make money. I've seen several people ruin their reputations that way.

SETTING YOURSELF APART

Beyond pure longevity, there are other things that set the highly paid *Second Life* DJs apart from those who don't make as much. Nexeus jokes that he could write a thesis on the differences that separate the good DJs from others. But he does say that there are two main factors that differentiate the good and the not-so-good: how well you interact with the crowd and how well you put your music together.

"You can't just put music together and mix it or make a playlist," says Nexeus. "You have to talk, interact, have fun with [the crowd], make them feel as if you are paying attention to what is going on in the event area." That means, he says, following the conversation that's going on, which isn't too hard, given that it's usually in text chat.

"Say there's a conversation going on about a certain dress or a particular topic," he explains. "I like to chime in with my own thoughts in between songs. Keeping that sort of interaction throughout an event is critical, almost more important than the music you're playing."

MARKETING YOUR DJ BUSINESS

Now that you've figured out what skills you need, when to play, how to pay royalties, and how much you'll need to invest to make a decent amount of money DJing in *Second Life*, you need to know how to get your name out there. To Nexeus, the first step is clear. "The best way to market yourself is by doing a few free gigs for people that you know or meet who have a club," he says. "Word of mouth works amazingly well in *Second Life*. A friend tells a friend who tells this club owner who tells this clothing designer." The next thing you know, people are showing up to your gigs because they've heard of you.

Nexeus says that once you start playing gigs in *Second Life*, you need to be consistent, because that's the only way for people to learn about you and know where and when to go to find you. "If you're going to do a gig at a club, don't just do one night," he says.

"Do the same night for a month. Or two months, so that people can expect to see you and will always know that you're around or always doing a gig."

THE HOT NIGHTCLUB OWNER: JENNA FAIRPLAY

CHAPTER 1
CHAPTER 2
CHAPTER 3
CHAPTER 4
CHAPTER 5
CHAPTER 6
CHAPTER 7
CHAPTER 8
CHAPTER 9

CHAPTER 10
CHAPTER 11
APPENDICES
INDEX

Figure 9.4: Jenna Fairplay (above) and her club (below), The Edge.

Every DJ needs an audience. For that, they turn mainly to nightclubs, where a potent mix of music, dancers, and social activity blend to bring together regular groups of *Second Life* residents. That's especially true at The Edge, one of the virtual world's oldest and most popular clubs. The Edge's success is due largely to the direction set by its founder and owner, Jenna Fairplay (Figure 9.4).

Jenna started The Edge in 2003 as her in-world home. Back then Linden Lab paid residents to host events, so she began doing so at her home as a way to raise some Linden dollars. "It grew as others wanted to host at my house and it grew and grew," she says, adding that she decided to transition her home into a full-fledged club "for the recognition of owning a club."

Unfortunately, Linden Lab eventually cut off the gravy train and stopped providing club owners with stipends for hosting events. And that, Jenna says, meant that entrepreneurs like her had to find new ways of funding their clubs.

CHAPTER 9

MUSIC:
DJs,
NIGHTCLUBS,
AND BARS

NEWS:
NEWSPAPERS,
MAGAZINES,
AND BLOGS

GAMES

THE FINANCIAL SIDE OF THE NIGHTCLUB BUSINESS

The truth is, Jenna says, that nightclubs in and of themselves are not a hugely profitable enterprise. In fact, it's likely that the DJs and dancers who get paid to perform at places like The Edge may well make more money than the club owners do. It's not that the clubs don't bring in very much. But to maintain a serious club, it's necessary to maintain a steady staff of managers, security, and other employees, as well as the DJs and dancers, with whom the clubs have to split tips and donations. Given that, some may wonder why clubs are included in a book about making money in *Second Life*.

The reality, explains Jenna, is that while the club itself may not be a huge profit center, it is a traffic draw that can lead to a great deal of successful business for nearby merchants. "Everybody thinks all I do is run a club," says Jenna, "but it's actually the other things I do that fund my club. A club does generate revenue, but it's a very tricky balancing game."

THE INVESTMENTS

Jenna says that the first thing an aspiring club owner needs to do is rent a plot of land. She encourages people to rent rather than buy because there's no prohibitive upfront cost and because you are not locked in. If you don't like the space, you can always move on.

She says that because of the substantial prim requirements and server pull of a nightclub, a new owner would really be doing themselves a disservice if they started with less than 16,384 square meters, or 1/4 of a sim. However, some people say starting with 4,096 square meters, or 1/16 of a sim, is enough.

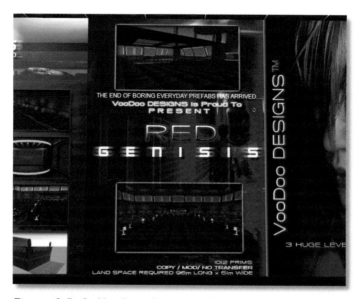

Figure 9.5: At VooDoo Designs, club owners can buy prefab nightclubs in many shapes and sizes.

To rent a 1/4-sim-sized parcel would likely cost you as much as US$120 per month, but if you bought the land, tier fees would only run around US$75 a month. If you're going to rent, Jenna says it's best to rent on an island because Class 4 and Class 5 island servers can hold more people than those on the mainland. (Class 5 is the highest class of three; the higher the class, the more powerful the server.)

Next, you'll need your club. One of the leaders in prefab nightclubs, VooDoo Designs (Figure 9.5), sells various configurations starting at L$5,000. If you decide to buy a custom club, you could end up paying more than L$50,000, Jenna points out. Although that's not even US$200, it might be more than you want or need to spend, especially given that there are plenty of prefab choices available.

Next, you have to stock up on the interior of your club. Jenna cautions buyers to do some comparison-shopping before plopping down their hard-earned Lindens. That's because, she says, there's often big-time buyer's remorse when someone goes into a shop and gets all the things for their club in that one place, and then later finds better or cheaper items at other stores.

"So make a list [of what you need] and look around," she says. "SL Exchange and [OnRez] are great ways to comparison-shop. [Club owners buy a] lot of stuff because they saw it in another club and saw people having fun." In fact, she says, that is a common effect at The Edge. People "assume if it is in The Edge and I have it, their club will rock," Jenna says.

MORE INFO

HOW TO STOCK YOUR NEW CLUB

Jenna says any new club owner will have to purchase the following things:

- A staff pay system, which can consist of a scripted payroll box
- Dance pads and camp pads
- Animation balls
- Raffle balls
- Décor, such as plants
- A dance machine
- A dance floor
- DJ equipment
- A scripted tip jar

CHAPTER 1
CHAPTER 2
CHAPTER 3
CHAPTER 4
CHAPTER 5
CHAPTER 6
CHAPTER 7
CHAPTER 8
CHAPTER 9

CHAPTER 10
CHAPTER 11
APPENDICES
INDEX

CHAPTER 9

MUSIC:
DJs,
NIGHTCLUBS,
AND BARS

NEWS:
NEWSPAPERS,
MAGAZINES,
AND BLOGS

GAMES

HIRING EMPLOYEES

Figure 9.6: At nightclubs like The Edge, hired dancers are always on hand to get the crowd worked up.

Figure 9.7: Scripted tip jars allow club patrons to give dancers, DJs, and event managers a little money for their efforts.

As a club owner, you'll need to hire a few people to work there. Over time, says Jenna, you'll need a more developed staff of managers and security personnel. In the short term, you will need to bring in some dancers (Figure 9.6) and some DJs.

"The best way to not lose money on dancers," says Jenna, "is to pay them L$30 per hour. Dancers are somewhat glorified campers, but they get paid more because it's their job to greet and interact with guests."

Next, you need DJs. As Nexeus Fatale said, pay varies widely depending on the DJ's experience. Expect to pay a new DJ around L$500 per hour. Jenna says she pays her DJs L$150 an hour, though that is for everyday music at The Edge, and not for special events, for which DJs can sometimes ask for more.

Either way, both dancers and DJs will get tips (Figure 9.7)—which is why you need to get a scripted tip jar. In many cases, club owners take a cut of that, often between 15 percent and 20 percent.

Finally, clubs need managers to host events. According to Deede Debs, the payroll manager for The Edge, managers there get paid between L$100 and L$300 per event they host. All told, Jenna says, The Edge hosts around 12 events every day, so that amount can add up quickly.

CHAPTER 1
CHAPTER 2
CHAPTER 3
CHAPTER 4
CHAPTER 5
CHAPTER 6
CHAPTER 7
CHAPTER 8
CHAPTER 9

CHAPTER 10
CHAPTER 11
APPENDICES
INDEX

REVENUE PRODUCERS

Figure 9.8: Nightclubs like The Edge bring in revenue by renting out vendor stalls to other Second Life merchants.

Figure 9.9: Another way nightclubs bring in revenue is with large billboards that rent for thousands of Lindens a week.

For club owners, says Jenna, there are many ways to bring in revenue. The first is vendor stalls (Figure 9.8), which a club can rent out to other Second Life merchants who hope to sell their goods in a popular venue. She recommends that any new club owner set aside half its prim limit for vendor stalls because they can produce a significant amount of revenue.

She says that on a 1/4-sim parcel, an owner could expect to rent out 30 or 40 stalls for between L$300 and L$600 per month per stall. That, she says, could cover the monthly tier fee on the land and even provide a bit of a cushion.

Another lucrative endeavor is selling advertising on billboards in the club and included in the DJ sets. The Edge, for example, has two giant billboards (Figure 9.9) and sells space on them for L$2,500 per week.

For L$4,000 a week, The Edge DJs will insert commercials between songs they play during events. Being able to sell such ads is important, given the cost of DJs, says Jenna. "You can't really recoup the cost of DJs [directly]," she says, "One way I manage to do it . . . is through commercials."

Planning

Because running a successful club is so dependent on the dancers, DJs, and managers who work there, Jenna says it's crucial to hire good people. "They need to be professional and leave their drama at the door," says Jenna.

She explains that she and her team try to interview managers using voice applications like TeamSpeak (www.goteamspeak.com) so that they can have a real conversation, unlike what is possible using *Second Life*'s text chat feature. Usually that's possible. But sometimes it's not, for example if the potential manager is playing a female in *Second Life* but actually is male, or vice versa. In such cases, the people involved often don't want to do voice interviews.

Either way, it's important to interview would-be managers carefully and make sure they're committed to the task and not just looking to take advantage of the popularity of the club. For example, managers must know how to take care of winners of contests—which The Edge has regularly—and also the losers. "When someone wins an event, you think it's all done," Jenna says. "No, the loser has something to say, and it's the manager who needs to work that situation out."

According to Deede, managers need to be able to explain things to visitors quickly and have it make sense. When it comes to DJs, though, she says you have to interview them with voice, rather than text. "If you don't, you're asking for problems," she says. "I've had DJs with heavy accents, bad microphones, etc. You need DJs with a good voice." Potential DJs should have large collections of music and a good personality. "Nobody wants to hear someone say, "And this is this [song] and that is that [song]," Deede says.

The Required Skills

Running a nightclub doesn't require the kinds of technical know-how—like mastery of Photoshop and Linden Scripting Language—that other *Second Life* industries do, but that doesn't mean no skills at all are needed. Jenna says you need to be a leader and have stellar people skills. Further, you need to have lots of free time to devote to the club and be good at time management. Although you probably won't be called on to do any serious building yourself—either one of your partners or someone you hire would likely do those kinds of things—it wouldn't hurt to know a little Photoshop or have a little experience with *Second Life*'s building tools.

For a club owner, marketing and building a name require some work. First, you're going to need to count on word of mouth. To get that, you must build a club that is fun for people, that has good DJs spinning good music, and that is the kind of place people will tell others about when they leave. You'll also want to buy a Classified ad, though Jenna cautions that getting a Classified ad that appears high up in search results can cost a lot because results are based on how much the advertisers are willing to pay.

Similarly, she suggests buying ad space in *Second Life* publications like the *Metaverse Messenger* or *Shout* magazine, and placing ads on SL Exchange and OnRez. At the same time, explains Jenna, you'll need to maximize your traffic, which means putting in traffic boosters.

Traffic boosters are things that draw traffic to your club, which in turn, drives more traffic. That second-level benefit is because of the aforementioned "green dot" effect, in which *Second Life* residents peruse the in-world map looking for where people are gathered. On the map, residents are indicated by little green dots.

Figure 9.10: A raffleball allows players to buy into a small raffle for the chance to win free Linden dollars or other prizes.

For example, Jenna and her team have installed several traffic boosters. Among them are raffle balls (Figure 9.10) and prize balls, objects that have been scripted to run a raffle or give a prize. These objects regularly reward residents with small sums of free Lindens or some small item. Raffleballs, for example, are good because people pay a small amount to play—a few Lindens—and can only win 50 Lindens or so. But the prospect of winning draws traffic.

Other things that can bring in people are money trees—which give out very small numbers of Lindens to new *Second Life* residents. She says she invests L$500 a week in money trees. And, although some people think camping chairs (Figure 9.11), which encourage residents to sit in them and earn small amounts of Lindens as they sit, are a bad thing to add to a venue because those using them act like "zombies," Jenna says they bring in traffic because of the green dots they generate.

MUSIC:
DJs,
NIGHTCLUBS,
AND BARS

NEWS:
NEWSPAPERS,
MAGAZINES,
AND BLOGS

GAMES

Figure 9.11: Although many people think camping chairs are a waste of time, some nightclubs use them to boost traffic.

Then there are events. According to Jenna, The Edge hosts around 12 events a day and, in each case, the club pays the event manager between L$100 and L$300 to host it. But the club also pays out a significant number of Lindens as prizes during the events. Jenna budgets L$11,000 a day for event prizes and manager pay. Ultimately, though, she says the payback is that significant numbers of people visit the club for the events, and they in turn bring in revenue.

Once the people show up, she says, your staffing choices will determine whether they'll stick around: Are your managers smart? Are your DJs good? Do you have outgoing dancers and fun hosts? "All of those are just to bring in the people," says Jenna. "If the staff and location are good and fun, you get your loyal guests who come a lot, who bring in their real-life friends to party at your club."

RESIDENTS SPEAK

JENNA FAIRPLAY ON CREATING A SUCCESSFUL VENUE

With more than three years as owner of one of the hottest nightclubs in Second Life, Jenna knows as much as anyone about what it takes to create a successful venue. Here, she shares her advice on some of the most important things to do when trying to start a new nightclub.

- **Make sure you plan well in the beginning so that you can recoup some of the cost of tier payments with vendor stalls.**

- **Make sure that for each expense you add, you try to find a means of offsetting it. For example, you might offset dancers' hourly pay with a percentage of their tips.**

- **Make sure you don't throw in too many traffic boosters, like camp chairs and raffleballs, and drain your supply of Linden dollars.**

> ● Make sure you have a loyal staff. Having volunteers doesn't hurt either.
>
> ● Utilize the marketing power of a good club by putting up ads and billboards to generate revenue.

CHAPTER 1
CHAPTER 2
CHAPTER 3
CHAPTER 4
CHAPTER 5
CHAPTER 6
CHAPTER 7
CHAPTER 8
CHAPTER 9

CHAPTER 10
CHAPTER 11
APPENDICES
INDEX

■ THE FAMOUS BAR OWNER: HAM RAMBLER

In many ways, running a bar in *Second Life* is much like running a nightclub, and the economics are similar, too. In some cases, however, a bar can be an opportunity to bring a little bit of real-world feel into *Second Life*.

Figure 9.12: The Blarney Stone, in the Dublin sim, is one of the most popular bars in **Second Life.**

Ham Rambler runs The Blarney Stone (Figure 9.12), which he designed as an authentic Irish pub in the center of the Dublin sim. Among the offerings there is piped-in live music being played by bands at a club in London, England. He says he'll occasionally host a simulcast of the band's performance if its members have *Second Life* avatars.

As a business, The Blarney Stone is Ham's marketing calling card to real-life Irish businesses, as well as to anyone who wants to set up shop in the Dublin sim. For residents, the lure is a spot in *SL* that evokes the joyous experience of being in a real Irish bar.

"First of all, it has to be a 'safe' place," says Ham, "where everyone can feel comfortable. So I banned pole dances, escorts, all that stuff. Secondly, everyone arriving should be made to feel welcome, whether they are a *Second Life* veteran or a newbie. Thirdly, it has to be entertaining, either through music or just good company. This should be the same experience in every Irish bar in the world."

CHAPTER 9

Music:
DJs,
Nightclubs,
and Bars

News:
Newspapers,
Magazines,
and Blogs

Games

TIP

To Trinity Cole, the longtime owner of the Witch's Brew, one key to growing a reputation as a place Second Life residents want to go is to focus on creating an energetic and welcoming atmosphere. That means presenting patrons with a personal welcome, someone to show them how to utilize the bar's dance features, and someone to explain about what an event is if there is one. In other words, Trinity says, the key is "taking time to treat your guests like friends."

That's Ham's business model for The Blarney Store. Similar to The Edge, the bar itself is a lure—a way to draw in people who then shop nearby or who themselves want to build a business that feeds off the bar's traffic. Ham knows that the bar itself may not bring in a large amount of revenue, but it's also a calling card that could bring in real-world business. "I can get drink manufacturers to use my bar for advertising purposes and charge them real-life fees," Ham says. "Building a city gave me a lot of options. For example, it was appropriate for me to include the Guinness Brewery in the build of Dublin, which I did. I then let Guinness know it was there. Their Digital Marketing team came and looked at Dublin and realized it was an 'appropriate' and 'contextual' way to use the growth of *Second Life* for brand marketing purposes. The Blarney Stone was the focal point, around which I built 'context,' and the surroundings made approaches to Irish and Dublin companies easier. The bar is in fact a replica of a real Dublin bar called Gogarty's. So I have now sent out a feeler to Gogarty's to see if they want me to rename the bar and have them use it for marketing purposes. I'd have to build another Blarney Stone, but that won't be an issue."

MORE INFO

 ### SPOTLIGHT ON HAM RAMBLER, OWNER OF THE BLARNEY STONE

In the center of the Dublin sim in Second Life, which is built to resemble the Irish city, sits an "authentic" Irish pub called The Blarney Stone. The bar is run by Ham Rambler, who built the sim and who set out to create an Irish experience, one that appeals to people interested in that country's culture and one that appeals to that country's businesses as well.

Already, he's gotten a public relations firm from the real Dublin to open a presence in the sim, and now he's reaching out to brewers and to real bar owners, hoping for sponsorship tie-ins. Ham sat down for an interview about The Blarney Stone and about how to run a bar in Second Life.

CHAPTER 1
CHAPTER 2
CHAPTER 3
CHAPTER 4
CHAPTER 5
CHAPTER 6
CHAPTER 7
CHAPTER 8
CHAPTER 9

CHAPTER 10
CHAPTER 11
APPENDICES
INDEX

Q: What is the history of The Blarney Stone?

HR: I first arrived in *Second Life* having read a story on BBC News about a woman hiring a private detective to check if her husband was having an affair there. It was an intriguing story. So I came in, and like everyone else, struggled to make any sense of it. I quickly realized that it lacked a good place to hang out, meet people, and listen to good music. Basically, an Irish bar. So I bought some land and opened the bar. Being Irish, and traveling a lot, I knew what a good Irish bar needed. So I replicated it as much as I could in *Second Life*.

Q: How do you make people feel welcome?

HR: I try to have a member of staff there to greet them by name and, if not, to just make the place welcoming.

Q: What else do you do to make it a welcoming, energetic experience?

HR: We set up some rules regarding behavior that everyone is given in the welcome pack. And believe it or not, we try to keep a level of appropriate realism. For example, you'll be asked to put a shirt on, if you walk into the bar without one. It's this level of "realism" that people feel comfortable with.

Q: How many people do you have working with you?

HR: Thirty. We have bar people, hosts, event managers, and team leaders.

Q: Are all these people paid?

HR: The bar people work for tips. But most bar people move up to hosting. My payroll bill is about US$150 a week. That includes paying the live musicians.

Q: For 30 people? That's not much.

HR: Well, a host gets L$500 for hosting a two-hour event, plus tips.

(Continued)

CHAPTER 9

● Music:
  DJs,
  Nightclubs,
  and Bars

● News:
  Newspapers,
  Magazines,
  and Blogs

● Games

> **Q:** Does the bar bring in much money? And, if so, how?
>
> **HR:** No, the bar doesn't bring any revenue. I have revenue from rentals. But my business drive has been to involve real life Irish or Dublin businesses. My medium-term objective was to have a "realistic" city build and high traffic. That makes the marketing to real-life businesses easier. So, I have made a long-term investment.

NEWS: NEWSPAPERS, MAGAZINES, AND BLOGS

Although much of the world gets its *Second Life* news only from mainstream publications, that reporting is often high-level material that focuses on business developments surrounding Linden Lab, the latest Fortune 500 company to set up a presence in-world, or issues related to its economy. But for news of the daily happenings in *Second Life*, residents are turning to a growing number of newspapers, magazines, and blogs that cover the virtual world with the precision of a local paper, and often a very professional editorial and design sensibility. For the residents, this is a welcome thing because it means they can have a much clearer sense of what is going on from day to day without having to go everywhere or talk to everyone. From the publishers' perspective, it's a good thing because it offers a blossoming business opportunity.

■ THE FAMOUS NEWSPAPER PUBLISHER: KATT KONGO

Figure 9.13: The AvaStar covers Second Life *inside and out.*

With the tremendous growth in the *Second Life* population has come plenty of resident-run news publications. Among them are the *AvaStar* (www.the-avastar.com), which you can pick up in several different locations throughout the virtual world (Figure 9.13). But the veteran of the *Second Life* newspaper business—and it's important to distinguish here between newspapers

CHAPTER 1
CHAPTER 2
CHAPTER 3
CHAPTER 4
CHAPTER 5
CHAPTER 6
CHAPTER 7
CHAPTER 8
CHAPTER 9

CHAPTER 10
CHAPTER 11
APPENDICES
INDEX

and blogs or magazines—is *The Metaverse Messenger* (www.metaversemessenger.com; Figure 9.14). Run by Katt Kongo, the *Metaverse Messenger*—also known as *M2*—publishes weekly in a Web-based PDF format.

Katt, who began in *Second Life* as an inveterate shopper, finally realized that she wanted to stop helping other people make money and decided to start her own business. But she had a problem at first: She didn't know what to do. "I can't script, create clothing, or build, so I was really scratching my head," says Katt. "I stopped thinking so much about what I couldn't do in *Second Life*, and thought of what I really enjoyed doing and what I was good at doing. The answer to both was a newspaper."

Figure 9.14: Katt Kongo (above) runs Metaverse Messenger (below), a weekly newspaper that covers Second Life.

Although a lot of people were already blogging about *Second Life*, and some people were putting out small "newspapers" on notecards, Katt felt that there wasn't anything available with much substance. So, she and a team of three others pooled their small *Second Life* resources; got a hold of copies of Quark, Acrobat Distiller, and Adobe Acrobat Professional; set to work; and before long had their first issue.

THE FINANCIAL SIDE OF THE NEWSPAPER BUSINESS

As with many *Second Life* businesses, *Metaverse Messenger* cost very little to get off the ground. Katt says that the paper started with a 512-square-meter land parcel, which she then sold for triple her cost, using the proceeds for the plot of land M2's headquarters are on now. She says she spent US$9 to register the paper's domain name and a small amount on hosting fees. She pays the paper's writers between L$250 and L$1,000 per article, though she says she is planning to begin paying experienced writers US$25 per article soon.

Music:
DJs,
Nightclubs,
and Bars

News:
Newspapers,
Magazines,
and Blogs

Games

SUBSTANTIAL AD RATES

Metaverse Messenger makes all its money from advertisements it sells. The paper accepts all ads that it can sell and then builds its editorial around that. That's important, because it lets Katt and her partners decide how much money they have to work with each issue and, therefore, how many stories they can afford to pay for. Because *M2* has a large number of readers—in May 2007, the paper was downloaded 81,285 times, according to its website—it can charge fairly high ad rates. *Second Life* businesses pay L$60 per column inch, while real-life companies with no *Second Life* presence pay US$5 per column inch, and those who do have an in-world presence pay US$3 per inch.

Katt and her team have to do very little advertiser outreach—at least in *Second Life*. Instead, most advertisers come to them. However, the paper is launching a new initiative aimed at getting real-world companies to advertise.

Given those ad rates and the number of copies *Second Life* residents read, it should come as little surprise that Katt says she now earns her full-time living with *Metaverse Messenger*. It didn't happen overnight, though, she says. It took her a year and a half of building the paper up from nothing before the income was enough to quit her previous job and focus entirely on *M2*.

THE REQUIRED SKILLS

There's no shortage of *Second Life* news publications, but those that stand out, like *Metaverse Messenger*, are staffed by people with solid skills. Those skills include high-quality writing and editing, a good design sense, excellent people skills, and being able to sell both the product and yourself. Also, Katt says that someone who wants to run a successful newspaper needs to have someone on staff who knows how to use pagination software.

Getting *Second Life* residents to open up about what's going on around them is also a crucial skill, but one that simply takes being curious. "I think people in *SL* are very excited about what they do here," says Katt. "Whereas in real life, a lot of stuff is done to pay the bills, here it's done for the enjoyment of doing that. So if a reporter appears genuinely interested, that's usually all it takes."

MARKETING YOUR NEWSPAPER

Despite *M2*'s substantial readership and the breadth of its coverage, Katt says she's sure there's room for more newspapers. "*Second Life* is huge and growing so fast that no one publication can possibly cover every single thing," she says. "And most people who read one *Second Life* publication will read others."

For those who want to get their paper off the ground, it won't be easy. Katt says any new publication will be competing with many of other publications, and so it's hard to get noticed. The way to stand out, she explains, is to be as visible and as active in the community as possible. To get where she is today, Katt did a lot of virtual pounding the pavement. She says that in the early days of *Metaverse Messenger*, she did most of its marketing on her own: "I went everywhere, and I told anyone who would listen about *M2*. I was always digging for interesting things to put into the paper, and so I met a lot of people who would then tell [others] about *M2*. Now, it's similar, but on a broader scale. All *M2* staff members are encouraged to be active in the *Second Life* community."

She says she also relies on some of the more traditional *Second Life* marketing methods: She advertises in high-traffic sims, maintains *M2* offices in several locations, and sponsors events. And, you can find *Metaverse Messenger* newspaper boxes—which residents click on to download the paper on PDF—in many locations throughout the virtual world.

RESIDENTS SPEAK

 ### KATT KONGO ON SUCCEEDING WITH A NEW PUBLICATION

Metaverse Messenger's Katt Kongo is one of the leading editorial voices in Second Life. *Here, she shares some advice on how to succeed with a new publication.*

- Learn *Second Life*.

- Find your niche.

- Be ethical, always.

- Think outside the box and the old journalism traditions and create your own rules.

- Network your butt off.

- Don't make the mistake of not thinking through a business plan. Someone who wants to start a new newspaper needs to have a clear idea of where revenue will come from.

- Don't just publish one viewpoint on issues

- Try to proofread carefully. You lose credibility when words are spelled wrong, etc.

- If you continually attack Linden Lab, it's really hard to get responses from them when you need one. At the same time, you can't be buddy-buddy with them. So just be aware of the relationship you are building with them.

CHAPTER 1
CHAPTER 2
CHAPTER 3
CHAPTER 4
CHAPTER 5
CHAPTER 6
CHAPTER 7
CHAPTER 8
CHAPTER 9

CHAPTER 10
CHAPTER 11
APPENDICES
INDEX

MUSIC:
DJS,
NIGHTCLUBS,
AND BARS

NEWS:
NEWSPAPERS,
MAGAZINES,
AND BLOGS

GAMES

A HIT IN FASHION MEDIA: CELEBRITY TROLLOP

Figure 9.15: Celebrity Trollop (above) is the managing editor of Second Style magazine (below).

For the most part, writing a *Second Life* blog or magazine is a way to gain recognition in the community, but not to make much money. There are a few people and organizations who earn substantial amounts of money blogging about *Second Life* and virtual worlds. Examples include 3pointD (http://3pointd.com/), *Second Life Herald* (www.secondlifeherald.com/) editor Mark Wallace, *New World Notes* (http://nwn.blogs.com/), and GigaOM (http://gigaom.com/) blogger Wagner James Au. However, Au and Wallace are both professional journalists who have been around for years, and both are blogging on multiple sites and writing books.

That doesn't mean that you can't earn something being a blogger or running a magazine in *Second Life*, especially if you write about a popular subject like fashion or, frankly, sex. That's why Celebrity Trollop (Figure 9.15) is a good person to

talk to about building a successful *Second Life* blog or magazine—because she has done both. As managing editor of *Second Style* magazine (www.secondstyle.com) and lead blogger on the magazine's blog, Fashionista, Celebrity has the experience to know what it takes.

CHAPTER 1
CHAPTER 2
CHAPTER 3
CHAPTER 4
CHAPTER 5
CHAPTER 6
CHAPTER 7
CHAPTER 8
CHAPTER 9

CHAPTER 10
CHAPTER 11
APPENDICES
INDEX

What Makes a Good Blog?

Celebrity looks for two elements in a good blog, one that she wants to read. And she should know. In addition to running one of the most popular fashion blogs, she also reads many others covering fashion and other issues. First, she says, a good blogger is someone who writes well and writes cleanly. Spelling and grammar count for lot. Someone once said that poor spelling or grammar feels to a reader like a sound boom sticking out of the top of the screen feels to a moviegoer. So, make sure your prose is polished. Next, be sure you have a point of view on issues and something to say about them. Even if readers disagree with you, they'll still come to see what you've written because it will interest them.

Once you've got their attention, you need to keep it, and that means posting at least a couple of times a week. Beyond that, you need to show a great deal more awareness of what's going on in *SL* than a reporter who just shows up to write one story.

"Bloggers who write about *Second Life* tend to spend a fair amount of time in-world, and so I think they have a deeper connection to the various cultures," says Celebrity. "Mainstream media types parachute in for a story and typically never come back."

Of course, publications like *Metaverse Messenger* have some similarities to the dedicated *Second Life* blogs. But Celebrity notes the differences between a blog and a newspaper, as well. The difference boils down to editorial bent: *M2* focuses on providing a balanced and objective view of issues, while a blog like Fashionista is the opposite.

"Bloggers really don't need to play it straight," Celebrity says. "Blogging inherently has a point of view. No one typically wants to read a 'he said, she said' kind of story on a blog unless it's a recap to [explain] some post you're about to make.... Bloggers are opinionated. Conceited, one might even argue. I mean, who died and appointed me the arbiter of good taste in [*Second Life*] fashion?"

NOTE

Celebrity says that the differences between blogging and writing a magazine are in the way you approach issues. That means, she says, when she writes for Second Style, she's thinking about themes and writing longer feature stories. (And that's because the magazine only comes out monthly.) But when writing Fashionista, she doesn't worry about themes and just covers what she wants.

Music:
DJs,
Nightclubs,
and Bars

News:
Newspapers,
Magazines,
and Blogs

Games

The Financial Side of Blogs and Magazines

The way to make money with blogs and magazines in *Second Life* is by building a big enough audience that you can charge good rates for your ads. Celebrity says that Fashionista advertisers pay about US$1 per thousand impressions. By comparison, *Second Style* advertisers pay US$25 for a full-page ad. A blogger starting out is not going to instantly get thousands of readers. But, over time, she says that a committed blogger with a unique writing style can develop a following, and it's easy to imagine them getting around 40,000 to 50,000 unique viewers per month. Ideally, it's best to aim for page views being at least twice the number of unique users if you want to be making money.

The Required Skills—Blogs

To make a successful blog or magazine, you need to develop a certain set of skills. First, says Celebrity, you need to be able to write. "You don't need to be Herman Melville or anything, just solid and with something to say," she says. "If your posts consist of quoting the [virtual world community blog] Terra Nova and then writing a paragraph, I don't think that's going to be very successful."

Beyond that, she says, you have to know how to sell yourself, your publication, and your readership—and be comfortable with doing so. You'll need to convince advertisers that they will do well by buying space in your publication. And, to make money, you need to be willing to put in the work, day in and day out, for months before your readership is big enough to pay off. "Don't blog to make money," says Celebrity. "Blog because you have a passion for your topic."

You'll also need to use blogging software, as you probably can't make a professional-looking blog that will make money using free tools like Blogger (www.blogger.com). Celebrity says she began using TypePad (www.typepad.com/), before converting to WordPress (http://wordpress.org/). "If you're technically clueless, then I'd say go for TypePad," she says. "At this point I recommend designers and others who want to start blogging sign up with WordPress, [because it offers superior support for] template, layout, ad serving software, ad placement on the page, CSS formatting, etc. If you don't care about that stuff, then TypePad rocks. Otherwise, you'll probably need to host your blog on your own server running WordPress."

As for serving ads, Celebrity uses Openads (www.openads.org/), because it allows Fashionista to serve much more contextual ads than Google can. "I only want to show my readers ads for specifically *Second Life* stuff," she says. "If I post about a top that comes in 'crème,' for example, I don't want Google Ads showing my readers ads for crème brûlée torches and stuff." And that, she says, is how Fashionista maintains a high click-through rate, which translates to a higher rate of pay-per-thousand clicks.

Finally, offer RSS feeds. That will make it easy for the growing number of people who use RSS readers to add your blog to their list of feeds.

THE REQUIRED SKILLS—MAGAZINES

CHAPTER 1
CHAPTER 2
CHAPTER 3
CHAPTER 4
CHAPTER 5
CHAPTER 6
CHAPTER 7
CHAPTER 8
CHAPTER 9

CHAPTER 10
CHAPTER 11
APPENDICES
INDEX

Many of the skills are the same for magazines as for blogs, particularly when it comes to writing and being able to sell yourself. But because a magazine needs to be well designed and laid out, you'll also need to know how to do that. "Magazines are a tremendously visual medium, so the budding publisher is going to need to be able to photograph her content well, lay it out attractively, and still write well enough to hold people's interest."

In many cases, that means working with others so that you and your team have all the required skills. It's not easy to find writers who know how to do page layout, which means using pagination software like Adobe InDesign (www.adobe.com/products/indesign/).

MARKETING YOUR BLOG OR MAGAZINE

As with so many other areas of *Second Life* business, one of the best ways to get the word out about your new publication is on the official forums (http://forums.secondlife.com/forumdisplay.php?f=128). Once there, post the URL and say a little bit about your blog or magazine. Then, says Celebrity, another good way to get noticed is to do link exchanges with other bloggers, which means adding a link to their site to your blogroll and asking them to do the same. Some bloggers may be reticent to add you to their lists of links until you have established your ability to be consistent, but Celebrity says many will be willing to make the exchange right away. After that, she says, "If you're feeling especially full of chutzpah, email more established bloggers and try to get them to link to your content or site in a post."

Finally, if you have budget for it, think about placing ads on other *Second Life* Web properties or publications. "*Metaverse Messenger* classifieds aren't *that* expensive," Celebrity says.

RESIDENTS SPEAK

CELEBRITY TROLLOP ON STARTING A BLOG OR MAGAZINE

As someone who helps run two of the most-read publications in Second Life, *Celebrity shares her wisdom on the most important things to do and to not do when starting a blog or magazine.*

FOR BLOGS

🔲 Blog about what you love.

🔲 Be patient. Readers take time to find you.

(Continued)

🔊 **Be fair-minded if/when people criticize you. Keep your blog demeanor professional and high minded.**

🔊 **Make sure you can sell your site and your audience to advertisers.**

🔊 **Keep on writing. Your first month's worth of posts will probably embarrass you.**

🔊 **Don't expect to be an overnight sensation.**

🔊 **Don't disrespect your readers' trust or intelligence.**

🔊 **Don't be resistant to self-promotion.**

🔊 **Don't post too much.**

🔊 **Don't post too little. You want to post enough to make things interesting, but not so much that you're not writing anything worth reading or people start tuning you out.**

For Magazines

🔊 **Create a unique visual style for your magazine layout.**

🔊 **Be comfortable photographing the content that you cover editorially.**

🔊 **Don't sell more ads than you have actual content for.**

🔊 **Have patience—magazines, like blogs, take time to find their readership.**

🔊 **Promote yourself and your magazine wherever you can.**

🔊 **Don't try to do too much yourself. Don't be afraid to find reliable help and delegate.**

🔊 **Make sure your layout is elegant. Ugly layouts aren't going to lead to success. If all you do is slap some words next to a photo and put a page number in the corner, that isn't going to impress readers or advertisers.**

🔊 **Don't be afraid to take some risks with your editorial.**

CHAPTER 1
CHAPTER 2
CHAPTER 3
CHAPTER 4
CHAPTER 5
CHAPTER 6
CHAPTER 7
CHAPTER 8
CHAPTER 9
CHAPTER 10
CHAPTER 11
APPENDICES
INDEX

- Make and keep your advertisers happy. It's definitely worth it in the long run to make them very happy. They place the ads in your publication.

- Try to be consistent about your publication schedule. It's challenging, but try your best to be consistent for readers.

GAMES

You'll hear it all the time: *Second Life* is not a game. However, there are plenty of games being created inside *Second Life*. Many of the games are free to play. Some charge a little money. Most aren't very good, but a few are. If you can create one of those few, you might achieve great success.

THE GAME INNOVATOR: KERMITT QUICK

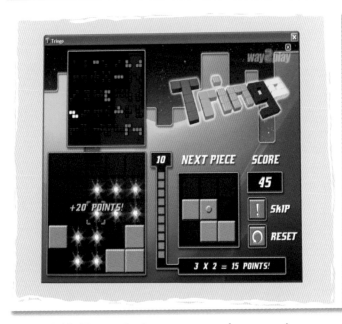

Figure 9.16: Tringo is the most popular game in Second Life's history.

Of all the *Second Life* success stories, there are few more famous than that of Kermitt Quick's Tringo (Figure 9.16). An entirely original game he created in-world, Tringo became a hit that still is found all over the virtual world. The game was so popular, in fact, that Kermitt ended up licensing the rights to a real-world company that wanted to produce Tringo for the Nintendo GBA. That deal brought Kermitt a great deal of attention (and a fair, though undisclosed, amount of money) because it was very likely the first case of a *Second Life* product becoming available in the real world.

239

🎵 Music:
DJs,
Nightclubs,
and Bars

📰 News:
Newspapers,
Magazines,
and Blogs

🎮 Games

Best of all for Kermitt, he didn't have to give up ownership of Tringo in *Second Life*. He is still free to develop and modify it there and to build his business around it. And that's what he's done, releasing a new version of the game and continuing to have the most popular and widely played game in *Second Life*. Because there are so few truly successful games in-world, I won't offer generalized tips for game development here. Instead, please refer to the "Spotlight on Kermitt Quick" sidebar for Kermitt's insights on Tringo's success.

MORE INFO

SPOTLIGHT ON KERMITT QUICK, INVENTOR OF TRINGO

Kermitt shares his thoughts on the creation of Tringo and what someone else wanting to develop a game business in Second Life *should think about.*

Q: How did you come up with the idea for Tringo?

KQ: The initial idea came from playing Bingo in *Second Life*. I was going to Bingo events quite a bit and liked the general structure of how the game was implemented, but it always bothered me how the winner is basically random. So I decided to make something original that involved a bit of skill. From there it was just a matter of putting together some general puzzle game ideas, and finding some rules that worked well with the features that were available in *Second Life*.

Q: Why did you design the game in *Second Life*?

KQ: More than anything, just to see if I could. I'd been in *Second Life* for six months or so and was looking for a larger project to work on and something like Tringo seemed like a good idea at the time. The ideas and rules came from *Second Life* itself in many ways. For example, the placement in Tringo is a simple click on the right square, and there's no ability to rotate the blocks. I did that because having more complex placement would increase lag and frustrate players, but things like that really became Tringo's defining points.

Q: What kind of technical skills were required to design the game?

KQ: There was definitely a lot of scripting required to make Tringo work. The current version has somewhere around 40 to 50 different scripts to make the whole thing work. Whenever I'm working on a *Second Life* project of that size I use SciTE-ez (`http://sl.sdfjkl.org/secondlife/scite/`) to edit my code, combined with lslint (`http://w-`

hat.com/lslint/) for syntax checking. For my second version of Tringo, I taught myself Ruby on Rails (www.rubyonrails.org/) and added a website which communicates with the Tringo boards in *Second Life* to display basic statistics and Tringo locations, etc. (http://tringoweb.com/). That included design of a MySQL database for the data storage. I also use Paint Shop Pro for creating textures, but none of them were incredibly complicated.

Q: **I realize that you made money by selling the out-of-*Second Life* rights to Tringo. But how did you make money with Tringo in-world?**

KQ: I picked a very basic sales model in *Second Life*. I simply sell Tringo boards for L$15,000 apiece, and once someone has purchased one they can set it up however and wherever they wish. After the initial purchase, I don't take any profits from the owner. I never really set out to make money from it, so I've always just looked at any income from there as being a bonus and never saw a need to complicate it.

Q: **What were the biggest challenges to making Tringo a hit in *Second Life*?**

KQ: Getting people to like Tringo wasn't really an issue. I pretty much relied on word of mouth and it spread like wildfire. So I think the biggest challenge would have to have been getting it to run consistent and stable so that it remained a hit. Since *Second Life* is a user-generated world, conditions can change drastically from place to place and sometimes caused the first version to be a little prone to freezing. Version 2 was when I moved to using SciTE-ez and settled into a much nicer code pattern so I could get all the scripts to work together much better.

For marketing, I set up some beta test games at one location while I finished off the first version, and by the time it was released everyone seemed to have heard of it already.

Q: **For someone wanting to create a new game in *Second Life* that they hoped to make money with, how long do you think it might take them to be ready to succeed?**

KQ: If they had some programming knowledge already, I'd think most people would find Linden Scripting Language (LSL) pretty easy to

(Continued)

CHAPTER 9

● MUSIC:
DJs,
NIGHTCLUBS,
AND BARS

● NEWS:
NEWSPAPERS,
MAGAZINES,
AND BLOGS

● GAMES

pick up. Based on my experience you could learn LSL and be able to make a game [within] six to 12 months, depending on prior knowledge. But it would take another year or so to understand the quirks of the language and get to know the community before you could do something like that really well. I think quite a few projects fail because people haven't spent enough time understanding the community and so they create something that doesn't "fit" right.

Q: **Do you have some suggestions for someone wanting to create a new game as a money-maker?**

KQ: ● First would have to be, don't just do it for the money. That may seem a bit contradictory, but I firmly believe that a better product usually comes from people that enjoy what they're doing, and the enjoyment of being able to create these things has always been my motivation.

● Learn all aspects of LSL and practice on lots of small projects before you embark on the big one. Then, you'll better know all the features that are available and how to use them the right way.

● Include building in your practice, because the way prims should be arranged and how they can be manipulated by script is also very important.

● Engage the community and make contacts. One of the major strengths of *Second Life* is being able to work alongside others and learn and, of course it's also important to know your audience so you can design something they want.

● Keep it simple. A lot of *Second Life* projects don't make it because people try to go too complex too quick. You'll get a much better end result if you start small and work your way up.

Q: **Any other *Second Life* games that you are particularly fond of?**

KQ: I seem to spend more time making things than playing games in *Second Life* these days. The two I've probably spent most time with would be **Bingo** and **DarkLife**.

CHAPTER 10

RUNNING A BUSINESS IN TEEN SECOND LIFE

Business is not just for adults anymore: This chapter takes a close look at the Teen grid and what business opportunities it offers its residents. From fashion to real estate to gadgets and building, the Teen grid abounds with successful businesses. But it also presents unique challenges, the most obvious of which is that teens have strict limits on how many Linden dollars they can buy. That means the economy is much smaller than the main grid's, and prices are usually low. This chapter talks about the skills you need to succeed as a Teen grid entrepreneur.

CONTENTS

CHAPTER 10

WHAT IS
TEEN SECOND
LIFE?

A BUSINESS
OPPORTUNITY
FOR TEENS

UNDERSTAND-
ING THE
FINANCIAL
ASPECT

OPPORTUNITY
ABOUNDS

THE
ECONOMY
AND
MARKETING

WHAT IS *TEEN SECOND LIFE?*

In August 2005, *Second Life* publisher Linden Lab opened *Teen Second Life*, an entirely separate grid of the virtual world just for those aged 13 to 17. The move was based on the idea that teens enjoyed using *Second Life* but weren't legitimately able to do so because it was limited to those 18 and older.

"It was pretty evident for us that *Second Life* was a terrific environment for kids," Robin Harper, Linden Lab's senior vice president of community, told CNET News.com in the first story about the new teens-only grid. "Every time a teen would sit down in front of *Second Life*, he or she would immediately get it."

The idea was to give teens a fully functional, adapted version of the virtual world—one in which they could live and socialize and in which they could start and maintain businesses. To get *Teen Second Life* started, Linden Lab convinced several adults on the main grid to donate content to make the new environment more attractive. Before long, more teens began to build and design, and the Teen grid began to resemble its older, more developed sibling. However, the Teen grid is nowhere near as big as the main grid. There are probably fewer than 10,000 active residents, and the total amount of land at this writing is less than that owned by only a couple of the main grid's biggest real-estate barons. Still, there is a bustling economy, and teens are building fashion, real estate, construction, and other businesses and earning profits.

The Teen grid serves as a kind of apprenticeship for entrepreneurs, in the sense that teens who learn how to run a business in their grid can take their skills with them when they turn 18 and graduate to the main grid. Because the technology behind the Teen grid is identical to the main grid—think of *Teen Second Life* as essentially an outlying (though unreachable) continent in the overall virtual world's geography—the structure is the same. What works in the main grid will work in the Teen grid, and vice versa. With the tips, tricks, and tools of running a successful *Teen Second Life* business, several residents quickly become profitable after moving to the main grid, earning even more money than they did before turning 18.

CHAPTER 1
CHAPTER 2
CHAPTER 3
CHAPTER 4
CHAPTER 5
CHAPTER 6
CHAPTER 7
CHAPTER 8
CHAPTER 9
CHAPTER 10
CHAPTER 11
APPENDICES
INDEX

A BUSINESS OPPORTUNITY FOR TEENS

The economic activities in the Teen grid are very similar to those on the main grid. Although *Teen Second Life* does restrict behavior to that appropriate for minors, its residents have just as much need and desire as adult *Second Life* residents to make themselves look good, to own a plot of land and a dwelling, and to have all kinds of toys to play with. Because such content is created by the users, there is ample opportunity for teens to create the content that fulfills those needs, and then to sell it to those who want to buy it, making a nice profit in the bargain.

Teen Second Life offers a way to experiment with entrepreneurship with minimal risk. Residents are limited to buying US$25 worth of Linden dollars per month. This is a nod to parents who want to be sure that their kids aren't haphazardly using credit cards and getting in financial trouble. Because the Linden purchase limits are low, if a teen starts a business, there's not a lot of initial capital on the line. Yet, if the business does well, the upside is substantial. Because the structural elements of running a business in the Teen grid are the same as they are on the main grid—they revolve around real-world business principles of risk versus reward, resource allocation, marketing, investment and reinvestment, and so on—*Teen Second Life* is a terrific place to learn about starting an enterprise. After all, it's an environment where innovation abounds and is rewarded, where a good idea mixed with the commitment and skills to carry it out can result in a product that everyone wants and will pay for, and where the most business-savvy residents can become celebrities—and score a nice, ongoing revenue stream.

Teen Second Life is an opportunity to learn some of what works and what doesn't work in business, how to innovate, how to hone marketing and customer service skills, and how to do so while having fun and without risking an arm and a leg. If you can master the art of building a business in the Teen grid, you will be in an ideal position to take your skills with you to the main grid when you turn 18 if you so choose, and take a crack at a much bigger market with fewer constraints on what you can do and more potential profit.

UNDERSTANDING THE FINANCIAL ASPECT

No one is going to promise that you'll make a lot of money with a business in *Teen Second Life*. In fact, as with any business environment, more ventures will fail than succeed. That's

Figure 10.1: Ming Chen ran one of the biggest and most successful Teen Second Life **businesses before he graduated to the main grid.**

just the way of the world, real or virtual. However, residents who do create businesses that stand out find that there's definitely money to be made, even though teens can buy only US$25 a month worth of Linden dollars and that Premium members get only L$300 a month as a stipend. How much a business earns depends entirely on how much time is put in, how valuable the product is considered by the community, and how good the business owner is at marketing it. Take the case of Ming Chen (Figure 10.1), who ran a Teen grid business called Dynamics Interactive Gadgets that sold all kinds of scripted toys and gadgets and games.

When Ming was able to concentrate on his store—usually during summers and times when school wasn't dominating his attention—he says he was able to pull in between US$400 and US$800 a month in pure profit. When school was in, or he was otherwise distracted, the products in his store still earned him US$100 to US$400 a month. Ming was on the upper end of profitability in the Teen grid, with only a few land barons and fashion designers making similar money. Among those were Wicked Loudon and Asuka Martin, both fashion designers who, according to fellow designer Anna Normandy, make in excess of US$300 a month. For her part, Anna says she earned about US$70 during summer 2006, before she put her store, Anna's, on hiatus for nearly a year.

More often, teens' ventures earn them enough to cover their own *Teen Second Life* costs and still have a little bit of spending money left over. Aesop Thatch, a designer of custom buildings for private residents and commercial venues, was one of those people. With his Teen grid business, Aura Architecture, Aesop developed a reputation as one of the more detail-oriented and high-quality builders. For that, he was often able to charge L$10,000 to L$15,000 for a build, though he generally wouldn't do much more business than that in a month. Aesop recently turned 18 and graduated to the main grid, where he began an entirely new business.

On the more casual end of the spectrum is someone like Kaeman Demar, whose Kaeman's Shop sells all kinds of scripted items like guns, armor, belts, and couches. He says his goal with his business—and one he has been achieving without too much effort—is to cover the expenses on his several shop locations in various locations around the Teen grid. That means, he says, it's necessary for him to earn just L$500 every couple of weeks to cover the rent.

As you plan for a new business, decide which category of earning is your goal. There are no guarantees that you'll get what you want, but without goals you won't be able to gauge how hard you have to work or how much business you need to do.

RESIDENTS SPEAK

CHAPTER 1
CHAPTER 2
CHAPTER 3
CHAPTER 4
CHAPTER 5
CHAPTER 6
CHAPTER 7
CHAPTER 8
CHAPTER 9
CHAPTER 10

CHAPTER 11
APPENDICES
INDEX

MING CHEN ON CREATING A NEW TEEN GRID BUSINESS

Ming Chen was one of the most successful entrepreneurs in Teen Second Life's *history. His gadgets business sold everything from toys and games to functional tools. Here's his advice on things to do and mistakes to avoid as you create a new business.*

- **Don't set time constraints on when a new project has to come out. A competitor may release theirs first, but teens want the better product and the cheaper product. Rushing through a product shows.**

- **Advertise on the forums and malls, and ask owners of popular places if you can advertise your product there.**

- **Try to make a product priced at under L$300. That is the stipend for Premium users—the majority of teen purchasers.**

- **Find or make unique ways to distribute your product. Things such as "virus-like" vendors, incentives, and promotions are great ways to drag in new customers. Remember, teens are compulsive buyers and buy what is cool at the time, but don't treat them that way: Make your product sound valuable so they don't have spender's guilt.**

- **Take advantage of the fact that** *Second Life's* **only cost of production is the time it takes to develop a product. After that, copying is instant and free. Give out some products, but make the receivers earn the free product. Making them tell all their friends to take a look at your business/product or having them sell your products can solve this.**

- **Never think your product is going to be the "next best thing" because doing so will make you rush through development and make you raise the price beyond a teen's Linden dollar balance.**

- **Avoid purchasing generic products that are related to helping your business in** *Second Life.* **Using a "starter kit" is a bad idea. Since people can see who created the original item in the kit, they will**

(Continued)

wonder why it wasn't you, and there's a much greater possibility people are using the same kit.

- Never, ever have "business partners." Using that phrase to refer to a friend or acquaintance will just make them think they will get an equal portion of the profit. Instead, refer to them as contractors or let them know that you just want them to make something. For instance, if you need a person who is good at branding or design, don't say, "You can be my business partner by making the signs or textures for my product." Instead, only ask them for what you want when you want it.

- Have your own plot of land, if possible, for the business. Avoid having just a few stalls in a high-popularity mall. If you don't have the money to buy your own land, rent it on a private island. By having no specific headquarters, people see your shop as just another attempt to earn some money. Having your own plot shows consumers that you plan and expect to earn money.

- Never, ever assume popular malls are the best places to sell your products. You can have your nice stall set up, but the neighboring stall may be [giving out] freebies. Instead, try renting stalls in malls next to or near successful businesses. The successful business will likely renew their rent and if they stop renewing it, it would be a good idea to do the same—because there is a likely chance they do not have sales coming through.

OPPORTUNITY ABOUNDS

From the perspective of a would-be *Teen Second Life* businessperson, opportunity abounds. What kind of business you choose to pursue depends on your interest and your skills. Your success depends in large part on whether you can follow some basic concepts. "To have a successful business in the Teen grid requires marketing to make it teen-worthy," says Ming Chen. "Overcome greed—don't make things too expensive—and offer the ability to update a product because teens want the latest and greatest, and they usually don't want to pay for it."

Figure 10.2: In **Teen Second Life**, residents can have almost any kind of store they want, including one that sells guitars.

Once you understand those basic tenets, it's time to think about what specific kind of business you want to go into. It's hard to measure exactly how big each area of the economy is, but it's safe to say that among the very biggest segments are fashion (clothing, skins, and hair); real estate; gadgets, musical instruments (Figure 10.2), games, and toys; and construction of residential and commercial buildings.

FASHION

Figure 10.3: The largest area of business in **Teen Second Life** is fashion. Teens everywhere want to look good.

It's no surprise that teens in *Second Life* want to look good and have a variety of outfits and looks for different occasions. Those who don't know how to create their own attire will end up buying what they want and need. Fashion in *Second Life* refers to clothing (Figure 10.3) and to avatars—residents can have multiple characters that they can switch among as they choose hair and skins. (They can buy more realistic skins to go under their clothing and to replace the bland, featureless skins avatars come with.)

In general, female residents are more likely to shop for fashion on a regular basis, so there's going to be more opportunity there than with male fashion. The same is true for skins, shapes, and hair. Because of the economic restraints on the Teen grid, pricing for these items is going to be low. According to Anna Normandy, most clothing sells for between L$15 and L$150, hair tends to go for around L$100 for packs of three, and skins go for around L$500 to L$625. To make money, you will need to sell a lot of product before the profits start to add up. But that's how the *Second Life* economy works, for the most part: It's a volume business, and the people who make money are the ones who create a wide variety of products for customers to buy and constantly update or put out new items.

Anna says that the things that set successful Teen grid fashion businesses apart from others is an emphasis on high-quality products and that she finds "bigger stores usually attract more people" (Figure 10.4). She also believes there is a need in the Teen grid for new styles, as many people buy their fashion from a small number of top designers.

Figure 10.4: Anna Normandy is one of the best-known fashion designers in Teen Second Life. Her store is known as Anna's.

To create high-quality fashions, you'll need to know how to use a 2D painting and texturing program like Photoshop and the *Second Life* building tools to manipulate prims. It's also a good idea to have, and know how to use, a 3D modeling program.

> **NOTE**
>
> *Much of what applies in the main grid applies in Teen Second Life. Chapter 4, "Walking the Runway: Fashion in Second Life" contains more details about the technical and marketing skills you'll need to run a successful fashion business in either grid.*

CHAPTER 1
CHAPTER 2
CHAPTER 3
CHAPTER 4
CHAPTER 5
CHAPTER 6
CHAPTER 7
CHAPTER 8
CHAPTER 9
CHAPTER 10

CHAPTER 11
APPENDICES
INDEX

RESIDENTS SPEAK

ANNA NORMANDY ON CREATING A TEEN GRID FASHION BUSINESS

Anna Normandy is one of the best-known fashion designers in **Teen Second Life,** *and she works hand in hand with some of the others, so she knows as much as anyone about what works and what doesn't when it comes to skins, clothing, and hair. Here she shares her advice for starting a successful fashion business.*

- **Make your store get noticed and known. Advertise.**

- **Don't slack off when making products. Quality is key.**

- **Don't be afraid to be unique, and to make something that no one has tried to make. We need variety in the Teen grid. Residents want new things.**

- **Try to add new items every so often. You don't want residents to get bored at your store and not want to come back.**

- **Ask fellow designers for help if needed. We don't bite.**

- **Don't copy other designers directly. That leads to trouble.**

- **Don't remake the same things over and over again, such as 10 flexi skirts in different styles, but with the same or similar textures.**

- **Don't ever spend more on rent than you make. This leads to bankruptcy.**

- **Don't think you're better than everyone else. People will start to dislike you and stop buying your products.**

- **Don't always work. Relaxation is just as important after you release a new line of products. If you work too much, you'll get uninspired.**

◾ REAL ESTATE

Like in the real world, *Second Life* residents want land. It's no different in the Teen grid, where people set up stores, libraries, art galleries (Figure 10.5), and their own personal dwellings.

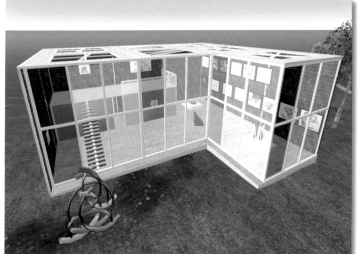

Figure 10.5: A library (above) and an art gallery (below) created by Jay Clostermann on Eye4You Alliance island, a popular hangout for **Teen Second Life** *residents.*

Of course, there has to be land to put those buildings on, and that's where the real-estate business comes into play. Any member willing to upgrade from a Basic to a Premium account (US$9.95 per month) has the right to own land in the Teen grid. For those who have the money to buy significant amounts of land, an opportunity opens up to become a *Teen Second Life* real-estate baron. Although there are already a few, such as Mercury Metropolitan, who dominate the business, it doesn't mean there isn't room for someone else who has business savvy to come in and take some of the business away. In real estate, there are really two different businesses: selling parcels directly to other residents and renting them out (Figure 10.6). You can do this with undeveloped land or with developed properties, such as mall storefronts.

As in the main grid real-estate business (see Chapter 5, "The *Second Life* Land Business"), you can't compete entirely on price. Instead, you'll want to focus on adding value by making your properties attractive, providing great customer service, offering customers privacy, and so on. Like other businesses in the Teen grid, real estate requires a bit of patience because your potential customers' spending is limited by restrictions on how many Lindens they can buy per month and their monthly stipends. Most will have only about L$300 to spend each month. "Top land prices in the Teen grid are about L$4 per square meter," says Aesop Thatch, "so if [a customer wants] to buy something that's 3,000 square meters, [they'll have] to wait two months" because it will take them that long to save the money.

Figure 10.6: A shop stall for rent

CHAPTER 1
CHAPTER 2
CHAPTER 3
CHAPTER 4
CHAPTER 5
CHAPTER 6
CHAPTER 7
CHAPTER 8
CHAPTER 9
CHAPTER 10

CHAPTER 11
APPENDICES
INDEX

In any case, if you want to go into the real-estate business you'll have to become very good at using the virtual world's estate and terraforming tools, at learning how to divide prims among parcels of land, and about how to deal with customers.

NOTE

For more information on the skills required to succeed in this business, see Chapter 5. Most of the business principles in the main grid also apply to the Teen grid.

BUILDING

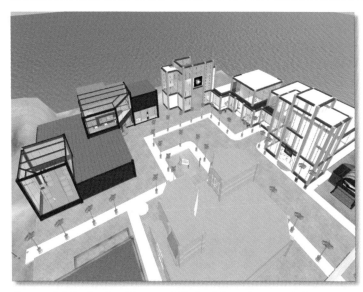

Figure 10.7: Asuka Martin, Wicked Loudon, and Anna Normandy—three of the best-known fashion designers in Teen Second Life—have their stores next to each other.

Although *Teen Second Life* is substantially smaller than the main grid, there's no shortage of residential and commercial development. Indeed, many teens have built attractive stores, houses, and other buildings (Figure 10.7).

Some residents have the skills to construct their own buildings. Many others either don't have the skills or the time, yet still want to have one, either for personal or business reasons. That's where builders like Aesop

CHAPTER 10

- WHAT IS
  TEEN SECOND
  LIFE?

- A BUSINESS
  OPPORTUNITY
  FOR TEENS

- UNDERSTAND-
  ING THE
  FINANCIAL
  ASPECT

- OPPORTUNITY
  ABOUNDS

- THE
  ECONOMY
  AND
  MARKETING

Figure 10.8: A sign advertising a prefab building for sale

Thatch come in, making money by creating custom buildings or prefabs for others. Custom jobs are, of course, more expensive because they require more time and attention to detail. However, many residents want custom work because it sets their space apart from others' and gives them a sense of being unique. Prefabs (Figure 10.8) sell for less, but can bring in more money over time because once you create one, you can sell it over and over again. Of course, if you design custom projects, you can also turn them into prefabs—as long as your customers don't mind.

Builders can make good money, depending on the quality and size of their creations. Aesop says that when he did custom jobs, he charged around L$1.50 per square foot, earning an average of L$5,000 per project. He says he also managed to find a customer wanting an L$10,000 or L$15,000 build about once a month.

Builders need a variety of skills to succeed. They definitely need to use software like Photoshop or something similar to design textures for interiors and exteriors, and they will have to master the *Second Life* building tools. Knowing how to use a 3D modeling program to create advanced lighting effects is also a useful skill, but it's not required.

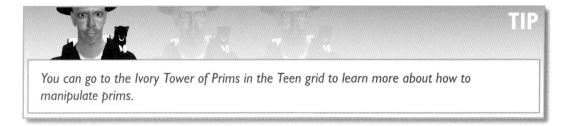

TIP

You can go to the Ivory Tower of Prims in the Teen grid to learn more about how to manipulate prims.

NOTE

Please see Chapter 6, "Construction Projects Big and Small," for much more information on the skills required for building.

CHAPTER 1
CHAPTER 2
CHAPTER 3
CHAPTER 4
CHAPTER 5
CHAPTER 6
CHAPTER 7
CHAPTER 8
CHAPTER 9
CHAPTER 10

■ EVERYTHING ELSE

In *Second Life*, people want toys, furniture, accessories, and all kinds of gadgets—and the Teen grid is no different. Fashion, real estate, and building are the three biggest and most visible areas of the Teen grid economy, and many businesses cater to these needs. Too many different opportunities fall into this category to discuss them all here, but suffice it to say that someone who specializes in one of these areas, builds high-quality products, and offers good customer service would be in a position to make some good money.

Figure 10.9: The Gizmo Vayu is a multi-gadget with more than 50 different features.

You probably won't make as much as the top fashion designers, real-estate barons, or builders, but it's not out of the realm of possibilities that you could earn US$100 a month or more. For example, in Kaeman's Shop, Kaeman Demar sells guns, armor, couches, belts, jetpacks, aircraft, and many other items. Prices for Kaeman's goods tend to be fairly low, so he has to sell lots of them to make money. His guns sell for at least L$100, and his aircraft for L$100. Another seller, Krypt Hax, sells the L$100 Gizmo Vayu

(Figure 10.9), a multi-gadget with more than 50 features, including the ability to trap people near you, to annoy them, to create a bubble shield around people, and much more.

Making objects—particularly ones that produce some kind of action—requires having good Linden Scripting Language (LSL) skills. You can learn a lot about how to use this language, which is *Second Life*'s native programming tool, at the LSL Portal (http://wiki.secondlife.com/wiki/LSL _ Portal). You also need to know how to use the *Second Life* building tools, especially if you are creating something like furniture. Additionally, you'll want to have some knowledge of a painting program like Photoshop. "Having skills in [Photoshop] is a plus because people are going to be interested in the nicest-looking stall, store, and mall first," says Ming Chen. "For scripting, there isn't software to make things easier, but I recommend reading up on another language such as C++," says Ming, "since it's very similar to LSL, and there are many books about C++ and exactly how it works."

Finally, Ming recommends using a program like OmniGraffle (Mac only, $80, http://www.omnigroup.com/applications/omnigraffle/) to plot out the scripts you'll write.

NOTE

Chapter 8, "Selling Objects from Toys to Weapons," provides much more information on the skills necessary to build a business selling objects, gadgets, furniture, and the like.

THE ECONOMY AND MARKETING

Running a business in *Teen Second Life* comes with special challenges that don't exist in the main grid. Of course, the main grid has its own set of hurdles, but it's worth mentioning what's different in the Teen grid.

THE ECONOMY

The biggest challenge of all is that residents have much less money to spend than their main-grid counterparts. "Teens can only buy US$25 worth of Lindens a month," says Aesop Thatch. That's "severely limiting."

Ming Chen agrees. He says that he built a Teen grid version of a multi-gadget available on the main grid that sold for L$750 and had to sell it for L$250, because of the limits on the money supply. Anna Normandy says the same is definitely true in fashion, where skins on the main grid can sell for up to L$2,000, but for only around L$600 in the Teen grid. Essentially, adds Ming, the reason teens have less money to spend is that many parents won't let their kids use credit cards to buy Linden dollars and, as a nod to those parents, Linden Lab set the monthly purchasing limit at US$25.

The lower prices means that you have to sell more to make money and that your earning power is limited. Unfortunately, there's not much you can do about the limited economy. However, if you build a business that sells products or services residents want, there's no limit to how many Lindens you can accumulate, and you can always trade them in for US dollars on the LindeX.

MARKETING

Although the economic situation in the Teen grid is markedly different from the main grid, marketing a business is pretty much the same. You still need to be proactive in marketing your new business because, as Anna Normandy says, "You could have amazing products, but if no one knows who you are, or where your store is, you won't make any money." She says that advertising your business in all the ways possible is crucial.

Teen Second Life is small enough that some people think Classifieds aren't really necessary. "When all the shops are [in] three places, you don't really need them," says Aesop Thatch. "Everyone is on Eden or Alcove or one of the islands." Anna does recommend using the Classifieds, but also emphasizes the importance of posting in the *Teen Second Life* forums about your business and your new products, making freebies to give away, and hosting events to bring people in.

Ming Chen says that business owners should offer one-to-one support for their products and be prepared to answer every question that comes up or respond to any incidents that occur. "Since money is scarce on the Teen grid," Ming says, "teens look for things like 'free support,' 'updates automatically,' and 'feature-filled.' If an owner doesn't answer a support request, it hurts the business because of the possibility of the requester not recommending the product to their friends."

Ming agrees with Anna that using the forums is essential, as is offering discounts or freebies, especially if someone is willing to do something to earn them—particularly because there's no production cost for additional items. "When I mention there is no cost of production," Ming says, "I stress that, but you can't make the receivers of the free products feel like your product is cheap. Make them work for the free product by going around and telling their friends about it, for example."

Finally, make sure that your products are high-quality, as teens are picky about what they'll spend their scarce Lindens on. One area where that's really important is the textures used to create many products. "Textures . . . are what makes or breaks a build," says Aesop. "I can have a totally awesome design, but if you put the wrong textures on it, it becomes so much mush."

RESIDENTS SPEAK

AESOP THATCH ON WHAT WORKS IN THE TEEN GRID

Aesop Thatch was one of the best-known Teen grid builders before he turned 18 and moved to the main grid. He still knows as much or more than most about what works and doesn't in the Teen grid, and he shares some of that expertise here.

- **Be good. Know what you are doing and stick to it. If you can build, build. And practice building. If you can script, it's the same.**

- **Know your market. Don't try to build things that are being built unless you can do it better *and* cheaper. Don't try to build your real-life home in *Second Life*. It just won't work.**

(Continued)

CHAPTER 1
CHAPTER 2
CHAPTER 3
CHAPTER 4
CHAPTER 5
CHAPTER 6
CHAPTER 7
CHAPTER 8
CHAPTER 9
CHAPTER 10

CHAPTER 11
APPENDICES
INDEX

- Ceilings should always be at least four meters high. Five is even better.

- Lie about what you make. If the [customer] thinks you're pulling in L$100,000 a month and compliments you on that, don't disabuse him of that notion. The customer will think he's getting a break.

- Don't lie about your age. It's not worth it, and it's a really good way to get banned.

- Don't build crap. Ever. And if you do, delete it before someone sees it. It only takes one of your builds looking bad to lose you a *lot* of business.

- Don't sell full permissions unless you're making more than [the reseller] ever will. I gave someone a freebie for a very specific use and he sold it for profit, after rebuilding it so he had the builder name.

- Don't stick to just one style. People who are paying you good money want something unique.

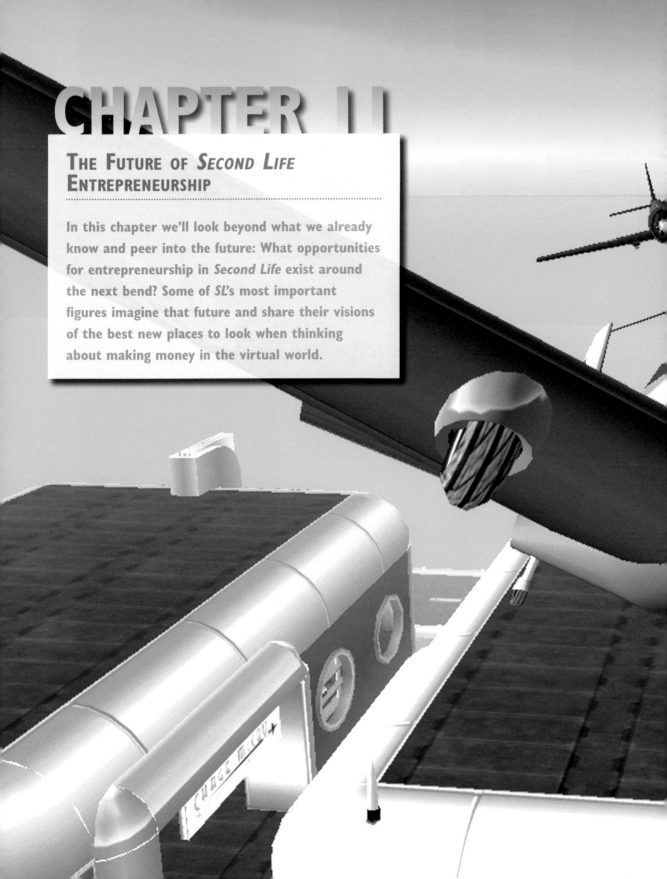

CHAPTER 11

THE FUTURE OF *SECOND LIFE* ENTREPRENEURSHIP

In this chapter we'll look beyond what we already know and peer into the future: What opportunities for entrepreneurship in *Second Life* exist around the next bend? Some of *SL*'s most important figures imagine that future and share their visions of the best new places to look when thinking about making money in the virtual world.

CONTENTS

CHAPTER 11

THE SKY'S
THE LIMIT

FUTURE
BUSINESS
OPPORTUNI-
TIES

THE SKY'S THE LIMIT

Second Life is more than four years old, and since its launch, the virtual world has grown to become a worldwide social and cultural phenomenon, a media favorite, and an economic marvel.

Thousands and thousands of people are making money in *Second Life*, from those earning enough with a small fashion boutique to cover all their expenses, to real-estate barons earning impressive full-time incomes. And there are many, many examples between those extremes.

Indeed, nearly everywhere you turn in *Second Life* there are signs of the strength of the economy: stores of all kinds are ubiquitous, the number of private sims is skyrocketing, and week in and week out, residents of the virtual world are trading millions of US dollars' worth of goods.

You've learned a lot about the many ways to make money in *Second Life*, what steps you must take to be a success, the technical skills you need, the ways to market your business, and much more. Now it's time to look forward. *Second Life* is changing rapidly, and we're at a crucial moment in its evolution: just as the population is exploding, there are several new tools and developments that will forever change the way things are done in the virtual world.

Among them are sculpted prims (http://wiki.secondlife.com/wiki/Sculpted_Prims)—which allow residents to create far more complex and organic shapes than are possible using traditional prims. In addition, *Second Life* residents now have access to integrated voice tools, meaning they can speak to each other naturally without the use of third-party software, and at long last, text chatting is an option, not a necessity. And finally, Linden Lab is allowing open-source development of the *Second Life* client software, meaning that the large developer community is now working on new approaches to the tools that we all use when we're in *Second Life*. The results of these innovations? No one knows for certain yet, but the sky is the limit.

To be sure, *Second Life* is still beset by seemingly never-ending bugs, crashes, rolling restarts, user-interface problems, and many other issues. And it is crucial for Linden Lab to continue to address those and others that arise if the virtual world is to reach its full potential. One thing seems clear, though: There is great opportunity for new businesses, and for more people to make money in *Second Life* than ever before. As the new technologies take hold and the population grows ever larger, those opportunities can only blossom.

FUTURE BUSINESS OPPORTUNITIES

To get a sense of what future business opportunities might exist in-world, I spoke with some of the most influential people in *Second Life*, asking each of them what they see coming next. What follows are my discussions with Linden Lab CTO Cory Ondrejka, Metaverse Roadmap co-director Jerry Paffendorf, and sculpted-prims creator Qarl Linden. To whet your appetite, here are some of the highlights:

- On-call language translation businesses
- Real-life product modeling
- Brick-and-mortar company customer service
- Design of real-world clothing
- New advertising, search, and communications tools
- Sims in a box
- Stores in a wand
- High-quality, realistic, complex objects and designs

THE EXECUTIVE: LINDEN LAB CTO CORY ONDREJKA

Since its founding in 1998, *Second Life* publisher Linden Lab has been led by two men: CEO Philip Rosedale and CTO Cory Ondrejka. While Rosedale gets most of the media attention, Ondrejka is an equally driving force behind *Second Life*'s development, and Rosedale's equal as a visionary.

Ondrejka (Figure 11.1) discussed with me the future of entrepreneurship in *Second Life*, and he had a lot to say on the matter.

Figure 11.1: Cory Ondrejka, Linden Lab's CTO

CHAPTER II

THE SKY'S
THE LIMIT

FUTURE
BUSINESS
OPPORTUNI-
TIES

Q: Why don't you start with some general thoughts on the future of entrepreneurship in _Second Life_?

CO: The first way to think about it is to consider how this is different than other communication options. The telephone has voice only, and doesn't work well for more than a few people. The Net is still mostly one-to-many and asynchronous. Video conferencing has weird properties because it is like having a plate of glass between you, and nobody looks at you correctly.

None of these really give you place. Even with video conferencing, you can't really get up, move around, pace, or do the things we do when we are together. And _Second Life_, while not the real world, helps with many of these. You have place, embodiment, and with the positionalized voice, a method for having real-world style conversations à la a cocktail party (i.e., multiple, parallel conversations). It is many-to-many and real-time.

Given all that, I think the first new opportunity is going to be helping companies that have dispersed work forces save money on recruiting, on-boarding, training, and collaboration. This is a lot like what IBM has said they are working on. But they are just scratching the surface. Think about companies with completely dispersed workforces. They could use _Second Life_ the way we do, to do collaborative/agile programming between developers scattered around the world. Because, after all, this is really about sharing culture, about allowing people to bridge the connections they make in the real world during the times they can't actually meet.

Next, you add in voice. You pick up this very high-bandwidth communication ability that we are used to in the real world. Except that you can be chatting with people anywhere with the added benefits to trust formation and social agency that avatars bring. Think about how many ways you could use translations if you could get a human to help you on a moment's notice from anywhere in the world. In the real world, if you want to do a business meeting, you'd hire a simultaneous translator. In _Second Life_, you could have a HUD attachment that allows you to request translation between language A and language B and which hits a web service, pages available translators, and tells you their rates per minute. They log in, stand with you, and now you conduct the meeting just like you would in the real world. But that would just be the start. What if you need a bit of a refresher before a trip or help understanding a foreign book or want to know how to say "thank you" in the country you are about to visit? In all of these cases, you need access to a native speaker, a way to pay them, and an environment where you'll be comfortable asking. _Second Life_ would rock for all of those.

And, as long as we are on foreign users, anywhere that you have broadband you have the ability to move Linden dollars in exchange for goods and services. Think about using _Second Life_ to set up a direct connection to tailors in Asia. You build the outfit you want in _Second Life_, they pull it from the client, combine it with your real-world dimensions, and FedEx you bespoke clothing. It could be cheap for you in terms of custom clothing—say US$100 an outfit—and still be very profitable for them. Plus, they could list all the outfits they've made.

CHAPTER 1
CHAPTER 2
CHAPTER 3
CHAPTER 4
CHAPTER 5
CHAPTER 6
CHAPTER 7
CHAPTER 8
CHAPTER 9
CHAPTER 10
CHAPTER 11

APPENDICES
INDEX

Q: I met someone who was using *Second Life* to model little toys and then he was building them in real life. Is that something you imagine seeing across broader ranges of products?

CO: Yes. Anything where visual representation, trust building, or easy payment become part of the equations.

Q: What limits are there on the kinds of products that could be modeled in *Second Life* and built in real life?

CO: Well, I think the question is: how do the strengths of *Second Life* help you in building your business? Modeling the product is only one dimension. One dimension, say for clothing, interior decorating—talk about another high-margin business where custom creations are valuable—then being able to model the item is very useful.

Q: How do you think sculpted prims will impact future entrepreneurial business in *Second Life*?

CO: Anything that adds to the fidelity of visual representation in *Second Life* simply broadens the opportunity space. Sculpties are a great part of that.

Q: Can you think of specific manifestations of business opportunities that sculpties offer that don't exist today? Or extensions to what does exist currently?

CO: I think for interior design—especially the creation of lighting elements, for example— sculpties will allow the generation of far more interesting objects.

Q: Are sculpties going to make it possible for a whole new kind of *Second Life* entrepreneur to create businesses in-world?

CO: I think that every new feature that expands the design space in *Second Life* will allow new entrepreneurs in. And, yes, this will help the 3D modeling pros.

Q: Will that hurt the existing business owners?

CO: Business in *Second Life* has always been competitive. This is just another change, but I think the businesses are used to the changing nature of competition and pace in *Second Life*.

Q: How will open source affect the entrepreneurial landscape?

CO: That opens an entirely new domain—the custom and modified *Second Life* client—and I don't think we've even seen the beginning there.

Q: Are there business opportunities there? Will people be able to sell their custom clients?

CO: That's one model, but there are many others. Think of all the businesses we've seen on the Web and Web 2.0. All of those could be blended into the client in various ways.

CHAPTER 11

🔹 THE SKY'S
THE LIMIT

🔹 FUTURE
BUSINESS
OPPORTUNI-
TIES

Q: Any specific examples?

CO: The obvious ones are advertising, search, and different communication tools. The more interesting are probably integration with other applications in ways we haven't thought about.

Q: What are some obstacles or challenges going forward that entrepreneurs should be wary of?

CO: They need to really understand *Second Life* and not just apply Web modes of thought, thinking that what matters is [page views], for example, is silly when you transition from one-to-many to many-to-many. Be ready for the speed and skill of competition. Think big, and realize that there are huge opportunities. Be aware of the practical limitations of *Second Life* and plan accordingly. You have to balance pie-in-the-sky with swinging for the fences. You know, worldwide, translations could be done today, easily, and could be a billion-US-dollar market? But doing a concert in *Second Life* for 10,000 people would be almost impossible.

Q: What are some mistakes entrepreneurs should avoid as they look to the future of business in *Second Life*?

CO: It's a bit like operating in a foreign country. Know the territory, the language. Don't sell the Chevy Nova in Spanish-speaking countries, that sort of thing. Know about Wednesday AM downtime—until we finally eliminate them.

Q: Can you imagine the rise of more Anshe Chungs? Or is that not possible anymore, given the size of the economy and the ecosystem?

CO: There is always room for great, competitive, flexible, innovative entrepreneurs to corner new and interesting ideas. And the larger the market, the more opportunities there are.

THE FUTURIST: METAVERSE ROADMAP CO-DIRECTOR JERRY PAFFENDORF

CHAPTER 1
CHAPTER 2
CHAPTER 3
CHAPTER 4
CHAPTER 5
CHAPTER 6
CHAPTER 7
CHAPTER 8
CHAPTER 9
CHAPTER 10
CHAPTER 11

APPENDICES

INDEX

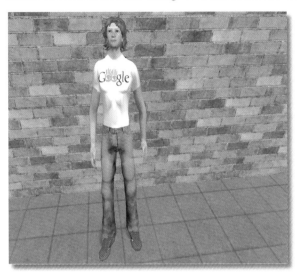

Figure 11.2: Jerry Paffendorf, one of the most active people in thinking about the future of *Second Life and 3D virtual worlds.*

Over the last couple of years, few people have had as much of an impact on 3D social virtual worlds and their communities as Jerry Paffendorf (Figure 11.2). Among his many roles are co-director of the Acceleration Studies Foundation's Metaverse Roadmap project and regular conference speaker on virtual worlds. He is also the former futurist-in-residence at The Electric Sheep Company.

Recently Paffendorf stepped down from his position at Electric Sheep to start his own company, but while he was busy putting that new project together, he took some time to talk about the future of entrepreneurship in *Second Life.*

Q: **What do new *Second Life* technologies mean for the future of entrepreneurship in the virtual world?**

JP: I think sculpted prims are the biggest innovation in *Second Life* for a while. We haven't seen the full extent of it yet, and there are a couple of things there. One, it throws open the content-creation market to a much larger group of people in the world who already use Maya. And since it reduces the number of prims needed to make complex objects, you can create new, more densely packed, and dynamic kinds of environments in *Second Life.*

My favorite thing in *Second Life* is still Starax's magic wand. It is no longer for sale, but [it] let you generate objects in the world by speaking a keyword. So you said "idea" and a light bulb falls. The thing with the wand was, the more items you rezzed, the slower things got, eventually crashing sims if you rezzed too many. Some of the things in the wand were pretty complex and prim-heavy, like a train with lots of cars, or the buffalo stampede.

When you start using sculpties, already you can generate a lot more content around you without taxing the system so much. It's hard to see outside the boundaries of what you can do right now, but that was a pretty encouraging step for *Second Life*, because now it's possible to constantly create and change more of the world around you. There's a pretty recent invention called "sim in a box" (http://youtube.com/watch?v=QcrgOj43wQI) that loads these huge sim-sized environments, so if you want

CHAPTER 11

THE SKY'S
THE LIMIT

FUTURE
BUSINESS
OPPORTUNI-
TIES

a shopping-mall sim or a forest sim or a racetrack you can click on this box and it generates the entire 16-acre layout. So as a trend riffing on sculpties, the wand, and sim in a box, I'm looking forward to opportunities in the content-creation market and also in new tools that allow non-builders in *Second Life* to easily conjure and customize really cool content.

Q: **So what kind of business opportunities are we looking at here?**

JP: I'm a big fan of generative content creation, and automating the process as much as possible. I know there are people out there using Maya to evolve themes and variations on their creations. So, say you make a rabbit and then you run 1,000 variations of that rabbit, with all the textures, facial expressions, and its size slightly varied. Then you slurp them into *Second Life*. So, the next step is giving people access to those kinds of content streams, like a wand that can conjure anything. Right now *Second Life* is set up so that you visit different destinations and see what's there. When people can bring the content to wherever they want, pull it out of their pocket, there'll be a lot happening with bringing the world to you, and a lot of that will come from the kinds of things you can do in outside building programs that just aren't possible with the internal *Second Life* building tools. If I was a Maya guru, I'd have a few ideas for *Second Life*.

Q: **What else might we see?**

JP: Starax started a pretty interesting model with the magic wand that we might see more of. He sold the wand for a high sum, US$55, but it was full of lots of content, and he was always adding new content to it, and there was also a way to add your own objects to it. So he was really selling a content stream that was easy to access.

Things like that could have effects on content creators and store owners. I can imagine people selling an entire for-purchase store in a wand. You're looking for shoes so you rez all of the shoes in its pool and then click and buy the ones you want before they disappear. *Second Life* really isn't at that stage yet, but between sculpties and an open wand system, you can really create tons more stuff and distribute it in streams right to users rather than making them go from store to store, place to place.

Q: **What do you think the effect of integrated voice in *Second Life* will be?**

JP: I think one of the greatest impacts of voice will be accelerating the development of the world. When you can talk to people hands-free you can converse while you build, and a lot more ideas flow into the world through what people are saying. There's also a lot to be done in *Second Life* with bots that can talk using text-to-speech that you can start having conversations with and giving verbal commands to. And I think new business opportunities will come from simply making things faster.

I'm a big fan of the *Second Life* machinimist Pierce Portacarrero, and I've gotten to see him work up-close. I didn't realize it before I saw his process, but he's obsessed with generativity and automation in the creative process. There's a kind of traditional way of building and editing in *Second Life* that can and has to change for people serious about making their living there, as far as I can see. One of the things I've learned from Pierce, to paraphrase him, is "*Second Life* is the best and fastest way in the world to generate novel imagery." When I watch his techniques I see what he means by that. He uses automated texture-creation tools, automated cameras, automated editing tools, automated music-creation tools, all that. He makes sure he's got control over the different palettes and then he just lets it run and assembles it. It lets him do things very quickly and generate lots of content like a one-man band. So if you take your time to set up your system, whether you're making objects, or machinima, or are podcasting, or whatever media you're creating, between sculpties and Maya and some of these outside editing programs, you can create much more high-quality content than people are generally doing right now.

I think some of these new changes in *Second Life* have opened things up for people with generative solutions to just make a killing in there if they have that attitude: "*Second Life* is the best and fastest way in the world to generate novel imagery," and not get so caught up on being precious and hand-crafting everything or getting every little cut or whatever perfect. With the right style, in the Pepsi challenge taste-test of how things are made, most of the time people can't even tell. So I'm waiting for the highly automated super builders and producers who basically just turn on the stream and never stop sending content into the world and making media out of it.

CHAPTER 1
CHAPTER 2
CHAPTER 3
CHAPTER 4
CHAPTER 5
CHAPTER 6
CHAPTER 7
CHAPTER 8
CHAPTER 9
CHAPTER 10
CHAPTER 11

APPENDICES
INDEX

RESIDENTS SPEAK

JERRY PAFFENDORF ON SUCCEEDING IN THE *SL* OF THE FUTURE

The following are some tips and suggestions from Jerry Paffendorf about how to succeed in the future Second Life *business landscape:*

- **Break out of the system of the way things are currently done.** *Second Life* **is [changing] and it's going to have to continue to change to stay relevant. It can be daunting to push the envelope sometimes because there's such a large and outspoken** *Second Life* **culture that demonizes things like CopyBot, and that's understandable. But to really move ahead you have to do things that disrupt business as usual.**

- **Find ways to generate and offer streams of new content with minimal editing and oversight. Fast is good! Variety is good! Automation is good! Think generative. Think "how can** *Second Life* **be the best tool in the world for generating novel content quickly?" and focus on the systems that do that.**

(Continued)

CHAPTER 11

THE SKY'S
THE LIMIT

FUTURE
BUSINESS
OPPORTUNI-
TIES

- Deliver things to people wherever they are—don't make them come to you or your sim. *Second Life* currently has technical issues with delivering media and objects and scripts wherever and whenever you want, but it makes sense to plan for the next era because it's inevitable and it's the one that way more people will really like.

- Don't be religious about keeping everything in *Second Life*. Tie it back out to the Web and other media and outside creation tools. *Second Life* is a sliver of the overall meta- and mediaverse.

- Don't bet on the future of the current in-world creation tool or scripting language (LSL), because they're weak and non-interoperable with the way that most everything outside of *Second Life* works. When you look at where *Second Life* has to get to and what kinds of things are going to have the greatest impact on the world and the experience within it, there are things like outside creation programs and scripting languages that allow you to do more. *Second Life* knows these things will be coming in from the outside—there are far too many people already trained in and using them, and there are far too many reasons to use them over *Second Life*'s proprietary tools once it becomes possible to.

- Don't get caught up in *Second Life* drama if someone doesn't like what you're doing in-world. I've seen that happen way too many times. It's tricky in *Second Life* because it seems like half the people are kind of roleplaying at any given time, even if they're not heavy roleplayers. It goes back to that difference between a world and a platform. There are ways to service both. I'm coming more from the platform side, but still respecting the world, the world part will always exist, so just don't listen to people when they storm you and say that if you do X you'll destroy the world.

- Don't build a business around a hack that Linden Lab will eventually have to fix unless you think you can build up a large enough community or user base or collection of data that you can redirect towards something else later on.

- Don't think that what happens in *Second Life* stays in *Second Life*—not just in using outside programs and the Web and doing mixed-reality projects that span multiple media channels, but if you start a business in *Second Life*, pay attention to how what you create can transfer to another kind of marketplace, and what kinds of lessons you can learn and things you can come up with in *Second Life* before it's possible to do them anywhere else.

THE SCULPTED-PRIMS CREATOR: LINDEN LAB ENGINEER QARL LINDEN

CHAPTER 1
CHAPTER 2
CHAPTER 3
CHAPTER 4
CHAPTER 5
CHAPTER 6
CHAPTER 7
CHAPTER 8
CHAPTER 9
CHAPTER 10
CHAPTER 11
APPENDICES
INDEX

Figure 11.3: Qarl Linden, the creator of sculpted prims

To many people, the most exciting *Second Life* technological innovation in recent memory is the sculpted prim (sculptie). That's because sculpties allow content creators to make objects and designs that are significantly higher-quality and more realistic than anything that was possible using traditional prims. It's still not entirely clear what effect the new tools will have on the future of business in *Second Life*, but it's almost certain to open the doors to entirely new types of content creators and new kinds of products.

For one person, sculpties are more than a great new arrow in the quiver. For Qarl Linden (Figure 11.3), who created sculpted prims, they are his baby. He took some time to talk about sculpties and how they'll change *Second Life*.

Q: **Where did the idea for sculpted prims come from?**

QL: They originated with an old computer-graphics trick called "displacement maps."

Q: **What's that?**

QL: Basically, you have this simple geometric shape. But you want to add surface detail to it. Like if you have the moon, which is a sphere, but you want to add craters. The shape of the surface is put into a texture map—grayscale—that says how high to make the surface of the moon at different spots. It's an easy idea, but once you use it a few times it becomes extremely powerful. For example, we used displacement maps—procedural ones—to animate the wheat fields for [the film] *300*. [Qarl worked on the film in real life.] But displacement maps are grayscale, so they can't hold the entire shape. With sculpt maps, we use all three channels (red, green, blue) for the position data.

Q: **How long did it take to make sculpties a reality?**

QL: Well, one of the nice things about the sculpties is that they were extremely easy to implement. I had a demo version up and running in only a couple days. We make our old prims by using trigonometric functions. So a torus is shaped with a bunch of calls

CHAPTER 11

THE SKY'S
THE LIMIT

FUTURE
BUSINESS
OPPORTUNI-
TIES

to `sin()` and `cos()`. A sculptie is made in exactly the same way, but each call to `sin()` is replaced by a call to a texture look-up. So that makes the core definition easy. The hardest part is the graphical user interface, and updating the geometry as the texture loads. But that's one reason why I like them so much. They're a simple concept.

Q: **How will sculpties affect the business dynamic in *Second Life*?**

QL: With sculpties you can create *much* more detailed items, like a realistic ant (Figure 11.4). It was done with sculpties. So I think the successful artists will want or need to use sculpties to make their work stand out.

Figure 11.4: This ant, created using sculpted prims, is much more realistic-looking than was possible before.

Q: **Do you think that sculpties will open up opportunities to a whole new kind of person, 3D designers who were staying away from *Second Life* before, but will now be able to come in and create good stuff?**

QL: Yes, absolutely. For example, that ant. The original was made by a 3D designer friend of mine years ago. With sculpties, I was able to import it without much effort. And my friend is, in fact, exactly that kind of person. He's staying away from *Second Life* until he can do these sorts of things. And in part, I made sculpties to try to draw him—and others like him—into *Second Life*. Meanwhile, I know the Electric Sheep are seriously looking at sculpties for their new projects. Projects that weren't possible before. But I don't think I can talk about that.

Q: **And over time, would you think that those not working in sculpties are going to have trouble selling things, particularly when others in the same field are?**

QL: Sadly, yes. I think that'll become more true.

Q: **Why sadly?**

QL: Because I think there are a bunch of aspiring *Second Life* artists who feel that sculpties are out of their reach.

Q: **What's your take on that?**

QL: I think they feel that programs like Maya and Blender are too hard to learn. But [*Second Life* designer] Ordinal Malaprop had an interesting take on that: "This not only allows other modelers to come in but also gives residents an incentive to learn skills which are useful outside of *Second Life*. I have been worried for a while that *Second Life* building would end up being some sort of ghetto." I tend to agree with her. There's a *huge* 3D world outside of *Second Life*, and I think we do our residents a service by encouraging them to "get out."

Q: **Do you have a few suggestions someone wanting to incorporate sculpties in their designs should follow?**

QL: First, bake lighting whenever possible. Second, don't go too crazy with detail. The prim should look good from all distances. If you need more detail, use more prims. Third, start with NURBS surfaces (http://en.wikipedia.org/wiki/NURBS) as your basic model type. Meshes are difficult to convert and maintain. And fourth, don't expect to automatically convert models you find on the Internet—it takes some finesse to make a sculptie.

Q: **As sculpties become more widely used, can you imagine there being a time when things designed pre-sculpties (or things designed without them) are simply seen as amateurish?**

QL: I think that's true of *everything* in *Second Life*. If you look at things made a year ago, or two, they really stick out. So yes, but it's not necessarily because of sculpties. It's because we're all getting better at making this world.

APPENDICES

SUPPLEMENTAL INFO

To wrap things up we'll provide some helpful *SL* reference materials, including good sources for additional information, market values for a variety of typical *Second Life* items, and the earning potentials for the primary *SL* business models. We'll also cover Linden Lab's community standards and intellectual property rules.

CONTENTS

APPENDICES

APPENDIX A:
OTHER
RESOURCES

APPENDIX B:
SECOND LIFE
ITEM PRICES

APPENDIX C:
EARNING
POTENTIAL
OF A
SECOND LIFE
ENTREPRENEUR

APPENDIX D:
SL
COMMUNITY
STANDARDS
AND
INTELLECTUAL
PROPERTY

APPENDIX A: OTHER RESOURCES

ARTICLES

"My Virtual Life" (*Business Week*, May 1, 2006), by Robert D. Hof:

www.businessweek.com/magazine/content/06 _ 18/b3982001.htm

This cover story in one of the leading business magazines is a broad look at *Second Life* in which the author discusses spending a good deal of time there and shares his insights on many of the elements of the virtual world. He goes into depth about the *Second Life* economy, including a look at Anshe Chung and her blossoming real-estate empire.

"Second Life: It's not a game" (*Fortune*, January 22, 2007), by David Kirkpatrick:

http://money.cnn.com/2007/01/22/magazines/fortune/whatsnext _ secondlife.
fortune/index.htm?cnn=yes

This article looks in some depth at IBM's efforts and investments in the virtual world, as well as the rationale behind the economy of *Second Life*.

"Making a Living in Second Life" (*Wired*, February 8, 2006), by Kathleen Craig:

www.wired.com/news/technology/1,70153-0.html

The first widely read article that looked at the way *Second Life* residents were using the virtual world to make real money. It investigates several ways that users were doing so, and features comments from users about their methods.

"Second Lifers get hands on code" (BBC News, January 9, 2007):

http://news.bbc.co.uk/2/hi/technology/6245599.stm

This British article examines the importance of Linden Lab's decision to open-source the *Second Life* client, and what that means for its residents, its economy, and more.

"Second Life Lessons" (*Business Week*, October 30, 2006), by Reena Jana and Aili McConnon:

www.businessweek.com/innovate/content/oct2006/id20061030 _ 869611.
htm?chan=innovation _ innovation+%2B+design _ innovation+and+design+lead

This *Business Week* article looks at what big companies interested in establishing a presence in *Second Life* needed to learn about doing so and how they could benefit. The article was one of the first on this topic, and presaged dozens of Fortune 500 companies entering the virtual world.

"The Virtual Rockefeller" (*Business 2.0*, December 1, 2005), by Paul Sloan:

http://money.cnn.com/magazines/business2/business2 _ archive/2005/12/01/
8364581/index.htm

This article discusses Anshe Chung, her *Second Life* real-estate empire, and the implications for the economy and residents of the virtual world.

"Your Second Life Is Ready" (*Popular Science*, September 2006), by Annalee Newitz:

http://www.popsci.com/popsci/technology/
7ba1af8f3812d010vgnvcm1000004eecbccdrcrd.html

This fairly broad article about *Second Life* looks at, among other things, the thousands of people who are earning substantial amounts of real money in the virtual world.

"The Second Life Economy" (*Second Life* blog, August 14, 2007), by Zee Linden:

http://blog.secondlife.com/2007/08/14/the-second-life-economy/

This entry on the official *Second Life* blog is an up-to-date discussion of the virtual world's economy, including a look at some of the most common questions about the economy.

■ BOOKS

Second Life: The Official Guide (Wiley, 2006), by Michael Rymaszewski, Wagner James Au, Mark Wallace, et al.

This guide is intended to teach users the basic aspects of *Second Life*—how to move around, how to communicate with others, how to customize the appearance of their avatars, how to build things, how to shop, and more. Essentially, it's a user's manual and general orientation guide.

CHAPTER 1
CHAPTER 2
CHAPTER 3
CHAPTER 4
CHAPTER 5
CHAPTER 6
CHAPTER 7
CHAPTER 8
CHAPTER 9
CHAPTER 10
CHAPTER 11
APPENDICES

INDEX

APPENDICES

APPENDIX A:
OTHER
RESOURCES

APPENDIX B:
SECOND LIFE
ITEM PRICES

APPENDIX C:
EARNING
POTENTIAL
OF A
SECOND LIFE
ENTREPRENEUR

APPENDIX D:
SL
COMMUNITY
STANDARDS
AND
INTELLECTUAL
PROPERTY

Creating Your World: The Official Guide to Advanced Content Creation for Second Life (Wiley, 2007), by Aimee Weber, Kimberly Rufer-Bach, and Richard Platel.

Creating Your World is the official guide to learning how to create advanced content in *Second Life*. The book is aimed at people who want to learn how to design things like clothing, buildings, avatars, and the like. It is a perfect complement to this book.

Play Money: Or, How I Quit My Day Job and Made Millions Trading Virtual Loot (Basic Books, 2006), by Julian Dibbell.

Play Money is about the author's attempt over a couple of years to make a living by illicitly buying and selling the virtual goods of the online game *Ultima Online.* Dibbell uses that story as a way to get into a sophisticated, almost academic, explanation of the way virtual economies like that of *Ultima Online, Second Life, World of Warcraft,* and other online worlds work.

Synthetic Worlds: The Business and Culture of Online Games (University of Chicago Press, 2006), by Edward Castronova.

Castronova is the leading expert on the economies of virtual worlds, and his book is an intelligent, thoughtful examination of how those worlds work, how their cultures develop, and how their economies flourish (or don't).

BLOGS AND OTHER NEWS SITES

Second Life Herald

www.secondlifeherald.com/

One of the oldest and most read *Second Life* blogs, the *Herald* covers the virtual world with a challenging, irreverent tone and with a healthy roster of plugged-in writers. It is among the first places to go to get the residents' perspective on the latest *Second Life* news and issues of the day.

3pointD

www.3pointd.com/

Edited by veteran journalist Mark Wallace, 3pointD is an informed, intelligent, and analytic take on the latest news of *Second Life* and other virtual worlds.

Clickable Culture

www.secretlair.com/index.php?/clickableculture/

Written by Tony Walsh, Clickable Culture focuses on news and other developments related to virtual worlds and interactive entertainment.

Reuters' *Second Life* News Center

http://secondlife.reuters.com/

Regular coverage of *Second Life* by one of the world's leading wire services.

CNET News.com's *Second Life* coverage

http://news.com.com/2990-5 _ 3-1.html?target=&query="Second%20Life"&tag=srch

The latest news articles and blog entries about *Second Life* from CNET News.com, one of the pioneers of covering the virtual world.

Second Style Fashionista

http://blog.secondstyle.com/

One of the leading blogs about *Second Life* fashion, Fashionista takes a regular look at the latest products, designers, and trends in the fashion industry.

Terra Nova

http://terranova.blogs.com/

The most influential academic blog about virtual worlds, Terra Nova is a collaboration by several of the leading researchers in the field and covers a broad spectrum of issues, including the economic, social, and intellectual elements of virtual worlds.

Linden Lab Blog

http://blog.secondlife.com/

The official *Second Life* blog, written by Linden Lab staff members.

CHAPTER 1
CHAPTER 2
CHAPTER 3
CHAPTER 4
CHAPTER 5
CHAPTER 6
CHAPTER 7
CHAPTER 8
CHAPTER 9
CHAPTER 10
CHAPTER 11
APPENDICES

INDEX

APPENDICES

APPENDIX A:
OTHER
RESOURCES

APPENDIX B:
SECOND LIFE
ITEM PRICES

APPENDIX C:
EARNING
POTENTIAL
OF A
SECOND LIFE
ENTREPRENEUR

APPENDIX D:
SL
COMMUNITY
STANDARDS
AND
INTELLECTUAL
PROPERTY

New World Notes

http://nwn.blogs.com/

The original *Second Life* blog, New World Notes is edited by veteran journalist Wagner James Au. It offers regular, on-the-ground coverage of the virtual world through the eyes of one of its most veteran observers.

The Metaverse Messenger

www.metaversemessenger.com/

A weekly *Second Life* newspaper covering events and news from inside the virtual world.

Second Life Forums

http://forums.secondlife.com/

The official community site for *Second Life* residents is a place where business owners can post their latest products and services and where residents can discuss the issues of the day.

Second Life Insider

www.secondlifeinsider.com/

A good, general-interest *Second Life* blog written by residents who are well-informed and who have valuable opinions.

CHAPTER 1
CHAPTER 2
CHAPTER 3
CHAPTER 4
CHAPTER 5
CHAPTER 6
CHAPTER 7
CHAPTER 8
CHAPTER 9
CHAPTER 10
CHAPTER 11
APPENDICES

INDEX

APPENDIX B: *SECOND LIFE* ITEM PRICES

As noted earlier in the book, the *Second Life* economy is a micro-economy. That is, even when things like clothing, cars, or swords cost several hundred or even a thousand Linden dollars, they're still only a few US dollars.

Prices can vary drastically in individual categories of items, and the differences have to do with quality, features, flexibility, and more. Generally, the cheaper items are no-frills, while the more expensive goods have wide varieties of extras, bonus features, flexibility, and such.

In general, prices listed here will be in Linden dollars, though when discussing real-estate pricing, it will be in US dollars.

It's important to remember that these prices are ranges, and that it is also possible to find things cheaper—generally very low-quality things—or more expensive than these ranges would indicate.

There are thousands upon thousands of different kinds of items for sale in *Second Life*, so it is impossible to provide an exhaustive list. The items listed here are just examples of what's available and what things cost.

REAL ESTATE

In *Second Life*, real estate is unlike any other category of business, as pricing is often in US dollars and can be much more expensive than the typical prices for fashion, gadgets, and the like.

That's because land is one of the few things in *Second Life* that has a real-world cost associated with it, given that it's based on actual server space.

Land is available in whole sims, as well as in fractions of sims. Also, there is property available on the islands and on the mainland, and pricing tends to be different for each.

- Whole islands for sale by Linden Lab: US$1,675 plus US$295 a month

- Mainland sims at auction: US$1,700–2,100 plus US$195 a month

- 1/128 of a sim for sale by a developer: US$10–15 plus US$3 a month

APPENDICES

APPENDIX A:
OTHER
RESOURCES

APPENDIX B:
SECOND LIFE
ITEM PRICES

APPENDIX C:
EARNING
POTENTIAL
OF A
SECOND LIFE
ENTREPRENEUR

APPENDIX D:
SL
COMMUNITY
STANDARDS
AND
INTELLECTUAL
PROPERTY

- 1/64 of a sim for sale by a developer: US$20–25 plus US$6 a month

- 1/32 of a sim for sale by a developer: US$45–50 plus US$12 a month

- 1/16 of a sim for sale by a developer: US$85–100 plus US$24 a month

- 1/8 of a sim for sale by a developer: US$175–200 plus US$45–50 a month

- 1/4 of a sim for sale by a developer: US$375–400 plus US$90–100 a month

- 1/2 of a sim for sale by a developer: US$750–800 plus US$150–175 a month

- Full sim for sale by a developer: US$1,500–1,600 plus US$325–350 a month

- 1/32 of a sim for rent by a developer: US$14–18 a month

- 1/16 of a sim for rent by a developer: US$26–32 a month

- 1/8 of a sim for rent by a developer: US$55–65 a month

- 1/4 of a sim for rent by a developer: US$110–125 a month

- 1/2 of a sim for rent by a developer: US$230–250 a month

- Full sim for rent by a developer: US$395–440 a month

■ FASHION

As discussed in Chapter 4, "Walking the Runway: Fashion in *Second Life*," fashion means many things. This section offers a cross-section of different categories of items and ranges of what things in those categories can cost, which should give you an idea of what you could charge for new items.

- Prim hair: L$100–600

- Day outfits, such as sundresses: L$200–300

- Special formal outfits, which will likely come with lots of extras like a hat, sword, or scripted item: L$800–1,500

- Regular shoes, such as loafers or leather slip-ons: L$400–800

- Boots: L$500–1,000

- Sandals and slip-on shoes: L$200–350

- Accessories like a fancy negligee with high-heeled slippers: L$650

- Typical full outfit, complete except for shoes, day or night: L$300–400

- Bathing suit: L$100–200

- Hand-drawn complete outfits: L$300–800

- Transformer avatar with wings: L$1,100–3,000

- Women's skins: L$600–3,000 depending on quality, detail, and whether they come with packages of multiple skins in different colors and shapes

- Men's skins: L$1,200–2,200

- Body shapes: L$400–3,000

- Tattoos: L$100–500

- T-shirts: L$50–150

- Pants: L$100–350

- Jackets: L$150–400

- Casual shirts: L$150–200

- Glasses: L$150–300

- Hats: L$50–300

CHAPTER 1
CHAPTER 2
CHAPTER 3
CHAPTER 4
CHAPTER 5
CHAPTER 6
CHAPTER 7
CHAPTER 8
CHAPTER 9
CHAPTER 10
CHAPTER 11
APPENDICES

INDEX

BUILDING

Second Life seems to have an almost limitless supply of buildings. Many were created by their owners, while many others were bought from the builders.

Of the latter category, some are prefab buildings, which tend to cost less up front, but which can be sold again and again and earn their builders more over time. Some are custom buildings, which are generally one-offs. Custom work also tends to pay an hourly rate, rather than a set fee.

This category also includes some of the building blocks, such as stairs, teleporters, and the like that make up buildings in *Second Life*.

- Custom work: US$15 and US$65 an hour, depending on your skills and how well known you are for the work

- Prefabs: Starting at a baseline of L$50–150 for the most simple prefab buildings

- A small prefab skybox: L$999

- A big, fancy modern house: L$4,500

- Gothic castles: $4,000–18,500, depending on quality, features, and many other factors

- Standard prefab houses: L$1,200–7,500, though specialty houses can go for much more

- A prefab store/shop: L$800–6,000, with most in the L$1,000 range

APPENDICES

APPENDIX A:
OTHER
RESOURCES

APPENDIX B:
SECOND LIFE
ITEM PRICES

APPENDIX C:
EARNING
POTENTIAL
OF A
SECOND LIFE
ENTREPRENEUR

APPENDIX D:
SL
COMMUNITY
STANDARDS
AND
INTELLECTUAL
PROPERTY

- Building packs (packages with windows, walls, and other building blocks): L$2,500–10,000

- Scripted stairs: L$800

- Scripted windows-building kit (allows buyer to build as many as they want): L$2,000

- Pools and spas: L$400–3,000

- Erupting-volcano kit: L$30,000

- Elevator-building script: L$3,800

- Teleporter script: L$50–1,000

ADULT-ORIENTED ITEMS

As is discussed in Chapter 7, "Making Money in the *Second Life* Sex Trade," there is a flourishing adult-oriented business in *Second Life*. The goods and services available in that genre may make some people blush, but for others, it's a great way to make money or a terrific way to spend it.

Here is a breakdown of some of the pricing for products and services available in this area.

- Adult-oriented fashion: L$1,000 or less, depending on the item; "Sexy Nurse" lingerie might go for L$400, for example

- A package of sexual sound effects: L$300

- A set of bath accessories that go with sexy bathroom furniture: L$300

- Strap-on male genitalia: L$1,000

- Male or female genitals: L$400–750

- Escorts who perform sexual services to paying clients: L$200–4,000 an hour, depending on the escort's experience, skill, wardrobe, and other factors

- A tickler and duster set: L$150

- Blindfolds: L$200

- Vibrators: L$175

- Paddles: L$150

- Sexual animations: L$250–500, depending on their complexity

- Sex beds: L$500–12,000, depending on features and number of included animations

- A St. Andrew's Cross: L$250.

- Slave crates: L$150

TOYS AND GADGETS

CHAPTER 1
CHAPTER 2
CHAPTER 3
CHAPTER 4
CHAPTER 5
CHAPTER 6
CHAPTER 7
CHAPTER 8
CHAPTER 9
CHAPTER 10
CHAPTER 11
APPENDICES

INDEX

Perhaps the most varied business category in *Second Life* is gadgets and toys. The nearly endless variety of products in this category, which is discussed in Chapter 8, "Selling Objects, from Toys to Weapons," commands an equally wide range of prices.

- Tiny animals, such as cats, rabbits, or dragons, that can be worn on the shoulder or chest: $L300

- Scripted animals like cats, chickens, turkeys, or ducks, that perform tricks on command: L$100–175

- Samurai swords: L$300–900

- A Colt .45 pistol: L$875

- Other handguns and machine guns: L$600–2,000

- Crossbows: L$400

- Flamethrowers: L$800

- Replicas of famous cars like the General Lee from *The Dukes of Hazzard*: L$700–1,200

- Sports cars: L$1,500

- Luxury cars: L$995–3,000

- Spaceships: L$1,000–2,000

- Military aircraft: L$2,200

- Elven Drums: L$1,500

- Pianos: L$200–950

- Catavina guitar with case: L$450

- Bagpipes: L$350

- Fender Deluxe White Stratocaster guitar: L$375

- Violin: L$400

- Drum and bass set: L$1,250

- Specialty furniture: L$400–600

- Household furniture: L$10–245

- Low-prim furniture: L$150–350

- Modern office furniture: L$100–500

- A wooden garden bridge: L$150

APPENDICES

APPENDIX A:
OTHER
RESOURCES

APPENDIX B:
SECOND LIFE
ITEM PRICES

APPENDIX C:
EARNING
POTENTIAL
OF A
SECOND LIFE
ENTREPRENEUR

APPENDIX D:
SL
COMMUNITY
STANDARDS
AND
INTELLECTUAL
PROPERTY

- A four-level bursting fountain: L$150

- A baby crib: L$150

- A Superman bunk bed: L$200

- An L-shaped kitchen unit: L$200

- A pool table: L$400

- A Gothic velvet bed: L$445

- A heads-up display (HUD) with many built-in animations: L$1,499

- Necklace and earring sets: L$300–500

- Emerald ring and bracelet sets: L$250

- Diamond earrings: L$200

- A color-changing necklace: L$399

- Men's twisted-link bracelets: L$225

- Men's rings, in gold, silver, diamonds, and other gems: L$125

- Specialty lunchboxes: L$350

- A birdwatcher set with binoculars: L$350

- A Soviet bookbag: L$900

APPENDIX C: EARNING POTENTIAL OF A *SECOND LIFE* ENTREPRENEUR

Since this is a book about entrepreneurship in *Second Life*, it's only natural that you will want to know how much you can make with a business in the virtual world. It's hard to answer exactly, however, because almost no successful *SL* entrepreneur will say precisely how much they make. For some it's a matter or privacy. For others it's about not bragging, or keeping competitors guessing.

Still, most of the entrepreneurs I talked to for this book were willing to discuss their earnings in some way. One thing is for sure: the most successful people in each area of the *Second Life* economy are doing very well. There's no question that many people are making full-time livings in this business, though of course a full-time living means different numbers in different parts of the world.

The lesson of the book, however, is that if you're smart about how you go about running your *Second Life* business, you can make money at it, whether it's enough to just cover your expenses or whether it's US$80,000 a year. It all depends on you.

REAL ESTATE

You may have heard that *Second Life* real-estate baroness Anshe Chung is a millionaire and that she makes several hundred thousand US dollars a year with her business. The truth is that no one except Anshe Chung and her business partner and husband really know, but there's no reason to doubt it, given her domination of the *SL* real-estate business.

Still, it's pretty unlikely that anyone new to the business is going to approach those figures, because Chung and the other leading entrepreneurs in the field control such a large percentage of the available land. However, that doesn't mean you can't make money in *Second Life* real estate. You'll just have to be willing to put up a lot of capital to get started (see Chapter 5, "The *Second Life* Land Business") and bide your time for eight months to a year to see the fruits of your investment.

As to how much you can make, it's hard to say. If you do put up the capital, have strong business skills, and are committed to your business, you could make several hundred US dollars a month on the low end to US$1,000 or more on the higher end. It all depends on the scale of the business you want to run and how good you are at it.

APPENDICES

APPENDIX A:
OTHER
RESOURCES

APPENDIX B:
SECOND LIFE
ITEM PRICES

APPENDIX C:
EARNING
POTENTIAL
OF A
SECOND LIFE
ENTREPRENEUR

APPENDIX D:
SL
COMMUNITY
STANDARDS
AND
INTELLECTUAL
PROPERTY

FASHION

As the most visible and active segment of the *Second Life* economy, it's no surprise that the most successful fashion designers are making a lot of money. The very top designers, in fact, are said to be making more than US$100,000 a year, though it must be noted that very, very few people will be able to approach this level. Others who are fully committed to their *SL* fashion businesses and who have great talent will be able to make more-modest livings, in the US$30,000 to US$60,000 range.

But these individuals represent the cream of the crop, and most people are not going to be able to do as well. Much more likely is that people who put 10 to 20 hours a week into their businesses and who are talented, innovative, and willing to stay abreast of the latest trends will see profits of between US$100 and US$1,000 per month.

Regardless, you'll be able to make money in *SL* only if you are able to sell a significant amount of product, because prices (see Appendix B) in this micro-economy are low.

BUILDING

For a small group of building success stories, *Second Life* has been the key to a full-time living. These are the people who are considered the leaders in their respective areas of building, whether it's in castles, office structures, or entire sims. All told, a handful of people make their entire living building in *SL*, and it's certainly possible that more people could join those ranks.

For those who focus on doing custom building, their earnings are going to be based on how well they're known. Pay for custom work ranges from US$15 to US$65 an hour, depending entirely on how well the builder is known and the quality of their work.

For prefab builders, there's no easy formula for understanding potential earnings, other than to say that talent plus commitment plus time equals good money. Someone new to the business who has skills and commitment could easily earn US$100 a month, or even US$500 to US$1,000.

But to make much more than that will require a notable level of skill, plus the time, commitment, and business skills to make high levels of sales.

ADULT-ORIENTED BUSINESSES

There are three areas of the adult-oriented *Second Life* business world where significant money can be made.

First is creating and building a well-known and well-regarded store that sells a wide variety of sex toys, genitalia, and other items. For those who are able to reach the top levels of this industry, it's easy to imagine making US$80,000 to US$100,000, given that there is a huge amount of interest. Still, this group is going to be limited to a small number of entrepreneurs, just as in other areas of the *SL* economy.

Second, and more commonly, people will start a business selling a highly regarded product line but they can't quite crack the top echelons, either in terms of quality and breadth of product line, or in terms of marketing skill. Still, these people could earn hundreds of US dollars each month, and possibly even US$1,000–2,000. For others whose skills aren't top-notch, the competition is fierce. Still, there is enough interest in adult-oriented products to imagine a lot of people being able to reach US$100 per month.

Third, escorts can do pretty well. The best ones are making around US$15–20 an hour without having to worry much about technical skills, operating a store, or any of the things that make other segments of the *SL* economy more complicated.

For those who are below the top tier, it's more common to be making much less, but still accumulating US$5–10 a day. Indeed, some say that escorting is the single easiest way to make money from the start in *SL*.

TOYS AND GADGETS

Given that there are so many different kinds of businesses that fall into this category, it's hard to sum it all up. In general, the profits in this segment of the economy will be lower than that of others, such as fashion, real estate, or the adult industry.

That's not to say that some people won't find a way to make significant amounts of money. However, if you want to be in this area, you should probably think about profits on the order of US$100–500 a month unless you're at the very top of the field.

Some jewelry designers are making enough money to earn a full-time living, although no one is yet making the kind of money the top fashion designers are pulling in.

INTERACTIVE OPPORTUNITIES

There are three lucrative interactive opportunities in *Second Life*.

DJING

The first is DJing, even though a plethora of people have chosen this route. The top DJs commonly get paid around US$35–50 per hour for high-profile gigs. Other well-known DJs can expect to earn around L$1,500 an hour (about US$5.50) for less-visible work. To make good money doing this kind of work, it's necessary to hustle and find a variety of employers. You also might want to run your own small club to DJ in when other work isn't available.

CHAPTER 1
CHAPTER 2
CHAPTER 3
CHAPTER 4
CHAPTER 5
CHAPTER 6
CHAPTER 7
CHAPTER 8
CHAPTER 9
CHAPTER 10
CHAPTER 11
APPENDICES

INDEX

APPENDICES

APPENDIX A:
OTHER
RESOURCES

APPENDIX B:
SECOND LIFE
ITEM PRICES

APPENDIX C:
EARNING
POTENTIAL
OF A
SECOND LIFE
ENTREPRENEUR

APPENDIX D:
SL
COMMUNITY
STANDARDS
AND
INTELLECTUAL
PROPERTY

However, clubs really only want DJs at night, which reduces the number of hours that can be worked. So, although it's possible there are a few DJs making a full-time living, the bulk of those working steadily are probably topping out at around US$2,000–3,000 a month.

DANCING

Club dancers can make steady money, even if it's not as good as the pay for DJing. Dancers usually get most of the tips left by patrons and also can get hourly pay from venue owners. This kind of work is easy, requires little investment, and can pay between US$500 and US$1,000 a month for the most talented and business-savvy performers.

NEWSPAPERS, MAGAZINES, AND BLOGS

There's certainly money to be made in this area, as demonstrated by the full-time living that *The Metaverse Messenger* founder Katt Kongo is earning with her work. However, there probably won't be many more people who earn a full-time living in this field—the competition is strong and the skills required to succeed are limiting.

Still, if what you want is to earn US$100 or a little more each month, this is probably a good industry to try out if you have some writing and editing skills, the ability to get others to work for you, and some business savvy.

TEEN SECOND LIFE

Teens are limited to buying only US$25 worth of Linden dollars a month and the population is much lower than in the main grid, so the economy of *Teen Second Life* is much smaller. Because the amount of money in the economy is simply far less, the earning potential also is lower. Still, there are teens making money in their grid.

The top earners—and it's a small group—are earning between US$400 and US$800 a month during summers, when school is out, and a little bit less when they're in classes.

More likely, teens who have some business skills and who commit to their businesses can expect to earn enough to pay for their *Second Life* expenses and perhaps have a little left over. It's certainly possible for those who do commit to the work to make US$100 a month or a little more.

Perhaps more important, developing skills in the teen grid puts entrepreneurs there in position to jump right into making much more money once they turn 18 and graduate to the main grid.

CHAPTER 1
CHAPTER 2
CHAPTER 3
CHAPTER 4
CHAPTER 5
CHAPTER 6
CHAPTER 7
CHAPTER 8
CHAPTER 9
CHAPTER 10
CHAPTER 11
APPENDICES

INDEX

APPENDIX D: *SL* COMMUNITY STANDARDS AND INTELLECTUAL PROPERTY

It's important to know *Second Life*'s community standards and excellent intellectual property policies. Here they are, and you can visit `http://secondlife.com/corporate/cs.php` to get the latest community standards and see Section 3.2 of the Terms of Service (`http://secondlife.com/corporate/tos.php`) for up-to-date intellectual property information.

COMMUNITY STANDARDS

Welcome to *Second Life*.

We hope you'll have a richly rewarding experience, filled with creativity, self expression, and fun.

The goals of the Community Standards are simple: treat each other with respect and without harassment, adhere to local standards as indicated by simulator ratings, and refrain from any hate activity which slurs a real-world individual or real-world community.

Within *Second Life*, we want to support Residents in shaping their specific experiences and making their own choices.

The Community Standards sets out six behaviors, the "**Big Six,**" that will result in suspension or, with repeated violations, expulsion from the *Second Life* Community.

All *Second Life* Community Standards apply to all areas of *Second Life*, the *Second Life* Forums, and the *Second Life* Website.

1. **Intolerance:** Combating intolerance is a cornerstone of *Second Life*'s Community Standards. Actions that marginalize, belittle, or defame individuals or groups inhibit the satisfying exchange of ideas and diminish the *Second Life* community as whole. The use of derogatory or demeaning language or images in reference to another Resident's race, ethnicity, gender, religion, or sexual orientation is never allowed in *Second Life*.

2. **Harassment:** Given the myriad capabilities of *Second Life*, harassment can take many forms. Communicating or behaving in a manner which is offensively coarse, intimidating or threatening, constitutes unwelcome sexual advances or requests for sexual favors, or is otherwise likely to cause annoyance or alarm is Harassment.

APPENDICES

APPENDIX A:
OTHER
RESOURCES

APPENDIX B:
SECOND LIFE
ITEM PRICES

APPENDIX C:
EARNING
POTENTIAL
OF A
SECOND LIFE
ENTREPRENEUR

APPENDIX D:
SL
COMMUNITY
STANDARDS
AND
INTELLECTUAL
PROPERTY

3. **Assault:** Most areas in *Second Life* are identified as Safe. Assault in *Second Life* means: shooting, pushing, or shoving another Resident in a Safe Area (see Global Standards below); creating or using scripted objects which singularly or persistently target another Resident in a manner which prevents their enjoyment of *Second Life*.

4. **Disclosure:** Residents are entitled to a reasonable level of privacy with regard to their Second Lives. Sharing personal information about a fellow Resident—including gender, religion, age, marital status, race, sexual preference, and real-world location beyond what is provided by the Resident in the First Life page of their Resident profile is a violation of that Resident's privacy. Remotely monitoring conversations, posting conversation logs, or sharing conversation logs without consent are all prohibited in *Second Life* and on the *Second Life* Forums.

5. **Indecency:** *Second Life* is an adult community, but Mature material is not necessarily appropriate in all areas (see Global Standards below). Content, communication, or behavior which involves intense language or expletives, nudity or sexual content, the depiction of sex or violence, or anything else broadly offensive must be contained within private land in areas rated Mature (M). Names of Residents, objects, places and groups are broadly viewable in *Second Life* directories and on the *Second Life* website, and must adhere to PG guidelines.

6. **Disturbing the Peace:** Every Resident has a right to live their Second Life. Disrupting scheduled events, repeated transmission of undesired advertising content, the use of repetitive sounds, following or self-spawning items, or other objects that intentionally slow server performance or inhibit another Resident's ability to enjoy *Second Life* are examples of Disturbing the Peace.

■ POLICIES AND POLICING

GLOBAL STANDARDS, LOCAL RATINGS

All areas of *Second Life*, including the www.secondlife.com website and the *Second Life* Forums, adhere to the same Community Standards. Locations within *Second Life* are noted as Safe or Unsafe and rated Mature (M) or non-Mature (PG), and behavior must conform to the local ratings. Any unrated area of *Second Life* or the *Second Life* website should be considered non-Mature (PG).

WARNING, SUSPENSION, BANISHMENT

Second Life is a complex society, and it can take some time for new Residents to gain a full understanding of local customs and mores. Generally, violations of the Community Standards will first result in a Warning, followed by Suspension and eventual Banishment from *Second Life*. In-World Representatives, called Liaisons, may occasionally address disciplinary problems with a temporary removal from *Second Life*.

GLOBAL ATTACKS

Objects, scripts, or actions which broadly interfere with or disrupt the *Second Life* community, the *Second Life* servers or other systems related to *Second Life* will not be tolerated in any form. We will hold you responsible for any actions you take, or that are taken by objects or scripts that belong to you. Sandboxes are available for testing objects and scripts that have components that may be unmanageable or whose behavior you may not be able to predict. If you choose to use a script that substantially disrupts the operation of *Second Life*, disciplinary actions will result in a minimum two-week suspension, the possible loss of in-world inventory, and a review of your account for probable expulsion from *Second Life*.

ALTERNATE ACCOUNTS

While Residents may choose to play *Second Life* with more than one account, specifically or consistently using an alternate account to harass other Residents or violate the Community Standards is not acceptable. Alternate accounts are generally treated as separate from a Resident's principal account, but misuse of alternate accounts can and will result in disciplinary action on the principal account.

BUYER BEWARE

Linden Lab does not exercise editorial control over the content of *Second Life*, and will make no specific efforts to review the textures, objects, sounds or other content created within *Second Life*. Additionally, Linden Lab does not certify or endorse the operation of in-world games, vending machines, or retail locations; refunds must be requested from the owners of these objects.

REPORTING ABUSE

Residents should report violations of the Community Standards using the Abuse Reporter tool located under the Help menu in the in-world tool bar. Every Abuse Report is individually investigated, and the identity of the reporter is kept strictly confidential. If you need immediate assistance, in-world Liaisons may be available to help. Look for Residents with the last name Linden.

INTELLECTUAL PROPERTY

You retain copyright and other intellectual property rights with respect to Content you create in *Second Life*, to the extent that you have such rights under applicable law. However, you must make certain representations and warranties, and provide certain license rights, forbearances and indemnification, to Linden Lab and to other users of *Second Life*.

Users of the Service can create Content on Linden Lab's servers in various forms. Linden Lab acknowledges and agrees that, subject to the terms and conditions of this Agreement, you will retain any and all applicable copyright and other intellectual property

CHAPTER 1
CHAPTER 2
CHAPTER 3
CHAPTER 4
CHAPTER 5
CHAPTER 6
CHAPTER 7
CHAPTER 8
CHAPTER 9
CHAPTER 10
CHAPTER 11
APPENDICES

INDEX

APPENDICES

APPENDIX A:
OTHER
RESOURCES

APPENDIX B:
SECOND LIFE
ITEM PRICES

APPENDIX C:
EARNING
POTENTIAL
OF A
SECOND LIFE
ENTREPRENEUR

APPENDIX D:
SL
COMMUNITY
STANDARDS
AND
INTELLECTUAL
PROPERTY

rights with respect to any Content you create using the Service, to the extent you have such rights under applicable law.

MORE INFO

WHAT ARE IP RIGHTS?

A thumbnail version of the *Second Life* intellectual property is (quoting from `http://secondlife.com/whatis/ip _ rights.php`): Linden Lab's Terms of Service agreement recognizes Residents' right to retain full intellectual property protection for the digital content they create in *Second Life*, including avatar characters, clothing, scripts, textures, objects, and designs. This right is enforceable and applicable both in-world and offline, both for non-profit and commercial ventures. You create it, you own it—and it's yours to do with as you please.

Notwithstanding the foregoing, you understand and agree that by submitting your Content to any area of the service, you automatically grant (and you represent and warrant that you have the right to grant) to Linden Lab: (a) a royalty-free, worldwide, fully paid-up, perpetual, irrevocable, non-exclusive right and license to (i) use, reproduce and distribute your Content within the Service as permitted by you through your interactions on the Service, and (ii) use and reproduce (and to authorize third parties to use and reproduce) any of your Content in any or all media for marketing and/or promotional purposes in connection with the Service, provided that in the event that your Content appears publicly in material under the control of Linden Lab, and you provide written notice to Linden Lab of your desire to discontinue the distribution of such Content in such material (with sufficient specificity to allow Linden Lab, in its sole discretion, to identify the relevant Content and materials), Linden Lab will make commercially reasonable efforts to cease its distribution of such Content following the receipt of such notice, although Linden Lab cannot provide any assurances regarding materials produced or distributed prior to the receipt of such notice; (b) the perpetual and irrevocable right to delete any or all of your Content from Linden Lab's servers and from the Service, whether intentionally or unintentionally, and for any reason or no reason, without any liability of any kind to you or any other party; and (c) a royalty-free, fully paid-up, perpetual, irrevocable, non-exclusive right and license to copy, analyze and use any of your Content as Linden Lab may deem necessary or desirable for purposes of debugging, testing and/or providing support services in connection with the Service. Further, you agree to grant to Linden Lab a royalty-free, worldwide, fully paid-up, perpetual, irrevocable, non-exclusive, sublicensable right and license to exercise the copyright, publicity, and database rights you have in your account information, including any data or other information generated by your account activity, in any media now known or not currently known, in accordance with our privacy policy as set forth below, including the incorporation by reference of terms posted at `http://secondlife.com/corporate/privacy.php`.

You also understand and agree that by submitting your Content to any area of the Service, you automatically grant (or you warrant that the owner of such Content has expressly granted) to Linden Lab and to all other users of the Service a non-exclusive, worldwide, fully paid-up, transferable, irrevocable, royalty-free and perpetual License, under any and all patent rights you may have or obtain with respect to your Content, to use your Content for all purposes within the Service. You further agree that you will not make any claims against Linden Lab or against other users of the Service based on any allegations that any activities by either of the foregoing within the Service infringe your (or anyone else's) patent rights.

You further understand and agree that: (i) you are solely responsible for understanding all copyright, patent, trademark, trade secret and other intellectual property or other laws that may apply to your Content hereunder; (ii) you are solely responsible for, and Linden Lab will have no liability in connection with, the legal consequences of any actions or failures to act on your part while using the Service, including without limitation any legal consequences relating to your intellectual property rights; and (iii) Linden Lab's acknowledgement hereunder of your intellectual property rights in your Content does not constitute a legal opinion or legal advice, but is intended solely as an expression of Linden Lab's intention not to require users of the Service to forego certain intellectual property rights with respect to Content they create using the Service, subject to the terms of this Agreement.

CHAPTER 1
CHAPTER 2
CHAPTER 3
CHAPTER 4
CHAPTER 5
CHAPTER 6
CHAPTER 7
CHAPTER 8
CHAPTER 9
CHAPTER 10
CHAPTER 11
APPENDICES

INDEX

Note to the Reader:
Throughout this index
boldfaced page numbers
indicate primary discussions
of a topic. *Italicized*
page numbers indicate
illustrations.

A

CHAPTER 1
CHAPTER 2
CHAPTER 3
CHAPTER 4
CHAPTER 5
CHAPTER 6
CHAPTER 7
CHAPTER 8
CHAPTER 9
CHAPTER 10
CHAPTER 11
APPENDICES
INDEX

CHAPTER 1
CHAPTER 2
CHAPTER 3
CHAPTER 4
CHAPTER 5
CHAPTER 6
CHAPTER 7
CHAPTER 8
CHAPTER 9
CHAPTER 10
CHAPTER 11
APPENDICES
INDEX

CHAPTER 1
CHAPTER 2
CHAPTER 3
CHAPTER 4
CHAPTER 5
CHAPTER 6
CHAPTER 7
CHAPTER 8
CHAPTER 9
CHAPTER 10
CHAPTER 11
APPENDICES
INDEX

CHAPTER 1
CHAPTER 2
CHAPTER 3
CHAPTER 4
CHAPTER 5
CHAPTER 6
CHAPTER 7
CHAPTER 8
CHAPTER 9
CHAPTER 10
CHAPTER 11
APPENDICES
INDEX

CHAPTER 1
CHAPTER 2
CHAPTER 3
CHAPTER 4
CHAPTER 5
CHAPTER 6
CHAPTER 7
CHAPTER 8
CHAPTER 9
CHAPTER 10
CHAPTER 11
APPENDICES

INDEX

T

prices, **287–288**
wearable pets, **187–188**, *187*
trading halts, 15
traffic
 land, **128**
 store locations, 53
traffic boosters for nightclubs, 225
training for outside clients, 142
transaction history, **31–33**, *31–32*
transfer fees, 111
Transfer permissions, 38, 97
transparencies, 81
transparency maps, 81
trends and issues in fashion, 98
Tringo game, **239–242**, *239*
Trinity Cole, 228
trust issues with employees, 127
tutorials, 25
 fashion, 78
 permissions, 206
 software, **204**
Twiddler Thereian
 business category selection, 28
 Classified ads, 63
 innovation, **61**
2D drawing programs, **145–146**
TypePad tool, 236

vendors
 automated systems for, **34–35**, *35*
 building, **45**
 fashion stores, 90
 objects, 205
Versu Richelieu, 117
vessels, 18
video card requirements, 22–23
voice applications
 future, 266
 nightclubs, 224
VooDoo Designs, 220, *220*
Voodoo Lunchbox, 198, *198*

script hiring by, 204
toy advice, **188–189**
wearable pets, **187–188**, *187*

CHAPTER 1
CHAPTER 2
CHAPTER 3
CHAPTER 4
CHAPTER 5
CHAPTER 6
CHAPTER 7
CHAPTER 8
CHAPTER 9
CHAPTER 10
CHAPTER 11
APPENDICES

INDEX